Letters to Dotty B

Letters to Dotty B

World War II in the South Pacific

Edited by

Frederick W. Lankard III

1531 Yuma • P. O. Box 1009 • Manhattan, Kansas 66505-1009 USA

Printed in the United States of America on acid-free paper.

ISBN 0-89745-218-6

Technical Editor Amie Goins

Layout by Lori L. Daniel

Just before the Battle, Dotty B, I am thinking most of Thee.

A snatch of verse, dashed off in dark blue ink on flimsy white paper and gracefully decorated with a dozen little musical notes, served notice to Dorothy Bonnette that, in the most personal way, World War II had begun.

Contents

Commander Paul C. Bonnette, probably early 1950s.

Acknowledgments

NO SINGLE SOURCE PROVIDES a completely detailed record of the *Louisville's* activities during Paul Bonnette's time aboard. "The Lady Lou And Her Valiant Crew," compiled by Irma Caluwe, wife of crew member Ted Caluwe, was a major source, as was *Man of War: Log of the USS Louisville* (Philadelphia: Dunlap Printing Co., 1946), compiled and edited in 1946 by two dozen of the *Louisville's* officers and crewmen.

Other sources, contributing to the attempts to clarify points in Paul's letters and establish the environment in which they were written, include the *History of the U.S.S. Louisville*; Samuel Eliot

Morison's *The Two-Ocean War* (Boston: Little, Brown, and Co., 1963); *The New York Times* files; the United States Postal Service; Kingfisher (Oklahoma) High School; *Kingfisher Times & Free Press*; Kenner, Louisiana, pharmacist John Bull; Oklahoma City dentist Dr. Dan Edwards; the Oklahoma Dental Association; the *Daily Oklahoman*; Northwestern University; the University of Michigan; the National Archives and Records Administration; the Naval Historical Center; the Admiral Chester W. Nimitz Museum in Fredericksburg, Texas; memorabilia from Sandra Sue (Stetler) Parsons and Fred Stetler; family albums; and personal memory. Another major reference, also provided by Ted and Irma Caluwe, was crew member Ralph F. "Red" Bender's log of the *Louisville's* arrivals and departures between September 29, 1943 and January 21, 1946.

The author, "Freddy" Lankard, with Aunt Dorothy and Uncle Paul Bonnette in Kingfisher, Oklahoma (*ca.* spring 1943).

But even the "Bender Log," the *Louisville's* deck log, newspaper accounts, and the official *History of the U.S.S. Louisville* are occasionally incomplete and do not in every instance match information in other credible sources or in Paul's letters. Where judgment calls have been necessary, I have made them based on the best information available. If that has resulted in errors, I apologize — especially to the brave sailors who were there and who know better.

Frederick W. Lankard III

Foreword

I HAD BEEN ALIVE for less than a year when my father's Uncle Paul died. Until I read his letters I knew him only as the hero of my father's war stories, told and retold during countless bedtimes. My father passed away about one week after finishing the rough draft of this manuscript. In it he left me far more than the isolated episodes of derring-do. He left the story of the great war told in simple words by an honest man. And through the tale we glimpse the teller. The words are not my father's, but they could be. My father was the hero of many of my bedtime stories — actual adventures of his, perhaps more than slightly embellished — but I think he always wished he could have been the hero of the

"Uncle Paul" stories. Part of that wish was fulfilled as my father found these letters, painstakingly researched the history they pointed to, and compiled them into the book you hold. This is not only a testimony to Uncle Paul, but also to my father.

Thank you, Dad, for giving me a great uncle I never knew, and for giving him and me a chance to establish this monument to you.

Wake Lankard
Oklahoma City, Oklahoma

Introduction

ON JANUARY 30, 1944, the heavy cruiser USS *Louisville* steamed to the Marshall Islands some 3,000 miles west-southwest of Hawaii. In the predawn heat and gloom, the *Louisville's* 8-inch guns were aimed at the Japanese garrison on Wotje Island.

Navy Reserve Lieutenant Paul C. Bonnette, an oral surgeon just three days past his 41st birthday, sat in his tiny cabin and hurriedly continued writing:

> Darling, the long awaited time is just about here. We had breakfast at 0315 and right after we went to G.Q. to

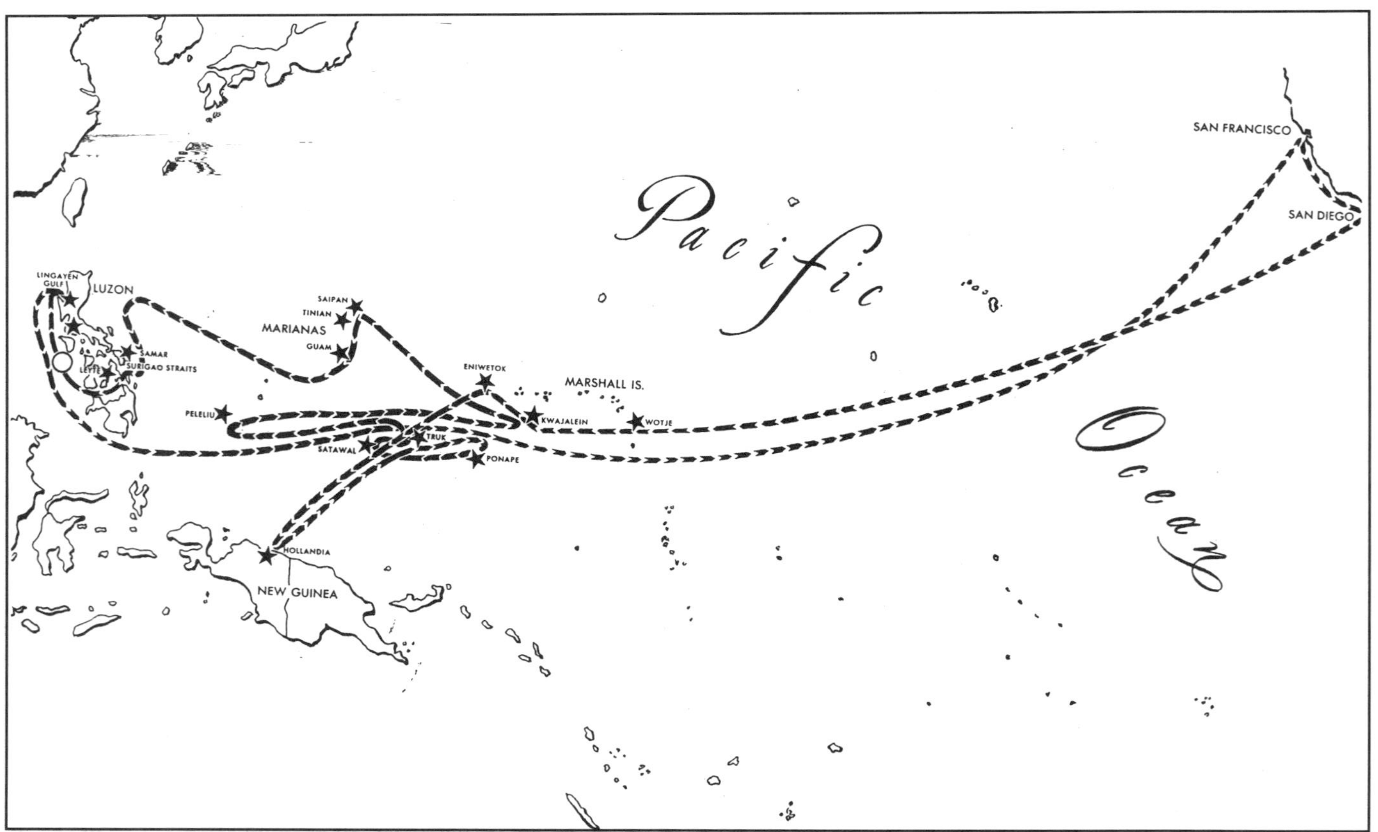

This map shows the USS *Louisville's* primary movements from December 1943 to February 1945 (from the USS *Louisville* association's *Lady Lou*).

> wait for the big blow off. Half hour before dawn we start bombarding — almost that time now, so if I sign off abruptly it won't mean anything has happened to us, just that there is too much going on. The number of shells and rate of fire is terrific, so with the jarring and din it will bc impossible to do anything but hang on.
>
> Apparently it's just another day — no fuss nor muss other than all available space is filled with live ammunition all set to go. Outside my door, it's piled high, only a small runway to my battle locker, operating table and sterilizer remains open.
>
> Hot! Jeepers! Not a dry stitch on us and it's still dark outside.

In 1944, Dr. Paul Christian Bonnette wrote his wife 249 letters from the Pacific. He marveled at glorious tropical sunsets and flying fish keeping pace as the *Louisville* cut through placid blue waters. He reported the horror of suicide air attacks and bloated body chunks bobbing in stinking, oily sea. He was appalled by the carnage on coral beaches. He worried about torpedoes in the night and watched Japanese and American airmen duel in the clouds. He chatted about island visits, pulling teeth, raucous parties, old friends rediscovered, and the endless "ding-ding-ding" call to General Quarters. He made an embarrassing joke about Eleanor Roosevelt and expressed a hearty dislike for General Douglas MacArthur. He smoked too much and grumbled about heat rash, broken glasses, boredom, and fouled mail delivery. He yearned for a real Pacific storm until a raging typhoon threatened to capsize the 9,050-ton *Lady Lou.*

Despite the danger, it was all exciting and fun and like a dime novel thriller in the way so many men and women experienced the great adventure of World War II, until a day came that was too awful for him to describe. Paul would leave the *Louisville* with seven combat stars and the Bronze Star Medal for "heroic and meritorious conduct."

"Dotty B," the former Dorothy Beatrice Lankard of Kingfisher, Oklahoma, saved each 1944 letter. There are also several letters from late 1943 when Paul first reported to the *Louisville*, and several more from the fateful month of January 1945.

My uncle Paul died in 1970. Before my Aunt Dorothy's death in 1987, she sent the box of letters to her sister-in-law, my mother. She died in 1992 and I discovered the sturdy, dusty box crammed tight with my uncle's story of his war.

As a Kingfisher teenager, Paul had worked as an ice man. With tongs and a leather sheet over his shoulder, he delivered blocks of ice to iceboxes through the small farming community. He loved baseball, tennis, and track and field, and in his later years he was an avid golfer.

Dorothy was a teacher as well as an amateur composer and short story writer. She spent many years as a Braille translator.

They had been sweethearts at Kingfisher High School and were married January 3, 1934, four years after Paul's graduation from the University of Michigan School of Dentistry. With a beloved terrier named "Geo. B.," they moved to Alpena in northeastern Michigan where Paul set up a dental practice.

In 1940, Paul earned his certification in oral surgery at Northwestern University. He and Dorothy returned to Oklahoma and Paul established an office in downtown Oklahoma City's Medical Arts Building.

A Navy Reservist, he requested active duty early in 1942, and by late summer 1943 Paul and Dorothy were at the Naval Training Station in Tucson, Arizona. When Paul went to sea, Dorothy moved into the Lankard family home — known as the "Big House" — on Seventh Street in Kingfisher. Early in 1944 she took an apartment on Northwest 17th Street in Oklahoma City, the same apartment she and Paul occupied in 1940-1942.

Paul and Dorothy had no children and were always close to their nieces and nephews. I was five during most of 1944 and spent happy afternoons in Aunt Dorothy's room at the Big House, fascinated with her new typewriter and her machine that created words in Braille. I often visited her in Oklahoma City, but it was not until I saw her address on Paul's letters that I was able to return 50 years later, to the 17th Street apartment.

Aunt Dorothy was an attractive brunette, intelligent, with a throaty laugh, an occasional smoker's cough, a quick wit, great curiosity, and high energy. She was self-confident and independent, which reflected — as it did for many women of that period — the sudden need to organize income tax material, pay bills, travel, and maintain an automobile (known as the "Jerk") with a husband 10,000 miles away.

Paul was handsome and athletic with a long, forceful stride, powerful arms, and large, strong hands. He taught me to play golf but always declined to risk his fingers by tossing a football or baseball. I remember him as a blend of sophistication and innocence. Although quick to smile, he could be gruff. He liked the security and periodic adventure of the military life.

Each of Paul's envelopes bears the initialed stamp of a shipboard censor whose duty was to make sure, as a matter of security, that such information as locations, destinations, plans, losses, and ship names did not become public knowledge. When kamikaze planes made their first appearance, Paul wrote freely about them. Later, he said reference to the suicide craft had been suddenly prohibited.

Paul and Dorothy followed the common practice of working out a code in advance of his first taste of sea duty. Its primary purpose was to help her track the *Louisville* on a large, detailed map. Combined with news reports, she could then have a reasonable idea where Paul had been and what action he had seen.

Their code was based on the names of friends, relatives, and familiar locations, which makes it difficult to tell when Paul is reminiscing about shared memories or giving Dorothy a coded message about where the *Louisville* will be next week. "Geo.," the terrier, was a location, as was "Mary Wilde" and "Ade." But in many instances it is a tough code to crack, and was even for Dorothy. Paul occasionally chides her for not being able to work out his cleverly constructed messages.

Deleted from the letters to Dotty B are random partial thoughts, uninteresting anecdotes, lengthy discussion of family matters, and information repeated in other letters.

Paul's letters should be read as much as possible from the perspective of 1944. Occasional racial slurs offensive to a more culturally sensitive time were, in 1944, the sort of comments that cropped up thoughtlessly in the conversation of a man whose whole experience had been in a firm, rarely questioned, segregated society.

But there is nothing thoughtless about his savage reference to the Japanese as he questioned their very humanity. They looked different, they talked different, they acted different, and they lived far away. All that made them easy to distrust. They had committed atrocities in China and they had brutally humiliated the United States at Pearl Harbor, and that made them easy to hate. Mitsubishis were not found on the streets of Kingfisher and Alpena; they dropped out of clouds, spitting flame, killing the boy next door. Bright young Japanese men were not neighbors in middle America; they hid in holes and caves on distant islands and they plunged bayonets into U.S. Marines. Japanese Americans in the United States were locked in concentration camps and Japanese in the Pacific were slaughtered. In 1944 the equation was simple: the Japanese started the whole thing and they deserved what they were getting. Paul Bonnette — however much he may have mellowed in later years — wholeheartedly agreed.

"So solly," he wrote, as enemy corpses drifted past the smoking guns of the USS *Louisville*.

The USS *Louisville*, the third U.S. Navy ship to be named for that Kentucky city, was a Northampton Class heavy cruiser bearing the Navy designation CA 28. Her overall length was 600 feet, 3 inches and she was 66 feet, 1 inch wide with a draft of 16 feet, 4 inches. She had eight boilers in four boiler rooms. Her turbines produced shaft horsepower of 107,000, and her four screws (propellers) could drive her through the water at 32.7 knots. Her standard displacement was 9,050 tons (12,000 tons loaded). She carried 3,064 tons of fuel oil, giving her an action radius of 13,000 miles at 15 knots. Her wartime complement was approximately 1,300 men.

The *Louisville's* teakwood deck bristled with 9 8-inch guns, 12 5-inch guns, and 16 40mm and 27 20mm anti-aircraft guns. The 8-inch guns were mounted in three triple turrets, two forward and one aft. Though no match for a battleship's raw power, the heavy cruiser's big guns were considered extremely accurate. She had been constructed with two triple torpedo tubes, but the Navy ordered these removed during a 1935 overhaul.

As a band played the "Star Spangled Banner" and "My Old Kentucky Home," the *Louisville* was launched September 1, 1930, 26 months after her keel was laid in drydock at Bremerton, Washington's Puget Sound Navy Yard. She was commissioned into the United States Navy on a rainy January 15, 1931.

The *Lady Lou* was a veteran ship by the time World War II began. For a decade she had traveled the Atlantic and Pacific, engaging in training exercises and "showing the flag" in Australia, New Zealand, Samoa, Pago Pago, Tasmania, Cuba, Haiti, Panama, Brazil, Uruguay, and Argentina.

Peacetime was not without exciting moments. In the predawn hours of May 30, 1931, the *Louisville* copied an SOS from the SS *Harvard*, a coastal vessel out of San Francisco carrying some 500 men, women, and children that had run onto submerged rocks off the coast of Santa Barbara, California. Racing through the night at 30 knots, the *Louisville* reached the rescue scene in less than five hours and took aboard several hundred of the *Harvard's* evacuating passengers.

In 1937, 800 miles off Hawaii, *Lady Lou* found eight passengers who had taken to life boats when their British ship caught fire. The following February in the Sydney, Australia, harbor, the *Louisville's* crew rescued 25 women from a capsized launch.

Her first feel for hostile waters came in early January 1941 when secret orders sent the *Louisville* to Simmonstown, South Africa. Europe was at war and the mission was to transport nearly $150 million in British gold bars to the Federal Reserve Bank in New York City. Pounded by storms and constantly alert for German submarines, it took the *Louisville* 22 days to cover the 6,800 miles.

The spring and summer of 1941 were devoted to amphibious exercises out of San Diego and gunnery training at Pearl Harbor.

On November 6, the *Louisville* was ordered to escort two transports carrying U.S. soldiers to the Philippines. On the return trip, loaded with American civilians headed home in the face of growing threats of war, *Lady Lou* received word of the attack on Pearl Harbor on December 7, 1941. The United States officially entered World War II the following day. The *Louisville* arrived there on December 16, where, according to the ship's history, "a heartsick crew viewed the disastrous results of the Japanese raid."

The *Louisville* returned to California's Mare Island Navy Yard to be fitted with radar and sonar before steaming to San Diego to join Task Force 17 that included the carriers *Enterprise* and *Yorktown*. Sporting a freshly painted camouflage design, the *Louisville* helped deliver troops to Samoa on January 22, 1942, then provided carrier support for raids against the Marshall and Gilbert Islands. During this, the Navy's first offensive action of the war, *Lady Lou* lost one of her planes and its pilot and radioman.

In mid-February she became part of Task Force 11, escorting troop ships and carriers to New Caledonia before racing northwestward across the Coral Sea to harass the Japanese on New Guinea.

May found the *Louisville* back at Mare Island to install modern anti-aircraft guns before being dispatched with Task Force 8 to the Aleutian Islands for four months of fog-bound patrolling and an August bombardment of Japanese facilities on the island of Kiska.

Warmer waters beckoned and November found the *Louisville* escorting troop transports and patrolling out of Espiritu Santo in the New Hebrides Islands. In late January 1943, as part of Task Force 16, she took part in the Battle of Rennell Island. In the darkness just south of Guadalcanal, the *Louisville* twisted and turned, dodging torpedo attacks that would claim a sister cruiser, the USS *Chicago*.

After rest and repairs in New Zealand and Pearl Harbor, it was back to the foggy, stormy Aleutians and the invasions of Attu and Kiska.

In early September, the *Louisville* steamed under the Golden Gate for overhaul at Mare Island. As she completed her preparations for a return to combat, the *Lady Lou* was boarded on November 15, 1943, by Navy Reserve Lieutenant Paul C. Bonnette of Kingfisher, Oklahoma. A log of his 16 months as her senior dental officer follows.

USS *Louisville* Log, September 1943 — April 1945

Date	Location	Arrive	At Sea	Departure
December 1943	San Francisco, California	Thur., Sept. 9		Sun., Dec. 26
	San Diego, California	Mon. 27		Tues. 28
January 1944	Long Beach, California	Mon. 3		Thur. 13
	Lahaina Roads, Territory of Hawaii	Fri. 21		Sat. 22
	Wotje, Marshall Islands	Sun. 30		Sun. 30
	Namur & Roi, Marshall Islands	Mon. 31		Wed., Feb. 2
February 1944	Kwajalein, Marshall Islands	Wed. 2		Sun. 6
	Majuro, Marshall Islands	Wed. 9		Tues. 15

USS *Louisville* Log, September 1943 — April 1945 *(continued)*

Date	Location	Arrive	At Sea	Departure
February 1944	Eniwetok, Marshall Islands	Thur. 17		Sun., Mar. 5
March 1944	Majuro, Marshall Islands	Tues. 7		Wed. 22
	Equator Crossing		Fri. 24	
	Raid Palau Islands		Wed. 29	
April 1944	Majuro, Marshall Islands	Thur. 6		Fri. 14
	Invade Hollandia, New Guinea		Sat. 22	
	Raid Truk, Caroline Islands		Sat. 29	
	Raid Satawan, Caroline Islands		Sun. 30	
May 1944	Majuro, Marshall Islands	Thur. 4		Tues., June 6
June 1944	Roi, Marshall Islands	Wed. 7		Sat. 10
	Saipan & Tinian, Mariana Islands	Wed. 14		Wed., Aug. 3
August 1944	Guam, Mariana Islands	Thur. 3		Wed. 9
	Eniwetok, Marshall Islands	Sat. 12		Sat. 19
	Espiritu Santo, New Hebrides Islands	Thur. 24		Sun. 27

USS *Louisville* Log, September 1943 — April 1945 *(continued)*

Date	Location	Arrive	At Sea	Departure
August 1944	Guadalcanal, Solomon Islands	Wed. 30		Wed., Sep. 7
September 1944	Peleliu & Arakabe-san, Palau Islands	Tues. 12		Mon. 25
	Hollandia, New Guinea	Wed. 27		Sat. 30
	Manus, Admiralty Islands	Sat. 30		Thur., Oct. 12
October 1944	Leyte, Philippine Islands	Wed. 18		Sun. 29
November 1944	Ulithi, Caroline Islands	Wed. 1		Fri. 3
	Raid Luzon, Philippine Islands		Sun. 5	
	Ulithi, Caroline Islands	Thur. 9		Fri. 17
	Hollandia, New Guinea	Sun. 19		Tues. 21
	Manus, Admiralty Islands	Wed. 22		Fri., Dec. 1
December 1944	Hollandia, New Guinea	Sat. 2		Thur. 7
	Manus, Admiralty Islands	Fri. 8		Fri. 8
	Leyte, Philippine Islands	Wed. 13		Tues. 26

USS *Louisville* Log, September 1943 — April 1945 *(continued)*

Date	Location	Arrive	At Sea	Departure
December 1944	Leyte, Philippine Islands	Fri. 29		Tues., Jan. 2
January 1945	Off Luzon, Philippine Islands		Fri. 5	
	Lingayen Gulf, Philippine Islands		Sat. 6	
	Leyte, Philippine Islands	Fri. 12		Sun. 14
	Manus, Admiralty Islands	Thur. 18		Sun. 21
	Pearl Harbor, Territory of Hawaii	Mon. 29		Wed. 31
February 1945	San Francisco, California	Tues. 6		Sun., Apr. 22
April 1945	San Diego, California	Sun. 22		Sun. 29

A prewar photo of the USS *Louisville* from a Lankard family album.

Chapter 1

Shrapnel Has No Conscience

DOTTY B WAS VISITING OKLAHOMA in September 1943 when Paul wrote from their home at the Naval Training Station in Tucson, Arizona, excitedly telling her of the assignment he had received from the Navy's Bureau of Personnel (BuPers). His concerns about having to find his new ship "somewhere in the Pacific" turned out to be unfounded; the *Louisville* had already arrived at Mare Island Navy Yard near San Francisco for overhaul.

Paul boarded the *Louisville* on November 15. Dorothy came to California, and on December 23 they had a farewell cup of coffee aboard ship and kissed goodbye. Three days later, the *Lady Lou* left San Francisco to spend the next two weeks in training off the Southern California coast.

After more than a year of suffering stinging losses in the Pacific (including the loss of the Philippines), the Allied forces slowly gained ground against General Hideki Tojo's military in 1943. The U.S. had taken Guadalcanal and met with success in driving the Japanese out of the Aleutian Islands off Alaska. In August, President Franklin D. Roosevelt and British Prime Minister Winston Churchill met in Quebec and agreed that the offensive strategy for the Pacific war would consist of two fronts — an island-hopping drive through the central Pacific, and an advance up the Solomons toward the Philippines.

By the time Paul boarded the *Louisville,* OPERATION GALVANIC was under way to take Tarawa in the Gilbert Islands. After intense fighting, U.S. forces successfully drove the Japanese out of Tarawa by the end of November 1943.

In early January 1944, the *Louisville* became the flagship of Rear Admiral Jesse B. Oldendorf, who, according to the ship's history, "was to command the great naval support group through all of the epic amphibious schedule ahead."

The first step in that schedule was the Marshall Islands, an 800-mile-long strip of over 1,000 flat, coral islands, most of them grouped into just over two dozen atolls and named for a British explorer, John Marshall.

After a brief stop off the Territory of Hawaii, the *Louisville* headed southwest with the Fast Carrier Force Pacific Fleet. As OPERATION FLINTLOCK, she took part in attacks on Japanese strongholds in the Marshalls, invading some, shelling some, bypassing others.

The *Louisville* first fired on tiny Wotje Island, then played a key role in the massive bombardment and invasions of Roi and Namur Islands in the northern sector of sprawling Kwajalein Atoll. Action then shifted to Eniwetok Atoll on the Marshalls' western edge, where the *Louisville* led the fire support group that bombarded Engebi, Eniwetok, and Parry Islands. Except for the occasional sniper, the islands were secured by February 22.

According to naval historian Samuel Eliot Morison, the Marshall Islands campaign enhanced the Navy's reputation by demonstrating "mastery of the art of amphibious warfare; of combining air, surface, submarine and ground forces to project fighting power irresistibly across the ocean."

Admiral Richard "Dick" Conolly, who earned the nickname "Close-in Conolly" for his bombardment tactics during the campaign, is quoted by Morison: "The Marshalls really cracked the Japanese shell."

27 Sept. 1943

Hello Darling,

What do you think of the old salt now? Things sure pop when the ball starts rolling.

My ship, the U.S.S. Louisville, is a heavy cruiser and a flagship. Talked with some of the Chiefs that have sailed on her and they say she is a beauty. She's over 600 feet long, carries four planes and is a fighting ship from stem to stern. Golly I'm tickled I got good duty. I'll be senior dental officer and may be a spot promotion. Won't that be something?

I'm to be detached on or about 8 November with 5 days delay. The Louisville is somewhere in the Pacific and I'll have to find her. That should be fun — don't know the first thing about going about it, but I'll find her. The consensus of opinion is I'll either go in a convoy or fly to Pearl Harbor and then fly to wherever she is from there. Sounds exciting, doesn't it?

We'll have to work out a code so I can tell you where I am — she has been in the Atlantic, Asiatic and Pacific fleets so I should see some of the world.

Tell everybody hello and all my love to you, honey.

Paul

PAUL WROTE DOROTHY all he felt he could get away with and she, no doubt, was alert to the hidden messages. He mentioned "birds" — other warships, no doubt — roosting on the *Louisville*. Then he recalled a "trip" through Tennessee, Maryland, and Colorado (all battleship names) and the fun he and Dorothy had in Saratoga and Lexington (both aircraft carriers). Either the censor who passed the letter wasn't paying attention, or he didn't have much of an eye for logical geography.

24 Dec. 1943

Hello My Honey —

Sure am spending a different Xmas Eve this year than ever before. We had movies aboard and then a hot cribbage match — Commander Bowers, Swain and myself. "Lud" and some of the gang were over in the corner with "a cord dean" and having a big time. We're all going to midnight mass and then call it quits for the night.

Sure was surprised this a.m. to find we had shoved off — good thing I'm not a sleep walker or I'd have wet my feet. We'll be around here a few hours tomorrow and then on down the avenue.

The night is clear — lights as far as you can see from our ten mile point.

Am making this letter short tonight. Four birds roosted on us today and they are tame, bet they stay with us for the duration. Have been thinking about our trip thru Tennessee, Maryland and Colorado and what fun we had in Saratoga and Lexington. Everything was so pretty that time of year.

All my love, honey
Paul

PAUL HAD LITTLE CONCERN for spelling and punctuation — in part, at least, because he had no idea anyone other than Dotty B would ever read his letters. Some of his abbreviations are clear, such as "rec'd," "thru," and "tho." Others are less clear, like "ont" and "int" for "onto" and "into." He made liberal use of dashes, often in place of periods.

26 Dec. 1943

Hello Honey,

We're finally on our way. Shoved off this morning and probably will see Comdr. Geo. [*San Diego*] tomorrow night. We had a hell of a rough sea this morning and a lot got seasick but so far I'm all right. Had a bad hour but it passed off as tho someone had pressed a button. Ate a good lunch, went to a show and now I'm swinging and swaying trying to write you a note. There is enough roll so chairs tip over, dishes slide around — funny sensation to reach for a knife and have it skid away from you. It's a great life and I get a big kick out of it.

Haven't been off the ship since I boarded her Thursday night [*December 23*]. Had too much fun in S.F. with you to try it myself so I'm saving it for when we get together again.

This sure is a hell of a sensation to try and write. First we roll to the right, then dip then roll left and then rare up — over and over again. We're pretty heavy and it's a slow pitch and roll-but good.

All my love to you honey — I love you gooooooood.

Paul

THE *LOUISVILLE'S* TRAINING maneuvers were conducted near San Clemente Island, about 60 miles off the California coast between the naval bases at Long Beach and San Diego.

29 Dec. 1943

Hello Leedle-wan.

Yesterday we were at it from 0800 until 2230 (10:30) and was it a day! Don't know where we were or are now, but tis somewhere between Hutset [*Long Beach*] and Comdr. George. There is a terrible land swell so we are not over a hundred miles out but everything is sliding around and my desk has a constant sway — not conducive to letter writing.

Had fun yesterday. Am an observer in Director One — way up as far as you can go — when the big guns go off it sure shocks the you-know-what out of you. It's hard work tho, last night I was so pooped I fell right to bed. We had a "general quarters" last night. The ship is blacked out and don't think I didn't have a hell of a time finding my way to the crows nest. Pitch dark, wind blowing ninety to nothing and colder than hell, but I made it before the boss got there.

Had our first casualty (?). Comdr. Towner broke two of his front teeth. He started to duck under a brace and the ship came up fast and met him tooth-on. Nothing serious, it just meant my racing from my perch down to sick bay and back again.

Ludlow happened to be watching a gull through his glasses today. A huge fish came up and swallowed him — the gull, not Lud.

As the old timers say, they'll be glad when they go to war — these maneuvers and training workouts are too tough.

All my love to you, honey.
Paul

30 Dec. 1943

Hello Honey,

Just finished main battery drill. Alarm came in twice — first time false alarm but we raced to our stations. It was raining and dark as hell — miserable I'd say. The second was at 2100 and we fired quite a few salvos. Cracked my head on a hatch and skinned a couple of fingers but don't rate a "purple heart". It's dark to start with — nary a light outside at all and when you first come out of a lighted room, you're blind as a bat.

Night firing is fun — they use radar to locate the target then shoot star shells to illuminate it and then fire — very pretty, but noisy.

Ship and plane maneuvers in this vicinity until "wedding day" and then we're off to raise a little hell of our own. Lou is getting on her toes and acts like she'd like to claw a few slant eyes.

They switched Admirals on us today, so Comdr Towner broke out a jar of homemade relish in celebration. He's a honey, that Towner man — is a hard worker and knows his stuff. Everyone sure has buckled down but they still are a grand bunch of fellows.

Must close. All my love to you, "leedle wan."

Paul

AT LEAST SOME of the coded language in Paul's first letter of 1944 is informal and easy to identify. "Basso" and "huge symphony" are gunnery practice. "Halls of Montezuma" has to be the Marines. The "operetta" is their upcoming operation. "Ade" is Hawaii — or, specifically, Pearl Harbor.

2 Jan. 1944

Good morning & Happy New Year Honey,

This is a hell of a time to be writing a letter, but this is a "simulated state of war" and we're in G. Q. (General Quarters). They broke us out at 0300 and it is going to be a long session. Wish I could tell you what is going on but it is too gigantic to pass along for fear something might happen. Yesterday, just sailing along tra la la la, today basso etc., a huge symphony and I mean a great beeg one with over 30,000 all boy chorus thrown in. From the "Halls of Montezuma" is a great song. Think this operetta will gain world wide recognition around my birthday [*January 27*].

How was your New Years — mine was very quiet but had fun watching people. The fleet was in — saw Lou and all her girl friends — talk about your 57 relatives, she has close to eighty and all present, all sizes, shapes and what have you.

Having a lot of fun — everyone is on edge and pooped — lots of gold braid aboard and we're all temporarily doubled up as to rooms — cots stuck around everywhere. Had abandon ship drill yesterday — they forgot to give me a station. Succeeded in getting one after convincing them it wouldn't be dignified for me to stand on deck attempting to thumb a ride. Got me a motor boat — Peabo, Sady, Johnson and myself plus some enlisted men go together. We have new fangled preservers — now know where all the fizzwater cartridges are.

All my love,
Paul

4 Jan. 1944

Hello Darling —

The whole fleet was in last night [*Long Beach*]. I've seen it in the movies but the real McCoy is something else again. We beached about

1945 — the ship is anchored about 20 minutes out and to get ashore we go by motor boat. It's quite a sight — all the white caps bobbing around — from where we docked there was a column of fours for as far as you could see.

The wives that remain are sure having a hell of a time — we never know when we will be in or for how long — you can't get a room and travel is so terrible that by the time word is gotten to them it's time to leave.

Tomorrow I have a busy day — starting my duty for sure — am booked solid so I'm staying [*on*] board tonight for a good rest. The past few days really have been rough ones. My shins are all banged up from skinning thru the scuttles (small opening in the hatches leading below) during water tight integrity. Things really move when g.q. is sounded and this is only the beginning.

It's chow time — I'm hungry so will sign off for now.

All my love to you, honey,
Paul

5 Jan. 1944

Hello and Goodby Honey —

This is my last letter for a time, from the U.S.A. — no liberty for anyone today for we're sailing on half hours notice or less. Can't actually believe we're really starting out to look for Japs. The war so far has been a vacation for both of us — pleasant tour of duty with pay. Now it's chop-chop.

Number one mess hall is loaded with ammunition and all other available space too. Looks like serious business for sure. Wonder what my reaction will be when I see my first "rising sun" and firing starts. Until now war has been just a rumor — something to read about in the papers. Wonder if the real McCoy will be like an over-rated first run.

We're having all kinds of drills today — just finished with a fire drill. Don't know what will come next.

Have some possible good news but don't say anything. My name has been sent to Washington for consideration to be promoted to Lt. Comdr. It's by board of selection now — no longer en-bloc but to be eligible you had to be a two striper on active duty June 15, 1942. Won't know for probably a couple of months but it is retroactive to Jan. 1, 1944.

My roommate has moved out, thank the Lord. I can [*breathe*] and write letters again. Most of the other single rooms have had bunks added but the ventilator pipes in mine prevents their addition so I'm secure.

All my love to you honey,
Paul

PAUL'S JANUARY 5 "last letter from the U.S.A." notwithstanding, the *Louisville* did not leave Long Beach until January 13.

7 Jan. 1944

My Darling,

We had an admiral detached and the new one came aboard — that called for much running around — in and out of blues, etc., etc. The detachment was on the order of the commissioning you saw but on a much more elaborate scale. Had bugle fare, side boys, admiral's staff plus all the ship's personnel. One "Ad" read his detachment orders supplemented by a short speech and then saluted, passed the word for his flag to be lowered and then walked off. He felt a little bad you could tell — said it was like leaving home for he'd been with us and she was an efficient ship.

Yesterday we had zone inspection. I was member of Wescott's party and we had all of top side. Lord, I didn't know there were so many compartments — know topside pretty well now.

We're having Captain's Inspection now — rated a 4.0 so I'm okay so far. Secure from Capt's Inspection just sounded so will light the smoking lamp. It's 1110 now and we've been at more or less attention since 0900. My office really looked nice, bulkheads painted bright, work area bright etc., etc.

Think of you all the time. Miss you loads, so keep up the letters.

All my love,
Paul

10 Jan. 1944

Hello Honey,

Had the medical watch yesterday — couple of temps came in but I fixed them up and they're all right today.

The main reason I didn't write — there were no censors aboard so the letter wouldn't go out.

Comdr. Towner is the hard luck boy so far. First he cracks his teeth and now he can barely walk. Woke up, kicked the covers back and stretched — bingo went his ankle — tore a ligament loose. I x-rayed it — no broken bones but he sure is disgusted.

Believe it or not [*I*] have some patients — one is due now so by by for now. Still looks like 13 is it. No more monkey business in these parts — boom boom for keeps — no more "pick up the marbles."

All my love
Paul

14 Jan. 1944

Hello Pretty One —

Had fun watching a school of porpoises frolicking in the water along side the ship as we sailed along. They kept in formation a la chorus girls — leap clear of the water, back in again as one, time and time again. Cute little (?) rascals.

If I could only describe the picture out there — it's "agin" the law. Thrilling? I should say so! Thought I had seen a lot but it was only a drop in the bucket. It's sinister, thrilling, awe inspiring and peaceful all at the same time. When one realizes our mission and the way we are gliding along quietly in formation, you have to pinch yourself to believe you are actually along and in on one of the greatest things in history. Small p-nuts to date — Ringling Bros are pikers.

I do love you loads honey,
Paul

15 Jan. 1944

Hello Honey,

The fellows are getting sunburned from standing watch. I'm going to start sun bathing myself ere long.

Had anti-aircraft firing drill this morning. Sure makes a racket when you're down below deck, but doesn't make you jump even when you're not expecting it. Guess it's because they let go anytime from now on and you are tuned to it.

Saw a good show a while ago — Fred Astaire and someone in "You Were Never Lovelier" — bright comedy and everyone enjoyed it.

Hit some rough weather yesterday and had to chase glasses, plates, chairs, etc., but still am hale and hearty.

We're having trouble impressing the crew that during drills they go forward on the starboard and aft on the port. A few have been banged up so Comdr. Towner composed a little verse: "Please send flowers to Johnnie McBride — he tried to go aft on the starboard side." Yes, Towner is still with us and he's a honey — the above jingle he had printed on the bottom of the day's work sheet for distribution.

Love you loads,
Paul

17 Jan. 1944

Hello Darling,

Had big doings yesterday evening. The wardroom was host to the Admiral and the Captain for dinner and what a meal! Started off with a shredded lettuce salad topped with a cracker and anchovy. Then stuffed olives and celery — puree of something soup. The main [*entree*] was filet [*mignon*] wrapped in bacon, french [*fries*] and lima beans. Then demitasse and apple pie a la mode — not bad, eh? Wonder what the poor people are doing — yea "noi-ve!"

Paid my ships service bill Saturday. My laundry bill was $1.32, that's sure a far cry from civilian or shore laundry. I always have six pairs socks, dozen hankies, khaki pants, 4 or five shirts, etc., each week — it's easy to keep clean. Sure pity the poor army fellows, especially the evacuation hospital. When I look at my office — it shines like a nigger's heel.

We still have our morning g.q. but it's worked a little differently now. They sound reveille fifteen minutes before and as Towner puts it, "Them that's up and wants it" can have a cupa coffee. We stay in until an hour after sun up, then secure and have breakfast — then the day's activities start. We used to have g.q. an hour before sun up and breakfast before that. We'd stay in six hours and it sure make a long hungry stretch. Am getting so I hit the deck before "Up! All bunks, hit the deck" is sounded so I avoid the rush.

Everything really is sliding around, worst we've had but it's fun — I don't even have that light feeling anymore so I guess I have my sea legs for sure.

There was a big crash, bang, thud just then — seemed like the whole cafeteria fell in, but it was only a dozen or so racks, trays etc. We must be inclining better than fifteen degrees each way so it starts things skidding.

Did I tell you about the destroyer that came alongside and picked up mail? Sure was a pretty sight, especially as she came ploughing up to us. Quite a trick throwing line and then transferring the mail bag. Am looking forward to refueling at sea — guess that is quite a trick — both ships lashed together and away they go.

Lot of firing yesterday at a sleeve dragged by plane. We led the procession. We're all in a single file and we blaze away and then it is taken up by the rest of the ships — noisy but good. You can see the shells flying thru the air and then the pattern as they burst in the air — at night it's [*supposed*] to be really something so I'm anxious to see it. Have seen some night firing but nothing compared to what it will be now.

My reaction to going into the actual battle has got me stopped. Had a lengthy x-ray session with Comdr. Bowers yesterday and asked him about what one's reaction should be going into combat. It seems like a big checker game — maneuvering of men until you wipe all off or bottle them up. He said it was more like chess — no one seems to worry about getting banged up or killed — just outsmarting the enemy. At chow in the evenings when we are all together, except the watch, you'd never know we were a fighting ship. Everyone has fun, lots of razzing, dominoes, cribbage — complete relaxation. They're on the beam all day but when they are off duty — they're nuts.

Am working up quite a practice — same old story: "Doc, that's the easiest I've ever had one pulled." Have synchronized my zig with the ship's zag and am having fun. Almost fall on my face a few times each day but it's all in the day's work.

Love you good, honey,
Paul

18 Jan. 1944

Hello My Sweet —

"Merrily we roll along"

Busy days but lots of fun — crash! bang! tud! again — seems as though every time I get ready to write to you we start rolling and tossing. The cafeteria starts moving. You can imagine the racket several hundred eating utensils make when they spill out on a steel deck. No place for a hangover.

I haven't heard from my promotion yet. All I ask is that I get it — out here it doesn't make any difference. Chances are we won't have liberty for a long time — at least until after the big push. They're not taking any chances of a leak so all hands remain aboard. Eddie Page was just in. He's a censor and was telling me about a letter he read last night — a kid writing to his folks — "Dear Mom, just got back from the dentist. Had two teeth pulled and some fillings. Best Dentist I've ever been to." How's that?

Gang of us took a sun bath on the prow of the ship yesterday. Was marvelous — sun hot and occasional salt spray doused us.

From 1630-2000 they have a phonograph hooked up on the address system. It's fun to loll on the well deck in the sun shine and balmy air and listen to the music. No war as yet. Still a Cook's tour but won't be long now.

All my love,
Paul

20 Jan. 1944

Hello My Honey,

Sure had a rough nite last night — busted dishes, drawers slammed open and contents spilled — sure a mess. From 0100 I was awake — chairs sliding around me barely able to stay in my bunk we were rolling so much. Barber & the Padre got their dinners in their laps and the rest of us slid clear against the bulkhead. It's fun tho and if it hadn't been for some heavy object over my head that would slide and then bang against the bulkhead and then roll back and bang, over and over again — couldn't sleep for it and I'm all pooped out today.

All my love,
Paul

PAUL GOT HIS first look at the Hawaiian Islands, but it was a short stay as the *Louisville* arrived at Lahaina Roads on the 21st and left the next day.

21 Jan. 1944

Well, Well, Honey,

Here we are and my first view of the "- - - -"s. It's really quite a picture, one especially stands out, it's really beautiful and looks like one of those dolled up post cards. Have been up in the fire control tower and looking over the country through binoculars — it's simply grand. It has California beat all hollow for beauty, at least from a distance. High mountains with low hanging clouds, green trees and fields of various shades of green and red, believe it or not. The water is calm — deep indigo and looks awfully inviting. At 1600 we're sounding "swim call" and all hands are going in. The sun is hot and a dip should set us up in business.

Some time during the wee hours we shove off again and the serious side of this tour has priorities. We're in enemy waters and anything can happen from now on. The magnitude of this operation is stupendous, we're just a part of it so when you read the papers "months" from now — remember your boy friend was in it. History will be made and that is for sure.

We're checking over our battle dressing stations, sterilizing, rearranging, etc., because after this p.m. all store rooms and compartments are sealed until after the big show. Looks like war, sure enough.

All My Love,
Paul

IN PAUL'S CODE a "Eugene Stetler" is an aircraft carrier and "Toby Cleaver" is the Marshall Islands.

22 Jan. 1944

Hello My Sweet,

Forty-five minutes until sailing time. Cancelled my last appointment so I could drop you a note and then watch them weigh anchor. Must get my last look at friendly shores — tomorrow we face the menace of subs and planes as we will be beyond the limits of our own bomber patrol. The fun is over for a while but as I always sez — "let's see what gives it."

Enjoyed our brief stay while here, even if we couldn't get ashore. It was interesting watching them refuel at sea — it's quite tricky and needless to say, the smoking lamp was out thru out the ship.

They had a half hour swim this morning — seems odd to have Marines posted with rifles and tommy guns to take care of inquisitive sharks and barracuda. Nice friendly atmosphere — sea food in reverse potential, nez pas?

Life goes on as usual aboard ship — we're having a movie after we get underway. The picture is "Always In My Heart", that's you little one. You sure are going with me — believe the picture is dedicated to you.

The galley is full of turkey so I guess we're going to have a final big meal — very shortly we will be at our battle stations and on a diet of sandwiches most of the time.

Must be off to Toby Cleaver's. Does 24 Eugene Stetlers mean anything to you? Quite a family I'd say.

Here's to you, honey. Wish I could kind a hug you but no can do so here's the next best —

All My Love To You,
Paul

25 Jan. 1944

Hello Darling —

Wrote you last, last Saturday just before shoving off for Japland and was going to take in a movie. Had seen it before — you and I, Kay Francis and Walter Huston in "You're Always In My Heart". Do you happen to remember the scene where they were having a harmonica concert? Anyhow, our five inch guns let go just at the time the director turned around and signaled for silence and held his ears — it was timed just right and sure brought the house down.

Went to church Sunday and enjoyed the services a lot. Ten minutes before time to start the organist was turned in with measles so we had to sing without benefit of music.

Started out with the Invocation, then song #89 or "Onward Christian Soldiers", then he read from the 33rd Psalm. That was followed by a short sermon and then "we will have a minute's silent prayer, each in his own way" — reminded me of the picture "Guadalcanal Diary". We closed by singing "God Bless America". Really enjoyed the service a lot. It was held in the port [*hangar*] — we rocked and swayed along but we were attentive. Seemed more impressive than in proper surroundings.

The boys are beginning to look rugged — the redness is turning to sun tan so we look sea going if nothing else. Can't seem to write legibly today. We're rolling quite a bit, but may be because I've been up since 0430. General quarters (g.q.) twice daily is a chore but we're getting it down pat now so we're a smooth functioning team.

Things can pop any minute now and it's exciting. Have moved a complete outfit of clothes to my battle station so if I have to make it in my p.j.s I can dress there and if it comes to abandoning ship I'll have what the "well dressed officer should wear."

Had good chow at noon — cold macaroni and ham mixed together, french fries, mixed pickles, ice tea and cake. Sure hit the spot. I like Sunday lunches — assorted cold meats, potato salad, baked beans, pickles and tea. In the evening we have our big meal followed by g.q., a hot game of dominoes or cribbage and then bed.

Chocolate floats are the craze now — loser buys. Just had a casualty — boot busted a tooth. When I say "roll", I mean roll-l-l.

All my love,
Paul

28 Jan. 1944

Hello Honey —

The censors have clamped down so I'm afraid to say much. We're all in the know and have seen maps, reliefs, etc., of all the islands and it's really marvelous how things are done. This aerial photography is really something — the recentness of the views — you wonder how they do it. Uncle Sam is a smart "wan" take it from me.

Had my birthday yesterday on account of it was the 27th — me and Gen. MacArthur. My battle dressing station gang gave me a beautifully non-skid, veri-tuff, anti-tear toilet paper wrapped box containing a cartoon, slightly used cork screw, sputum cup and some so called personalized stationery.

It's mighty pretty out here. The nights are awfully dark but the stars are so bright and close by. We like dark nights at this stage of the game — they learned a lesson at Tarawa [*in November 1943*].

Don't say too much about the contents of this letter. We came into enemy bomber and submarine range yesterday and we're still moving at 13 knots day and night. It's a monotonous speed but we have many dozens of whatchamacallits that can't travel faster and we are one happy family so we stick together. Lou leads the pack and we are the smart ones — the picture never changes and it could be we haven't moved out of our tracks.

From sunup tomorrow until Lord only knows when, we expect action as we are within their territory but so far everything is quiet and serene. Hard to believe they are actually lurking under and over us and liable to let go any minute but we are having a grand time and every one is in the best humor. It's a strain all right — but good. It's hotter than hell and we sweat right thru our clothes so tonight Swanson and I dug out "Jingle Bells" and played it. It went over big and everyone had a good time.

Everyone is getting a good sun tan — after hours we all strip down and climb into shorts and lay out on the deck — would never know there was grim business ahead from the horse play that goes on. As I've often said, I'm with the grandest group of fellows and sure am thankful I'm with them during this party. We're on our toes but we still have time to frog around. We all have semi-boot hair cuts, wear no ties and would be wearing shorts if it wasn't for the danger of blast burns.

Night before last could hardly stay in my bunk and I was all banged up and pooped out the next morning. Didn't say anything until everyone was showing their bruises so I displayed mine. The bunks are narrow and when we'd roll, I'd bang against the bulkhead with my elbow and knees. I finally stuffed my blankets along the ledge and thus I remained intact. Just discovered today there are dashboards or side boards that pull up to help hold you in-situ. Also by sleeping on one's stomach one is more apt to stay put. Maybe I'll be cured of snoring by the time I get home.

My domino partner says Wrigley [*the code for Guam*] may be next host after Toby.

May get you a plane or sub in few hours.

All my love,
Paul

30 Jan. 1944

Hello Honey —

"Just before the Battle, Dotty B, I am thinking most of Thee" —

Darling, the long awaited time is just about here. We had breakfast at 0315 and right after we went to G.Q. to wait for the big blow off. Half hour before dawn we start bombarding — almost that time now, so if I sign off abruptly it won't mean anything has happened to us just that there is too much going on — the number of shells and the rate of fire is terrific so with the jarring and din it will be impossible to do anything but hang on.

Apparently it's just another day — no fuss or muss other than all available space is filled with live ammunition all set to go. Outside my door it's piled high, only a small runway open to my battle locker, operating table & sterilizer remains open.

Hot! Jeepers! Not a dry stitch on us and it's still dark outside.

Had fun listening to the radio yesterday. Some of the atolls were being hammered and we could hear the spotter call the shots — went something like this — "down a hair, over a hair, up five — boy! oh boy! a beauty — get a cigar for that one — now let's get that block house — up a hair — over a hair — Oh Baby! — new target — let's get this one now" and so on. Like listening to a prize fight — he's up! he's down!

Sh!! We're less than five miles off the island so will sneak top side and see what gives it when day light comes.

Had fun playing bridge last night. Hahn (chief aviator), Al Williams, Trammel Smith and I played a wicked few rubbers. Hahn and I whipped the pants off Williams and Smithy. It's to be continued tonight — this is if Hahn gets back. He takes off at 0615 to spot for us — kind of ticklish job but good. He's a lot of fun and it's a riot to hear him describe — "Hahn comes in at the terrific speed of 75 knots, unloads his one 100-pound bomb and races for the clouds at 120 knots — the enemy Zeros never had a chance."

Everyone sure has a bad case of nerves — Tiger Wallace, one of the chiefs & myself are the only ones awake in this space — the rest are all sound asleep on the deck or standing in a corner — know what they mean when they say a sailor can sleep anywhere. Call just came thru — "Fresh water will be cut in for fifteen minutes" so I'd better get mine — may be the last for some time — zero hour is at hand so here we go kids — hold your hats — all my love to you, honey — don't worry about me, am having fun and thinking about you.

More love,
Paul

31 Jan. 1944

Hello Darling,

Your boy friend is now a veteran of one engagement and still hale and hearty. It's quite a deal — not my being hale and hearty — but war. Nothing nice about it all, it's a bloody mess.

Lou is still the Lucky Lady — shells whizzed over and around us — the nearest was ten yards and the runner-up twenty yards short, but, as they say in the "awl country", a miss is as good as a mile.

We're in g.q. again this a.m. and number two will get underway in just a little while — have two more and then the scene changes. Where to I don't know, but it's all the same.

One of our group took a shell — killed six including the captain and wounded nineteen. They transferred the more seriously wounded to our ship and Johnson and I had a field day. Never worked so hard in all my life. Missed noon chow and sure was hungry and pooped when we finished just before evening chow and g.q. All patients are fine this morning and yesterday's little deal was worth a million to me. Always wondered what my reaction would be in a wholesale bloody mess but there's nothing to it but pitch in and work like hell with what little common sense you might have.

The wounded sure were swell — nary a whimper out of any of them. All they had was morphine. Shrapnel has no conscience at all for it sure raised hell with them. Fingers & toes shot off — rather torn off — deep penetrating wounds — some thru and thru. No fractured jaws, but one had a hole torn thru his cheek, took out four teeth, burrowed thru his tongue and then out into the great open spaces. the worst or nastiest case I believe, was the kid that was all shot to hell but one piece of shell had the audacity to penetrate his rectum, rupture his urethra and then lodge against the pubic bone.

Barber didn't do a damn thing, goody, so Johnson and I did it all — gained a lot of experience — even gave plasma, my first and unaided too. By the way, "no eyes on cheek" as yet.

Honey — the word was just passed that fresh water will be turned on for 15 minutes. That's our cue to get our last drink before we go into action so here goes. I love you good and am impatiently waiting for mail. It's more important than boom-boom.

All My Love To You, Luddle Wan,
Paul

2 Feb. 1944

Hello My Sweet —

Lou got "hurted" but she's still lucky.

Monday started off with a "Bang" — we started firing from about 14,000 yards and then moved in to within a couple hundred yards of the island. Could see the coconut trees, buildings, pill boxes, etc., just as plain — the island's only about 1400 by 1100 yards and with several ships firing on it continuously for 72 hours you wouldn't think there could be a survivor on it but the little bastards were dug in so deep, they were still alive to come out and meet the landing force!

Am getting ahead of my story so will go back to Monday's party. Well, we banged away and banged away all kinds of explosions rent the air — smoke and flame would rise thousands of feet in the air — planes crashing — ammunition dumps exploding. It was beautiful — we started the best one — blew it up early Monday a.m. and it burned, and I do mean burned, until this a.m. Must have been one of their main fuel supplies. Monday was a day of methodical bombarding and was fun but yesterday (Tuesday) was the all high.

Remember it had been bombarded 48 hours straight and the island was nothing but flame and smoke — thought it was all cleaned out, but No! Thought I had seen explosions and heard noise but WOW! The U.S.S. "- - - -" scored on a target that must have been pure nitro or at least gun powder but a sheet of flame and smoke shot miles into the air — according to our fliers, they were plenty high and away off to the side but they were showered by dirt and had to dodge coconut trees as they went by. We could see the debris flying from where we were and felt the concussion. The fliers said it went clean thru the island — all that remains in that area is a huge crater filled with water.

Dive bombers are fun to watch. They come straight down, but fast, drop their load and away they go. Mighty pretty and effective — it's a sight to watch them in the evening when they return to their carriers. The sky is beautiful — sunset — clouds — tropical evening — the planes are in formation and then they circle and one by one set down. We have lost very, very few planes and those not by enemy gun fire. It was due to the violent explosions and they would get tossed together or torn apart.

We were awful close to the islands yesterday — even I could have "swimmed" it — at times we were dead in the water — just sitting and firing to beat the hell and watching shells drop all around us — it was fun until one hit us — but that comes later, Tee! Hee!

All ships intensified their fire and made ready for the landing parties and it was mighty spectacular. We ceased fire and watched them storm the beach and believe it or not — there were Japs there to meet them! After 72 hours of concentrated fire, the "- - - -"s were still alive! They dig in deep and set thru all we have and when we're sure they are all blown to hell and start to land — out they come. They're plenty tricky. They have a cute trick — when a shell hits, they set off a smoke pot so we think we blew the target up and move to another and they thumb their nose at us. Their barracks, caches, etc., are buried yards under the ground and are reinforced by concrete and steel and withstand a terrific bombardment. The fliers observed as many as five direct hits by our largest shells before they hit pay dirt — each hit would cause a crater, each one a little deeper until the target was exposed and then let go blam! The pill boxes are so constructed that the shells glance off without damage — Hahn saw a shell go in the door and about twenty Japs came out in a hurry. He and Trinkle have killed several hundred Japs themselves. They fly over the trenches at about fifty feet and machine gun hell out of them. Trinkle came in last night with his wings and gas tank full of holes but it managed for about 300 yellow bellies on that foray.

Gosh! I'm getting wet — the sea is coming in my port but it's cool. In just a little while we are going to steam into the lagoon — a bloody battle is raging and I think they are expecting submarines to come in so we want to get there first in order to keep them out and prevent help reaching the Japs. Supposed to be around 30 lurking in these waters so we may have an interesting night — we're spending the night there so we all have our fingers crossed.

Saw by the Louisville's paper (we have our own News Digest) that this battle of the Marshall Islands has been made public — supposed to be the store house for the Japs Mid Pacific forces — dozens of islands but the ones we were in were the main supply and air field — lots of fun. Must close and get my ringside seat — no dentistry these days — all my love, honey. Will give you more dope tomorrow.

Paul

BOMBARDMENT, followed by 4th Marine Division landings, secured the small, connected islands of Roi and Namur by Wednesday evening, February 2. Historian Samuel Eliot Morison characterized the once lush islands as "a stinking mess of debris and dead Japanese."

3 Feb. 1944

My Honey —

It's hot — we're setting out here like ducks on a pond — if you're topside and in the breeze, it's nice but down below it is quite tepid.

Had fun yesterday — no firing by us or our group. We steamed into the lagoon in the midst of all these islands or atolls. I spent most of my time in the fire control tower looking thru binoculars and watching the Marines on the islands — they were having a big time and they sure are black from the sun. Most of them were swimming or just messing around but some were busy taking two islands. They were really busy and interesting to watch — gunfire wasn't very heavy but it kept up until quite late at night. It's too quiet — something has to happen and soon. The Japs can't afford to lose an important group of islands as they apparently did without some sort of reprisal. Got a good look at the air field and it's huge — all shot to hell but the seabees will have it in shape before long.

It's beautiful out here. The islands are dense with coconut trees and undergrowth. Even have buzzards for you can see them circling around over the smaller islands that have been taken and secured. Wonder how they like Jap meat?

There's just a narrow channel for us to pass thru — numerous reefs and sand bars that cause the water to take on all colors — has green-yellow-violet and various shades of blue. Velly pletty.

Had the fun of waiting for enemy aircraft — alarm sounded they were sighted but [*none came to*] get us. Submarines contacted within seven miles but so far haven't bothered us. Must finish in a hurry — the censors have assembled so that means mail is going out and I want this to go.

We did get hit Tuesday about eleven o'clock back on the starboard side in Johnson's dressing station. Have a twelve-foot dent and twenty holes in the bulkhead and deck. Three got slightly injured — one pharmacist mate had the back of his chair shot off — two large holes in the chair seat and all he got was a small hole thru his ear and a shrapnel burn on his hip. I was topside talking to the gunner when it hit — we were watching the shells drop all around us when blam one got us. Sure staggered the ship but Lou is still lucky. We sailed along with a ten-degree list — something like a dog running on three legs — to keep water out and we're making temporary repairs. Wonder it didn't kill Johnson and his gang — exploded within two feet of them. I'm still not scared and am having fun and looking for mail from you.

All my love,
Paul

THE "HIT" DESCRIBED ABOVE was an eight-inch shell fired by another heavy cruiser, the USS *Indianapolis,* that ricocheted off the island into the *Louisville.*

In the following letter, "Clapper" refers to Scripps-Howard war correspondent Raymond Clapper. He died when the Navy plane in which he was riding collided with another aircraft as it was returning to its carrier.

The foc'sle, or forecastle, became one of Paul's favorite spots on the ship for "bull slinging" and "spectating." It is the forward area of the main deck — or, as Paul later described it, "the very tip of the ship where the anchors are."

4 Feb. 1944

Hello Honey,

We're sure leading a quiet and peaceful life these days — movies in the afternoon and evenings — bridge, dominoes or cribbage and a "soda" after the show. We're not careless by any means — we are on the alert and the guns are manned at all times by the watch but the remainder are relaxing.

I have my dental schedule down pat now — I fill and extract all morning and my corpsman cleans teeth all afternoon. That gives me my afternoons to mess around and at the same time we're keeping the chair hot and turning out a lot of work.

Some of the fellows got to go over on the island today and they said it was terrible. Bodies and parts of bodies strewn all over the place and hardly a square yard that wasn't pitted by shells. The stink was awful and several got sick. Most were killed by the bombardment. There's hardly a branch left on the trees but there still are Jap snipers — they're in the sewers and drains doing their dirty work.

Thought the fire we set last Monday had burned out but it's still going strong. It's so hot they can't get near it — it's coming from some sort of concrete structure and was an oil storage.

Still can't figure out why the Japs haven't sent planes or ships after us — maybe they think they'll lull us into a sense of security and then jump us — it isn't quite full moon yet so there still is plenty of time.

Too bad about Clapper wasn't it? It happened out there in this gang — we have quite a few big shots with us.

Trinkle [*flier*] has been recommended for the air medal for his strafing and killing all those Japs.

Good night, Sweet Heart,

All my love,
Paul

9 Feb. 1944

Hello Honey —

Dentistry has picked up — did a little orthodontia but they were mostly laterals involved. Have a number of impacted third molars scheduled, some are going to be meaner than any I have ever had and probably hope to have due to the bony structure around them. That's one thing in the Navy, you see all kinds of teeth.

Well, Honey — are you still with me — all hundred & twenty-eight pounds of loveliness? Sure would like to see you and make your ribs crackle.

Feel like filling some teeth so will go to work.

All my love, darling
Paul

10 Feb. 1944

Hello My Pet —

Have seen three good shows in a row. At least they are good out here aboard ship. Saw "Kid Glove Killer", "All By Myself", and "Sunday Punch". Last night was "All By Myself" and it sure left a good taste. In addition to the feature they had a community sing affair — you know, one of those deals where they show the words on the screen and everyone sings. One of the songs was "When The Lights Go On Again" — some parts everyone sings — then just the girls and then the boys, they again all join in. It was so darn funny when "just the girls" part came in, without a hitch everyone sang falsetto and it was a riot. Sure a bunch of screw balls.

Had a new thrill the other night — we took a several hundred mile jaunt unescorted [*to Majuro*] and in enemy waters and at a favorite Jap time for dirty work. We're standing by now for anything to happen as word has been passed that "enemy surface force" has been contacted. It's thrilling and if you knew the set up you'd be thrilled too.

Went fishing off the fan tail — saw a lot of fish, sharks to jelly fish, but didn't get a nibble. Fishing in 90 fathoms of water is slightly over my head. Comdr. Swain caught a beautiful something and had it for breakfast. As of now he hasn't food poisoning so I guess it was edible, digestible and compatible.

Love you and miss you
Paul

12 Feb. 1944

Hello Darling —

Nothing new has happened. We're just enjoying life — such as it is without mail. We haven't had any since we left the States, month tomorrow. The Admiral & Captain are sore about it so they sent out dispatches today to find out why in hell we haven't [*gotten*] any. Isn't fair — that's for sure.

Have been reading quite a bit — just finished "Reprisal" by Ethal Vance and have started "Adventures All" by John Buchan. It promises to be quite good.

Honey, must climb in and close one eye — traipsing around at 0200 in one's pajamas "ain't" becoming to an officer and I don't want it to happen again tonight.

Night, Honey
Paul

13 Feb. 1944

Darling —

Today we had the prettiest and most welcome of all bugle calls — Mail

Call! Tra la la la! Golly! What a thrill! — they brought up a batch of officers mail — was worse than bank night with a $1,000 prize. But — no mail for little Paulie — sob, sob. The next batch came up — Bonnette scored twice (thrill, thrill), 3rd batch and I scored four times (pinch, pinch), 4th batch, scored one (whoops) and the fifth batch brought me three more (tra la la).

Gee, Honey your letters were swell.

Will have my advance sea pay paid up shortly and then I'll send you some money to pay up my bills. I haven't had more than a couple of dollars since you left but I haven't needed it. Cigarettes, cokes, laundry, etc., runs about ten bucks a month — I bought 1/2 dozen shirts, underwear and K pants which has kept me broke but there's no place to go so I'm alright. The $25 you sent me will come in handy for more K pants and a wind break if & when I get to P.H. I now have four pairs of pants and in this weather you need a change every day. Thanks a lot.

Comdr. Towner (boo hoo) got his orders today — reports to "Hotel [*Bellevue*]" when relieved for further orders.

Can't think what I wrote to Ma to mystify her other than "when I was a kid I wanted to go to sea and finally got there." I have written her about airmail and will send her some stamps. V-mail is so unsatisfactory.

Honey, did enjoy hearing from you so much — I do love you, more than you'll ever know and when this is all over with - - - - - - - -.

All my love,
Paul

V-MAIL MAY HAVE BEEN "so unsatisfactory" to Paul, but it was widely used.

World War II produced vast amounts of mail flowing to and from millions of American servicemen and women around the world. According to a Post Office Department advisory of June 13, 1942, V-Mail was being established "to facilitate the transmission of letters . . . and reduce the weight and space of mail. . . ."

The basic procedure was for V-Mail letters to be written on special forms and mailed in special envelopes. At a central point they would be opened, censored, reduced to microfilm, then transported as reels of film. Near final destination photographic enlargements were made from the film and printed on continuous strips of sensitized paper. The paper strips were then cut into individual letters. These reproductions of the original letters were folded, inserted into uniform window envelopes and sent to their final destinations.

As might be suspected, the name "V-Mail" stood for "Victory Mail." A hyphen was commonly used between V and Mail but the official name used the Morse Code for V — three dots and a dash.

By February 1944, the U.S. Army Signal Corps and Post Office were handling 25,000,000 V-Mail letters each month.

17 Feb. 1944

Hello Darling —

Pretty soon it gives "ding, ding, ding, ding" and we are off in a cloud of cordite and another "star in our bar" — I don't mean crown or Curley's Bar, but a campaign bar.

Had a delicious breakfast and our chow last night was superb — they always put the frills on before we go into action — the mess caterer must have a conscience.

You wouldn't know we were playing "marbles for keeps" by the discussion at the breakfast table (whoops! there goes the alarm and the "patter of little feet" fills the air.) Anyhow, the discussion was conscription of labor and unions — Barber takes an awful beating at all meals — Towner always eggs him on with some sort of outlandish statement and Barber always takes the bait — never a dull moment.

It's been awfully quiet lately — maybe the calm before the storm, who knows. We've been left strictly alone by the - - - - and they sure won't leave us alone for ever. They can't afford to.

All My Love,
Paul

19 Feb. 1944

Hello My Honey —

Feel so smart and clean, had one of the mess boys scrub and clean my room — it sure needed it. My room used to be the poker players room and last week when we were laying it, they had several afternoons of games. That messed it up and then several days of firing finished it.

Don't know where all the dirt comes from. It sure isn't dusty out there, but everything gets covered with chipped paint, powder smoke, broken glass, etc. Sure would hate to be the electrician or pipefitter aboard ship — light fixtures and water lines are always jarring loose.

No — I don't play poker and don't intend to. Smith lost $125 one afternoon — he claims to be a gambler but I guess he gambles like he drinks, not very "gracefully".

[*Peabo*] and I were up in the main battery director this afternoon watching the Marines take another island — sure busy people & were doing all right. The glass up there has 17 magnification so we were actually riding in the landing barges — that is, seems so.

Saw the most gorgeous sunset Thursday night I have ever seen. Made me kind of ache it was so pretty. Maybe why it struck me was the fact we had been bombarding all day, killing people and destroying property and at the close of day the scene was so peaceful. Can't give the details or background but you've seen birds come in to roost no doubt — silhouettes on deep blue water and a golden sunset — just enough clouds to break up the rays into something that I sure can't describe — it was breathtakingly beautiful.

All my love, leedle wan,
Paul

20 Feb. 1944

Hello Darling —

Last week we had a visiting chaplain — a Lt. Shears from the U.S.S. - - - -, a Marine transport. He was a nice looking chap — [*curly*] haired, tanned and dressed in khaki clothes, no tie and a pair of "dainty" unfinished high top horse hide shoes. He brought a band of seven Marines and a soloist with him — they too were dressed in their fighting clothes, complete with camouflaged helmets, life belts, etc. Their instrument cases were so battered and the instruments themselves were beat up but boy howdy, they produced swell music. Everyone sang "out loud" because it didn't matter if you weren't on the beam — the band helped you out and forgave you. The chaplain delivered a hell of a good sermon and it seemed more like should be out here — the soloist had a swell tenor voice, and all in all everyone said it was swell.

After the services we gave them all the ice cream they could eat and the party was a grand success.

You remember what the port [*hangar*] looks like, don't you? [*That*] is where we have divine services, picture shows, etc. For services, the bulkheads are draped with flags, an altar set up and of course backed by the American flag. What attempt there is to hide the implements of war, sure isn't adequate for you still have bombs, propellers, spare wings, etc., staring you in the eye. Can still see those poor Marines, still wet from their trip over (rough sea) and really giving forth. Everything is serious and I honestly believe one really gets something out of it. Just a few days before, the lagoon was a Jap stronghold and then there we were — big as life and twice as natural, holding church services without a qualm. These American kids really are something and I'm proud to be one of them — but older.

From last Sunday to today — what a change! The Marine party of last week, safe and secure on Lou — today they are fighting for all they are worth several hundred miles away but just a mile or so from us, if you follow me. We're again sitting in a lagoon but there is a constant bombardment going on. It's our turn now and we're pouring it on — it's been going on night and day — the night show is beautiful — again words fail me and I can't describe it. You've seen state fair exhibitions so you have an idea.

It's more like an [*airdrome*] theater — news reels only — we sun [*bathe*] out on the foc'sle — play cribbage — drink cokes and watch the show. It's a funny war so far — more like a rehearsal than the real McCoy. So far it's been smooth sailing but it won't keep up.

All my love,
Paul

23 Feb. 1944

Hello My Pet —

Everyone is pooped out today. Lot of razzing about "operational fatigue". This last operation started last Thursday and the island was secured last night. Still some fighting going on but mostly machine guns and mortars. The big guns are quiet and it seems funny to have it so still and calm.

Yesterday was the all high to date — saw war in all its mercilessness and ruthlessness. Saw planes explode in air & plunge into the water, ships get shelled by big guns — tanks crawling along and firing — men falling, etc — it really was something. Wonder what the sons of the rising sun think now.

Yesterday morning the first shell hit just as the sun peeked over the island. Really was beautiful, but that was the signal for hell to cut loose.

Honey it was the most awesome thing I have ever witnessed — you had to see it to believe it. We were in close enough that we all were black with powder smoke, fire smoke and dirt from the island — it was terrible. It kept up a solid three hours and then the Marines went in — watched them thru glasses. By rights there shouldn't have been a soul left alive after the pounding they were given, but the s of bs were there to meet the landing force! They are dug in so deep and cleverly — they can take all we give them and stand up under it. Don't broadcast what I saw, someone might jump on us. The fox holes are all buried deep, just a small dome shows above ground — everything has connecting tunnels and outlets so they just move around to keep out of the way. But there wasn't a square yard of ground that wasn't blasted. How they can take it I sure don't know. They must be doped up.

The exploding bombs and shells jarred the ship all to hell and we could feel the concussion on our faces and [*it*] would even beat or whip our clothes against us. We were less than a mile out but that is far enough to lessen the shock a lot and to think having them pop right in your lap. After the landing we had to bombard again but now all that is going on is rousting out the remaining Japs and killing them. They stick a flame thrower in one opening — fire and smoke comes out at varying distances thru hidden outlets. Takes hand grenades and smoke to finally run them out. As far as I can learn only one prisoner was taken and he swam out to one of our ships thru shark infested waters.

We had been watching the tip of the island thru glasses — at first there were six Japs trying to hide. A few bursts of shell fire and then there were only three left. We watched them several hours and they finally dug into the sand and remained so until too dark to see any longer. One of the three reached our ship (not the Lou) but don't know what happened to the other two — whether they were shot, drowned or the sharks got them. Felt sorry for them — you could see them just as plain — ducking in and out of bushes, behind coconut trees, etc. Was a losing game for them. If we'd have been three weeks later getting here we never could have gotten them out. That is dope taken from the captured plans and documents. If it's this tough here — what will it be like when we really crowd them and step on their toes?

It will be many moons before this little deal is over — take it from me.

All my love,
Paul

27 Feb. 1944

Hello Darling —

All is quiet — once in a while at night you can hear a shot and a Marine bites the "dust". There still are snipers around. Where they hang out is a mystery, but it isn't safe to be out by yourself at night.

Had the misfortune of having my varsity glasses fall apart — the frame broke at the nose piece so Murphy sent them to his wife in Honolulu to be fixed. Thought it quicker than sending them clear to the States. [*Paul often used the word "varsity" to indicate something was "first team" or "the best."*]

Have been real busy — keep my mornings filled. This morning I did nothing but extract teeth and had some dandies. Missed church as a result. I was wringing wet and couldn't get cooled off by the time church call sounded.

Standing in like this, I get a lot of business from smaller ships — the enclosed 50-yen piece and beer label were given to me by one of the fellows — taken off a dead Jap and the label was picked up in a pill box.

Dr. Barber got to go ashore the other day, brought back a few stinking souvenirs. The Japs had been dead over five days and the weather down here isn't conducive to the preservation of dead bodies. The Marines get all the good trophies such as rifles, glasses, knives, etc.

We've been expecting mail every day now but no good yet. We are the mail boat for the Marines, soldiers and other ships here. Got 6500 lbs of mail and not a speck for ourselves. The Admiral sent out a message yesterday as to why in hell the Louisville's mail isn't sent up so we may get some tomorrow.

Peterson just came in and left — just got back from one of the islands — no souvenirs other than a song book, writing pad & account book. Said lots of dead Japs & flies — terrible stink. Should be my turn to go ashore after the next engagement — they say once is enough, but I won't be satisfied until I go at least that — once.

Love you good, Honey,
Paul

29 Feb. 1944

Hello My Honey —

No mail and everybody is getting pretty "miffed" about it. The soldiers & Marines all have theirs, but the war ships have been passed up. Everything is so secretive even the P.O. doesn't know where we are — hell to be lost that way.

Being Grand Central Station is quite interesting — sure see a lot of soldiers, Marines, war correspondents and Navy personnel. They are transient on their way to various stations and were dropped off here by plane or boat — no, no trains or stage coaches. They sure look beat up, so dirty and pooped out — sure glad I'm a Naval officer and on good old Lou. We furnish food, baths, and bed — should see their eyes bug out when they see our chow — the poor devils have been on rations for weeks and even months. They go nuts when they find they can have coca colas and ice cream. Never realized what a morale builder they are. They have interesting tales to tell (not the cokes). Hope I can remember some of them.

There still are snipers about — few of our boys knocked off every night. Two Jap medicos were captured last night — sh-sh! There is an epidemic of typhus fever on one of the islands [*that*] had caused a lot of Jap deaths.

Several Jap women and native women were found killed on the islands — they were in fox holes and pill boxes with the soldiers.

You should see the flies out here — those pretty black ones — they're so fat from feeding on Japs they don't even fly when you shoo them. Must be terrible on the island — they are quite plentiful on board so you can imagine what gives it on the beach. They're just about thru burying Japs now — they dig a deep hole with their bulldozers and dump the bodies in — some fun, eh?

Sure different out here the way military personnel look than in the States. There they all look romantic — spic and span — here, wow! See all kinds — some of the most fantastic whisker dos — hair, etc. — some haven't had hair cuts in months and shaves I figger are unheard of — quite a contrast on Lou. We all keep our hair trimmed, freshly shaven and bathed and at evening chow all put on clean uniforms — movies, good food & a sody fountain.

All My Love,
Paul

1 March 1944

Hello Darling —

This afternoon we are having holiday routine (a la peacetime) — some are swimming, some playing deck tennis — others volley ball — I chose to drop you a small note.

Had an interesting morning, went ashore! Brown, Grubb, Johnson and myself were allowed to go to the last bombarded island [*Parry Island*] — Brown on business — the rest of us, morbid public. It was interesting but what a mess — no dead bodies laying around, but flies! Millions of them and awfully tenacious. We all piled under the shower and really scrubbed, shampoo on down. The only souvenirs we got were Japanese medicines, charts, [*restraining*] straps and a dinner bucket (don't think I'll use the bucket for grub.) Was offered a Jap flag, but there was a catch to it — all he wanted was a hundred dollars for it. He kept it.

The sand is a foot deep — everything pulverized from shelling. The ground is literally strewn with coconuts — and the poor trees, they're all shot to hell. In places the stink is terrible from bodies in fox holes that haven't been dug out yet. There isn't a building of any kind left — all blasted in a million pieces & flush with the ground — hardly a yard without a bomb or shell crater.

The soldiers, Marines and seabees sure look like hell — dirty and all cloaked with flies. Some running around naked, others in trunks and some fully dressed. The medical department is pitiful — no facilities whatever. The severely wounded were placed on a hospital ship immediately — it now has pulled out so new casualties are left up to them and our ship. Still have Japs left and each day they get a few of our boys. This morning just before we got there, a Jap [*committed*] suicide in sight of the so called hospital — they are afraid to surrender, fear torture at our hands.

The favorite pastime seems to be digging up fox holes looking for bodies and souvenirs — flies and stink — wow! Watched them dig one — found a beautiful silk robe of some kind but it was stained, badly shot up and [*odoriferous*] — left it. Lots of grenades and duds lying around. Time was short so we keep pretty well to the beaten path. Were in a jeep and those boogers really are rough rides. Don't feel as tho' I'll ever get clean again, and again I say, I'm glad I'm in the Navy — the lowest seaman is better than being on one of these invaded islands — awful.

All my love,
Paul

3 March 1944

Hello Darling —

Murphy, Yeager and I hitchhiked over to another one of the recently acquired islands.

Hitchhiking in the mid Pacific is something new in my life, but good. We made the island okay — didn't know where to start so we walked clear to one end, sand and dust up to our knees, sweat pouring off us and flies so thick they actually aided us in walking by lifting us. Had fun climbing thru craters, under brush etc., and finally reached the tip. There we saw one of the prettiest little scenes — a small island as green as could be, beautiful beach surrounded by multi-colored water and in the center was our flag and surrounded by our implements. Always get a kick out of seeing our flag run up over enemy territory — guess it's one of those unexplainable things that happens to a fellow.

We explored that end of the island, examined different corals, shell, etc., and worked our way towards the other end where the worst resistance was met by our landing forces and where the native village used to be.

It was a long ways up there so we bummed a ride in a jeep and made it swell. It turned out the jeep stayed with us all afternoon and we really got around. We had one interesting experience — the damn jeep went every place and away back in the wilds we ran across two Jap tanks that had been shelled and burned. Murphy and I crawled into one and found two helmets — we stirred around a little more and, what you know, Joe, there were the Japs — nicely barbecued!

My pen pooped out so I will to — be continued. Did the boys get back to the ship? Read next week's chapter.

All My Love,
Paul

Chapter 2

Jammed a Paint Brush Down My Throat

THE *LOUISVILLE* LEFT ENIWETOK on March 5 angling southwest across the Marshalls to spend two weeks in the large lagoon of Majuro Atoll.

Scores of tiny islands form the lagoon that stretches over 20 miles long and 5 miles wide. Undefended by the Japanese, Majuro had been quickly occupied by U.S. forces on January 31.

In 1889, Robert Louis Stevenson dubbed Majuro the "Pearl of the Pacific." Some 55 years later Samuel Eliot Morison described it as "a paradise for American soldiers and sailors."

On March 22, the *Louisville* packed up and joined Task Force 58, a fast carrier group heading west to raid the Palau Islands (the actual invasion of the Palaus would not come until September).

En route the force dipped south, prompting the traditional initiation ceremonies for those crossing the equator for the first time. Paul had difficulty spelling "shillelagh" as he described his transition from "polly wog" to "shell back," but he never forgot the clubbing he received that left him with permanent lower back problems.

General Douglas MacArthur's strategy was to leapfrog along New Guinea's north coast, bypassing, isolating, and therefore neutralizing entrenched enemy strongholds. One surprise invasion came at the old colonial seaport of Hollandia. Five Japanese airfields clustered in the area were so pulverized by massive carrier-based air strikes that there was little air resistance for the April 22 invasion. The airfields were secured by May 3 with a loss of only 152 American lives. The *Louisville* was on hand to support the landings and, with no enemy fliers to meet them, Paul reported that D-day at Hollandia was "more like a pleasure cruise."

Returning to Majuro, the task force paused in the Caroline Islands for raids on Truk (April 29) and Satawan (April 30).

The *Louisville* returned to Majuro on May 4 to spend over a month in the busy, peaceful lagoon before again sailing west, this time to the carnage of the Mariana Islands.

5 March 1944

Hello My Sweet —

Goody! We're on our way again — hoisted anchor at 1440 today and are now zig-zagging our way to a rendezvous. There is some excitement in the air — contacted an enemy sub and the U.S.S. - - - -s are dropping depth charges.

Have seen a lot of good shows — enjoyed today's "Juke Box Genny" — they try to show light & airy pictures, I guess for morale's sake. Everyone perks up when we get underway and especially leaving the flies behind. They drive you nuts.

The old ship is really rocking & rolling. We're pretty light — low on ammunition and provisions so we're really reeling. We had rain, wind and huge white caps — waves would break over the deck and wash it clean.

Wish I knew where we will wind up. What news do you hear over the radio — do you know where we are?

Don't forget to keep loving me, honey — I miss you so much.

All My Love,
Paul

6 March 1944

Hello Darling —

Had general quarters this morning but nothing happened — more sub contacts have been made and charges fired but no results as yet. Kind of like g.q. — we get up early and get to see the sun rise — it's beautiful. Tonight we have a peculiar sky — we're heading into a storm, it's raining now. The western horizon looked like a huge forest fire, even to the black pall of smoke over it.

Had a tetanus shot today — arm sore as hell but I'll survive. They moved the time up on us, we're heading for some new battles and they want to be sure our anti-tetanus is working — good idea.

Cleaned Cmdr. Towners's teeth today — he's just like a kid. I did a good job on him and tonight when he came in for chow everyone he'd come to, he'd stick his teeth out at them. He is so tanned, his pearly whites really loom out. I plan on polishing all officers teeth before we hit P.H. (if and when). Everyone is so tan, I think they will look quite stylish.

Thought I was in dutch when I returned from the island the other day. Bowers jumped all over me, said I was a disgrace to the Louisville etc., etc. Had me scared, didn't know what possibly could have happened, so I just passed it off. Finally at dinner it came out — I had refused a drink of bourbon whiskey while on the island. Murphy had told him how the medic had broken out a bottle of Old Hermitage & I turned it down. Guess it takes a global war to straighten me out.

Good night, honey & think about me real often.

All My Love,
Paul

9 March 1944

Hello My Darling —

If and when I get to P.H. I'll do my best to get you some hose (size 9?) — I'll have Murphy ask his wife and have her send you some.

Comdr. Towner left today — kind of sad — everyone (enlisted too) was topside to see him off — gave him three big cheers and bye bye. He had tears in his eyes, hated to leave but he was headed up the ladder.

Had a beautiful experience this p.m. — flew all afternoon — honey, it was a regular fairy land. At first we practiced dive bombing & strafing, then sight seeing. We went up above the clouds and then dived in and out of them. It was the most gorgeous sight I have ever seen. The atoll with the numerous small islands — the different colored waters — coral heads, etc. The clouds were like spun sugar — whipped cream — cotton — blue sky — blue, green, yellow and white water and even a rainbow thrown in. Ran into a tropical squall and that caused various color schemes too. Went low over the main native village — lots of cute thatched roof houses — canoes etc. A relief to see beautiful coconut trees, green under growth — birds flying, etc — instead of shell craters and blasted trees. War "ain't" pretty, honey.

All My Love,
Paul

10 March 1944

Hello Little Girl —

Visited a hospital ship the other day. What a relief to be on a combat ship. I met the dentists — they have four of them and they do operative dentistry, prosthetics and some surgery. Had a nice talk with the senior dentist — he is a full commander and a surgery specialist — was glad to learn my theories of treatments and surgery were the same as his. Life is sort of hum drum with them — no excitement and the ship usually sits around.

The Padre is flying this afternoon — he is scared but when I raved how beautiful it was he went up. It won't be as pretty, not enough clouds but the islands and water will be pretty.

The planes are diving on us so must go out and see the Padre land — may have to change him for the planes come down awful close.

All My Love Honey,
Paul

12 March 1944

Hello My Sweet —

Am too excited and my mind is going around in circles — I got mail today!

Gee, Honey — I did so enjoy all your letters. I want to read them a few more times and then I'll do my comments. I'm pooped tonight. I was elected to go along on a liberty party to a couple of islands — six officers and about a hundred men. I didn't much want to go but felt I should as they had asked for me. Had my day all planned, had a beautiful morning of nothing but extractions, was wringing wet when I finished so I bathed, shampooed my hair and put on a clean uniform. Was going to write you a nice big juicy letter and take it easy the rest of the afternoon. But no — had to go [*picnicking*]! to be truthful, I did have fun — Yeager, Mills, the Padre and I stayed together and had a lot of fun. We all went over on a barge. I do believe a garbage barge because it was lightly odoriferous. The barge couldn't get up to the beach so we had to jump overboard and wade in — was fun.

The four of us walked around the entire island and then went interior. It was quite pretty — huge coconut trees and other trees we didn't recognize, bushes, etc. We climbed coconut trees, drank the milk and ate the nut. Didn't see any birds which was a disappointment.

It was a treat to be on an island that wasn't all battle scarred — shelling sure plays havoc. Gathered a lot of shells — chose small ones and will send them to you. Had a whole pocket full of them — when I got back to the ship and dumped them out, damned if there wasn't a live one! Thought I had felt something wriggle but thought it was sand or water — in true picnic fashion we had a terrific cloud burst and we were all soaked — but that is the tropics for you.

There were no native huts or inhabitants — that was another disappointment.

All My Love,
Paul

16 March 1944

Hello Darling —

Seventy-five bags of mail were just brought aboard — Oh Happy Day! Must be some for me. Must go and caress the bags with my eyes — will be some time before it's sorted. Sure has been a bottle neck somewhere.

Have had the Admiral in my power several times lately — first he dropped his uppers — then he broke his lowers so now he is having new ones made on the hospital ship. He's not a bad fellow, but couldn't pull, grind or scare a damn thing out of him as far as information is concerned. He doesn't know — probably here one day and gone the next — we stand in thirty minute notice.

All My Love,
Paul

17 March 1944

Hello My Sweet —

Our new Exec seems to be all right — more of a stickler for regulations — has been at the Academy so it makes a difference. I don't mind at all — in fact I'm glad. We are to have weekly inspections — just finished one and enjoyed it a lot. The ship is divided in zones and then inspecting parties are designated — I'm group three and we inspected Zone II B. — after engine room, evaporators, etc. I'd never been down there before and it was fun. Gives you a chance to see every part of the ship — it's amazing, the so-called bowels of a ship.

Soon will have completed 2 years of active duty — doesn't seem that long. Soon be a long three months you have been away — that's the only hard part of sea duty. Swell if it wasn't for that.

Love You Loads
Paul

19 March 1944

Hello Honey —

We're sitting on our fat fannies just marking time.

Had Captain's inspection yesterday on top of zone inspection the day before. Everything looked good — they really went over the dental office and the captain said it was "very good".

We're getting more regulation every day, but I don't mind — after all we are primarily a military organization so why not turn to and be one.

Didn't you say you saw "No Time For Love"? We sure got a bang out of it. You can tell the fellows have been out a long time — every time they show a girl's knee they go wild — nice girls better stay in when they do go ashore.

Can't make up my mind what to do this afternoon — there's a recreation party going out but don't think I'll go. We got in a bunch of magazines at Ship's Service and I laid in a supply so may read. Am reading "The Robe" — good isn't it? Have read a lot of books but still like my Westerns — Cosmo & American.

For lunch we are to have "curry" — can't stand the smell of it any more so I'm going to skip lunch even if we are having the Admiral & Captain as guests. Turkey tonight — it's good but we have it every Sunday. We still have the best steaks in the world — not one each for 60 cents but all we can eat for our $25 per.

All My Love,
Paul

20 March 1944

Hello Honey —

Have heard of running warm water into cavities while drilling — I always let saliva run in with about the same results. Kind of knocks "rubber damn to keep the field dry" exponents in the head. [*The use of "rubber dam to keep the field dry" is the common procedure in modern dentistry.*]

Have you put anything in the papers as yet? Don't know what to tell you other than I'm somewhere in the Pacific on a combat ship and having my share of excitement — everybody hale & hearty and morale is high — can't beat the spirit of Americans.

My dental appointments are getting ahead of me — lots of ticklish work. I'm going to work morning & evenings & let my corpsman work afternoons. Got hold of some penicillium and will try it on these next operations instead of sulfathiazole — really tuff ones coming up but I'm sure they'll turn out all right.

Take care of yourself, honey, and don't worry about me.

I Love You,
Paul

20 March 1944

Darling —

It's a pitch dark night only it isn't dark either — paradoxical statement — but it's true. The sky is so black and the water too, but there are a million and four stars out — little bitty ones and huge ones and so bright. I stood out on the foc'sle and just kind of took it all in — the stars seemed to reflect in the water. It's cool out and quite a breeze blowing that causes little white caps to come in — they are phosphorescent due to fungi and they sparkle like diamonds. As you look down over the side it's really beautiful — the breakers as they hit the side of the ship are broken up into thousands of spangles — all seem to be chasing each other. Silhouettes galore — all sizes and shapes — each showing one or two rubies — it's really a picture and don't believe I'll ever forget it.

Betcha this time next week I won't be sitting calmly by and writing you a letter — I'll sure be thinking of you though. I'm looking forward to the big deal but I'm going to have all my gear laid out so I can grab it in a hurry. Read up on my swimming and have plenty of "cotton" so I'm all set.

Well honey girl — am going topside & take another peep at my friends the stars and then climb into my little basket. Sleep tight little one — love you.

That's for sure
Paul

23 March 1944

Hello Honey Girl —

This letter may be awful short — "King Neptune" is holding court in the wardroom and us poor polly-wogs are in for a tuff time. It's been going on all day — tomorrow is the last of it — we'll be across then. College initiations were never like this — several in sick bay already. They took the "shalayes" away today because it got out of hand but tomorrow — wow! I won't have to comb my hair for a long time — got my preliminary haircut today and they didn't leave much — tomorrow I have to visit the Royal Barber and I'm afraid there won't be a mustache or hair left.

Just got back from trip #1 from the court — am accused of forgery — exhibit A was a Shell-Back certificate stating I crossed the equator in 1904 in the U.S.S. Never Sail — signed P.C. Bonnette Boilermaker 4/c — penalty, double dose.

They'll be here for me in a few minutes so must get set. All my love to you on your birthday — hope we will be together for all the remaining ones and lots of them.

Lot & Lots of Love
Paul (Polly Wog)

25 March 1944

Hello Honey —

Whew! I'm a full fledged Shell-Back now — my poor rear will remind me of it for some time to come. I'm going to have photostatic copies made of my card so I'll always have one handy.

It's a lot of fun but I'm glad it's over with — we're all pooped out —

general quarters at 0430 and then the initiation — we're all ready for our sacks, so this letter will be short again. Will tell you about it as I get over my aches & pains.

A few pictures were made, will send you some when they are ready. Would like one of my "hair do" — have an air strip down the center and two tufts (look like coconut trees) on each side at the rear. My knowledge bump is a series of beautiful terraces — very becoming. Monday will have my hair clipped but not shaved. From the looks of things we'll be out here a long time so it should be grown out by the time I see you again.

Crossed the line at 1355 today — announced it over the loud speaker but I couldn't see it — we had just rec'd a coat of grease & feathers so our vision was somewhat obscured.

Was looking thru a Feb. 15 Navy something and saw in the list of promotions from Lt. Cmdr. to Comdrs [*names deleted*] dates back to 1942. I'm very ill humored over it — why those S.B.s were relieved of their pants and damn near court martialed and still they get promoted. Beats hell, doesn't it. Nothing's been done about Lts. to Lt. Comdr as yet but expect it any day. If I don't get it — they can shove the whole business for all of me.

The time is all screwed up out here — we completely scratched Friday the 24th off — so today naturally is Sat. 25th. It's hotter than hell out here — must be a lake or something near here for it's a bit humid.

We're sitting on a keg of dynamite — contact subs regularly but so far, "knock knock", we zip a little and step on the gas. No one seems to be alarmed — have been ordered to have our life belts with us at all times and we do.

Everything seems so quiet & pretty but beauty is only skin deep I guess, even out here for below the surface there are some bad boys.

All My Love,
Paul (Shell-Back)

27 March 1944

Hello Darling —

How's my "one & only" tonight? Should say, "How are you last night or yesterday"?

Am suffering insult on injury these days. I have some heat rash on my "you know what" and it's so sore from the beating I got the other day I can't scratch it, so I ask you — what to do?

Had quite a day, general quarters most of the morning, movie at 1300, sun bathed an hour or so and then sat on the foc'sle the rest of the time — did take time out for dinner tho. It's only 97 degrees but there sure is a lot of heat in it. It was marvelous out on the deck however — ran into a lot of squalls and it was nice & cool. It rains so easily out here, no full nor muss, just upsy daisy, does its little job and it's over with. We sat outside until after dusk, the sky and water were so beautiful in an ominous way. Can't tell you where we are, but we're not in a bomb shelter, that's for sure!

Anything can happen any second — we have been sighted twice so they know we are around — they can't afford not to make some kind of pass at us — we're all hoping they do and soon. Everyone is in good spirits — can't get over what a swell bunch of fellows I'm with — they are 4.0.

Ran into a school of porpoises this evening about sun down. There were hundreds of them — quite a sight to see that large a number jumping out of the water. They swim and leap in formation and it's really something.

The water has been so calm — we all maintain the same speed and it appears we are standing still. At sun down it's especially pretty — "birds" coming home to roost — lost one tonight — saved two of the crew and one missing.

All My Love
Paul

28 March 1944

Hello Honey —

The air sure is charged, wouldn't be surprised if something let go between now & dark. Honey, something just has to. We're in their front yard, have made numerous contacts so it's just a question of hours.

It's really quite thrilling — much more so than here to fore — makes your nerves tingle and on the alert — wouldn't miss it for anything. Wouldn't be bad swimming today but I hope we don't have to.

All My Love,
Paul

29 March 1944

Hello Darling —

It's 0330 where you are and 2130 plus a day where I am — slightly different conditions too, I betcha. We're in general quarters and I do mean g.q. for sure — hell is being raised topside and we are zigging and zagging at a fast clip. It's dark as hell out, just came from topside but it's too hard to find your way around. I was glad to get back to my station. Lots of fireworks and several planes burning — may last all night. Hope they save some for day time so I can see. Our new exec is quite "regulation" and I'd hate to get lost and not be available in case he checked up on stations.

Last night was quiet — several contacts made & depth charges fired but we're getting used to them so it's a "quiet watch". Two large groups of enemy planes are over us now and it's quite exciting.

From the main deck to the horizon it is eight miles, so therefore we're sitting on a mirror 16 miles in diameter — no buildings to break the line so the sky makes a perfect dome — we have silhouettes but would be telling if I told you what they were. The clouds are slow and stacked on each other which accounts for the fantastic colors at sunset. Last night the gray, winter scene gave way to the most beautiful [*fiery*] one I've ever seen.

This water tight integrity is hard on bladders, etc. — had beans for breakfast and they are adding to my [*discomfiture*]. All water & ventilation is cut off so just have to sit tight.

It's sort of hard to write, we're "wiggling" so — think I'll take another gander topside & see what gives it.

All My Love,
Paul

31 March 1944

Hello Darling —

Started to write last night but it was so noisy and we were cutting capers in the water so I just didn't get the job done.

This afternoon [*Friday*] is the first time I've had my clothes off since

Tuesday night — took a little nap and then showered — now I feel like a "quarter" of a million dollars.

The days have been quite quiet in the immediate area — a few depth charges have to be set off but no planes bothered us. They were shot down before they reached us. At night is when we have our fun — they come in low and are on us before we can see them — of course we know about where they are due to our "instruments" so we're not caught napping. Beats any 4th of July you ever saw — sizes of guns blasting away and then watch the burning flame of the planes — they all seem to explode & then down they come — pretty awful to think about but they asked for it.

Our losses are very, very light. Saw a fatal crash this morning just off our port beam. Had been watching the planes take off — after a while I noticed one that seemed to be in trouble. He circled the carrier a few times and then unloaded his auxiliary gas tank — the carrier turned into the wind to receive him but as he came alongside preparatory to turn in — it dived straight into the sea and "busted" all to hell. A destroyer came alongside but didn't get him. The pathetic sight was to see his buddy in another plane, circling and diving over the spot to mark it — just like a papa bird.

Never a dull moment these days — love to watch the planes return at night — something fascinating about the way they circle & join up — then just like clock work they come in & set down — must be something to count noses & check to see if all returned safe.

Lot of contacts made of enemy planes — they seem to be snooping around the edges and no doubt will hit us full force tonight after sun down. It's their favorite sport — Lou and her cosmetics plus the wake she leaves makes her stand out like a sore thumb in this moonlight. Oh well — we have gone thru two nights of battle and nary a scratch so we will be all right tonight again. Have memorized the chapter on how to swim while holding one's nose so don't worry about me.

Happy Easter to you, honey — all my love — would like to grab you up and hug hell out of you — really make your ribs crack, that's for sure.

Love,
Paul

LIEUTENANT PAUL C. BONNETTE (Dental Corp) U.S. Navy Reserve, was not a big fan of General of the Army Douglas MacArthur, Supreme Allied Commander Southwest Pacific. Paul was certainly no military strategist so he must have picked up wardroom talk that MacArthur had "spoiled" the hunting. Paul also felt that MacArthur did not give enough credit to the Navy.

2 April 1944

Hello Honey —

We have been having a heavy sea and we have been fanning the breeze — cutting capers and what have you. It's been a lot of fun but MacArthur spoiled really good hunting for us — won't vote for him for president.

We have been playing a lot of "hearts" lately — really cut throat and that's for sure. All ship's work has been knocked off due to "extenuating circumstances" so to pass away the time, we indulge in mass "Hearts". Don't play for stakes other than a "jug" of root beer or Coke — aren't we devils? Good, clean fun for America's "fighting forces", sez eye. It's true our games were interrupted a few times, but no one seemed to mind — after all we're not paid to play hearts or cribbage.

Had a big thrill yesterday at noon chow — just getting ready to sit down when the bugler sounded "all anti-aircraft personnel man your stations" — boy, oh boy! Things really hum then! Two large groups of enemy planes were bearing down on us to attack but they gave it up as a bad job and went back. Can't figure out their tactics — they are either a lot weaker than we know or else have something planned. We cleaned their plows on this deal — you probably have read about it by now and I can't tell you, but in Navy parlance "well done" covers it.

It's fun listening to the Tokyo radio — especially Tokyo Rose. The latest word is "The Americans have been driven from the Pacific — the Marshalls safe." We retreated at great loss of American lives and very minor casualties of Japanese. Their tone of voice is such as one would use in placating a child or telling a bedtime story. If I hadn't been thru those operations and knew different, I'd damn well believe them myself.

All My Love
Paul

APRIL 5 WAS a Wednesday, the third day of a storm Paul calls a "lulu." The *Lady Lou* was retracing her route back to Majuro, where she was to spend the next week.

5 April 1944

Hello Honey —

Whew! What a life — am seeing the rugged life of a sailor these days. We have been in a storm since Sunday night and it's a lulu. Should have suspected something when we had those calms — it's monsoon season here and they are hell. On top of that, we are having two Wednesdays so the dates have been screwed up and the weather too.

If it doesn't quit raining we're sure to have a "flood" — the "ocean" is rising rapidly — in fact everything is inundated as if it were. Talk about rain and wind — visibility zero "minus" and blowing a good thirty-five knots — you can imagine what that does to the sea and poor Lou sure is kicking up her heels. Don't believe any of us will ever walk on an even keel again — talk about the poor hogs in Arkansas — they only wobble up and down but we roll and bob in all directions. It's inebriation without benefit of alcohol — talk about blind staggers and what have you — wow! The head is away forward in the ship — we're pitching and rolling so the deck actually goes out from under you — most disconcerting when one has a "job" to do.

Love You Loads, Honey
Paul

6 April 1944

Hello Darling —

It's still raining to beat hell and we can't get out often, but we at least can have our ports open and get some fresh air. Pretty bad when everything is closed — smells worse than a Chinese laundry.

Wish I could tell you what "confronts the eye" here — it's mighty "outstanding" as Lowell Thomas would say.

Don't believe I told you much about the initiation, or have I? Can't always remember what I say in my letters so if there is a lot of repetition don't hold it agin, plees.

It started out with quarters for muster — only it was in reverse, most of the officers were polly-wogs so we had to get in the ranks and the enlisted personnel held sway. First we had to get down on our knees and touch our foreheads to the deck and moan, then straighten yup, then down, then up, then down — not a half dozen times but damn near an hour straight! In the mean time they played a fire hose on us and drowned us with salt water — they stuck it in your face, belly and all over — when I say drowned us I mean drowned. As we were on the down beat they'd slug us with a "shalayli" (my own spelling) made by making a slender canvas bag 2-3 inches in diameter and a foot or so long. They'd stuff it crammed full of rags and then soak the whole thing in salt water for several days with the result it was as delicate & harmless as a length of gas pipe. Our clothes were dripping wet and when that club would land on our bottom it felt like a mule kick — lost track of the number of times I got slugged but my left cheek was beat to a pulp — none landed on my right — tried to turn the other cheek in the accepted quaker fashion but was ignored. The clubbing & drenching kept on about an hour and we were allowed to eat. We sure looked like hell and parts of us were "pulsating with pleasure" but we ate. The food was regulation much to my surprise. Barely finished lunch and they started us on the final phase of the ceremony. Of course it started out with more salt water and a lot more hefty slugs, but insult was added to injury — we got a coat of oil & feathers, eggs, jam and whatever else they could lay their hands on — was a mess & you know what wet feathers smell like. That kept up for some time and we were finally ordered to the well deck where King Neptune & his court were hold forth. Don't remember much how they looked but they were really dressed up — we were too busy jumping around, prodded on by two fellows dressed in red devil clothes and armed with Neptune's Fork that was charged with 115 volt current — sure knocked hell out of you due to the salt water soaked clothes. We were sentenced. I had to have my appendix out by the Royal Doctor — had to climb up on an "operating table" that was charged and the doctor had the electric knife. The table was wet of course and when the juice was turned on — wow! Had a hell of a time getting on because just as you placed your hands & got ready to jump on they either jab you with the charged fork or the table would short and it would knock you flat — finally got on, had my operation and when they said get off — I didn't need any aid — the current literally knocked you off. Had to visit the royal dentist — slammed me in a chair, opened my mouth and jammed a paint brush down my throat — the solution was lubricating oil and quinine — the solution container was an old garbage can. Aseptic technique? We had other little [*niceties*] bestowed upon us, like climbing into a wooden coffin, lid closed down on you and then the hose inserted thru a slit and the water turned on — quite a feeling. We wound up by running the gauntlet — had to crawl thru a tow sleeve on our hands and knees and then run like hell thru a million shell backs — all swinging clubs and our fannies were sorry sights — that's for sure. Some of the fellows had to stand Davey Jones watches — they would dress in arctic clothes consisting of thick leather, fleece lined boots, trousers, coats and helmets — had to wear them for two hours in this heat! I escaped that thank the Lord. [*Name deleted*] turned out to be a heel of the first order — he was a polly wog but a damn poor one. He gets more disgusting every day — they call him "big & dirty" — rightfully so. With his shaved head, and his general build & posture — you can imagine. I'm no beauty with my head shaved so I guess I'd better shut up.

Thought you might be interested in the transition of a polly wog to a shell-back.

All My Love
Paul

9 April 1944

Hello "Sweetie-Face"

Three months tomorrow since I left terra firma, outside my "unarmed" jaunts into Jap land — no beer, rum or whiskey, not even the desire outside of occasional longing for a couple of cold Budweisers on these hot days.

Went to Easter services today — decided to wear tan trousers, shirt & accessories — got tired of khaki. Seems as tho everyone else had the same idea so after all, I wasn't "outstanding". We even had lilies on the altar —

one of the fellows made two cute brass vases and some paper lilies so we really had the spirit.

Nighty-Night Darling
Paul

10 April 1944

Hello My Darling —

Seems we are losing several of the enlisted men — sexual perverts — quite a stink. It's a general court martial offense. One was caught so several more fessed up and are taking bad conduct discharges. Keep it under your hat, eh?

Am sending along three snaps of the "polly wogs". They are all the same and have written in the names of the fellows on the back of one — can you find "I" without peeking?

Aren't our hair cuts the damndest things you ever saw — they cut a furrow down the center and all the back so I just had the two tufts left in front. Poor Gandy had just a beret left, the rest was shaved. He landed in a coconut tree with his plane day before yesterday but didn't muss his hair.

We have lost two planes so far — crashed into the side of the ship and sunk — exciting but no one hurt.

One severe casualty as a result of the initiation — a kid got slugged across the kidneys and he is paralyzed from the hips down — injured his plumbing too so he has to be catheterized each time he has to wetty. He has been transferred to a hospital ship, prognosis bad!

All My Love
Paul

"EARHART" in the following letter is, of course, famed pilot Amelia Earhart. She and navigator Fred Noonan left New Guinea on July 2, 1937, in a twin-engine Lockheed Electra headed northeast toward Howland Island. They never arrived and their fate remains a mystery.

By today's standards, their navigation and communication capabilities were primitive, especially over the vast expanse of the Pacific, so it is possible Earhart and Noonan simply became lost, ran out of fuel, crashed into the sea, and sank. A more dramatic theory is that they were shot down while spying on the Japanese military buildup.

Records are filled with supposedly eyewitness and secondhand accounts of Earhart's plane crash landing on or near a number of small islands. These accounts are intriguing but often vague and contradictory.

One such scenario has Earhart and Noonan well northeast of their intended course, coming down at Mili Atoll's Barre Island in the Marshalls. There they were captured by the Japanese and later transferred to Saipan where they died.

Paul doesn't say what island he was on where Earhart was reported to have "gone native," but Mili Atoll was one of those spared bombardment and it is very possible Paul visited there.

11 April 1944

Hello Darling —

I'll be eligible for an Admiralcy by the time my Lt. Comdrship catches up with me. If you hear I am a Lt. Comdr. please let me know, will you?

Did you ever receive my letter requesting your various & sundry sizes? Thought if ever I hit a port I'd like to send you a garment or two — prices are outrageous at home & maybe I can find as pretty out here one of these days — at least it might be different.

Can't figure out why we should owe the bank $1.50 — I was late but I'm pretty sure I have paid them all — some time look thru the money order stubs and check up.

Costs about $50 a month aboard ship — that takes in mess bill, ships service and cigar mess and those are the only places you can spend money. I've been drawing $61 a month, after this month it will be, or should be $110 — should be able to lay away $50 a month towards something. Want to save enough so if we hit the States I can fly home — if it's just for a day — got to see you at the earliest and in the quickest time. If I ever get my promotion I'll raise the allotment to $300 and let you handle it any way you want to.

Am looking forward to receiving my package of magazines — it was awfully sweet of you to think of it, but honey, we have been getting in a big supply of all kinds in Ships Service so don't bother about sending any. The supply ships bring them & they are fairly recent issues — what I do wish you would send some time — a couple cans of "de odo" every once in a while. Mine's all gone and in this climate one is susceptible to B.O. and I hate it. No matter how often you bathe, your clothes are wringing wet in no time and the "delicate perfume" of de odo [*permeates*] the clothes and keeps one sweet.

We get mail spasmodically but it will be better now that we have bases established out here. Before we were busy taking them over and of course the outcome of the venture had to be established. For a while we didn't drop anchor — just a force without a port or harbor but there have "been some changes made". Do you know the differences between amphibious & Task Forces — look it up some time — have been both & in that order — both are fun but Task Force is more fun & spectacular.

Continue sending the clippings — the one about Earhart was interesting because I first heard it when I was on the island she was supposed to be on and wondered if the story reached the States. They swear up and down it's the truth — she was supposed to be wild — gone native, so maybe they suppressed the news and let it die rather than spoil a noble air adventure. Meant to tell you but during the excitement of boom-boom, I forgot.

Got to get to bed. Take care of yourself, honey. Hold your hats, here we go again.

All My Love
Paul

12 Apr. 1944

Hello Pretty One —

Enclosed find a couple of snaps — "Change of Command" when Admiral Wright stepped out and Oldendorf took over — Wright has his back to the camera. I have marked an X on the back to indicate where I stand.

Don't know the Admiral's name but [*he*] inspected us — wasn't Nimitz but he was here the other day.

Everyone is buzzing around "packing" — a hunting we will go — it's great to be on the move again. You have done a swell job on following the Fleet — can't tell you how close you really are. Everyone is in high spirits — you'd think we were starting off on a summer's vacation. Think about me on your birthday plus a month minus two days — won't be able to hear you cause I'll have cotton in my ears.

All My Love
Paul

MOST OF PAUL'S LETTERS were sent by air mail. The majority carried a red 6-cent stamp bearing a twin-engine transport plane or the combination of a blue 5-cent stamp with the profile of James Monroe and a green 1-cent stamp showing the Statue of Liberty with the words "INDUSTRY-AGRICULTURE FOR DEFENSE." Where the stamp would have been on this second April 12 "sneaker," Paul wrote "Free." It went by ship.

12 Apr. 1944

Surprise, Surprise! Hello Darling —

Thought I'd send a little sneaker along to fill in the blank spaces — sent a v-mail the other day — it will drift home one of these days too.

Saw a good show tonight — "A Guy Named Joe" — Spencer Tracy & Irene Dunne. Enjoyed it a lot — be sure to see it. Have had a lot of good ones lately — "Charlie's Aunt" with Jack Benny was good.

Lot of last minute letter writing this evening — don't know whether it will do any good or not but everyone is thinking of their girls — I know I am.

We are seven hours behind you "as of now," so you are safe in your little basket and may be thinking about getting up or at least it's time to turn over for another forty winks.

There isn't any news — nothing new or startling — just was thinking about you & lonesome for you — this note will bob up when you least expect it — on account of it is sent "for free" — thought you might enjoy one via-freighter, tanker or what have you. Bye Bye Darling.

All My Love
Paul

18 Apr. 1944

Hello Darling —

It's been very quiet these days — up until tonight the sea has been very calm & pacified but it let go just before dark. The sky sure looked mean but beautiful, and the water was purple and then went into a black black. The sky looked like there was a twister sure enough, black funnel shaped clouds and looked like a stage drop. Just as the storm hit we had to recover a plane that had been on submarine patrol. It really was thrilling and he made a beautiful landing in spite of the gale, rain and speeding ship. In ordinary weather it's quite a trick but when there is a storm and a lot of white caps — that's a pig of a different bristle.

Another man overboard last night and wasn't recovered.

Several Jap planes started in today but our fighter planes drove them off — we had an alarm of course and the anti-aircraft crews manned their guns, but no firing.

The paper weight with your picture sure is a handy gadget — have to have my fan going all the time so you're setting right by me all the time — your cheerful grin is a morale keeper upper for sure.

Sure got a bang out of "Blondie", especially the one where the pups got into the Easter hat.

All My Love
Paul

19 Apr. 1944

Hello Darling —

Tired boy tonight — had two g.q.s last night or rather early this morning. When I get out of the Navy, I'm going to join the fire department for

UNITED STATES NAVY

12 Apr. 1944

Surprise, Surprise! Hello Darling—
Thought I'd
send a little sneaker along to fill in the
blank spaces—sent a V-mail the ~~other~~ other day,
it will drift home one of these days too.
~~A guy named~~
Saw a good show tonight—
Joe—Spencer Tracy & Irene Dunne. Enjoyed it
a lot—be sure to see it. Have had a lot
of good ones lately—Charlie's Aunt & Jack Benny's
was good.
Lot of last minute letter writing this evening—
don't know whether it will do any good or not
but everybody is thinking of their girls—
I know I am.
We are seven hours behind you as of now, so
you are safe in your little basket and may
be thinking about getting ~~up or at least~~ its
time to turn over for another forty winks.
There isn't any news—nothing new or startling—
just was thinking about you & lonesome
for you—this note will bob up when you least
expect it—on account of it is sent for free—
thought you might enjoy one via freighter,
tanker or what have you. Bye Bye Darling
all my love
Paul

AIR MAIL

I can dress and get to where I'm supposed to be "at" in nothing flat. The alarm at one thirty this morning was a false alarm — a short circuit, but we didn't know that until we did our stuff and went to our battle stations. The one at 0330 was the real McCoy but they turned the planes back — came within eight miles of us.

Shot one down this afternoon — other than that, it's very quiet.

The [*skies*] are still overcast and raining so maybe we can slip in on them — it's hard for them to find us when it's so nasty. Will sleep in my [*skivvies*] tonight and for the next week or so — when you gotta go, you gotta go — that alarm doesn't fool. Also will stuff some socks in my pocket on account of I hate to pad around [*bare*] or bare feet in shoes — not good.

Wish I could tell you what goes on but no can do until I see you — hope I can remember.

Saw a huge whale that had been hit & split open by a destroyer — sure stunk.

No news about my half stripe — probably won't hear until after this operation. It really doesn't make any difference out here any how, so why warra?

Can't think of a thing to say, so I'll put it to bed and sleep with one eye open and both ears at attention. With this polly wog haircut they appear to be at attention all the time. Feel kind of silly getting haircuts these days but I warn them not to take any off the top or spend too much time looking for it. It's coming in gray. Must be a shellayla hit a "gray nerve" during initiation. Love you loads & take care of yourself.

Paul

20 Apr. 1944

Hello Best Girl —

We're having field day throughout the ship and g.q. for the gun crews, so I thought I'd clean my quarters and look respectable again for a change. Things sure accumulate way out here and I've thrown out a lot of junk, papers etc. — it gives me great pleasure to say — "nary a bottle did have to cart out." Rearranged my safe and looked at the pint I have stashed away.

If there are some ups & downs in this letter, think nothing of it — this is one of those days. We're in a hornet's nest and we are constantly making emergency turns and changing course — those dull booms and heavy jars you feel are depth charges going off. When we make those turns — that's when things really skid and crash. Was taking a shower just a few minutes ago when we were doing a series of them — had a hell of a time trying to soap myself etc., and hang on, but here I am all dry (?) and clean — nothing hit us — would have been embarrassed to have had to abandon ship in that state of dress, or rather undress. Seems foolish to bathe — the perspiration is fairly rolling off me and I'll be smelling bad again in a few minutes. Anything can happen any minute, so, as the gun boss (Bowers) says, he always cleans up on "this day" — might save the doctors a lot of trouble. Wish I could tell you what goes on but will suffice to say, it's many times bigger than our last venture.

Comdr. Bowers and I have a lot of fun — he's swell and to think they were scared of him at first. He and I are always first out in the morning for g.q. and have a cup of coffee together — this morning I was "tardy" so he came in to see if I had overslept or what was wrong. Tee, hee, I had been communing with nature, first "good bath" in several days but we had our coffee.

The exec usually drops in a close third so we have a little bull session before the alarm sounds. He's all right but not a Towner by a long ways — he has been awfully nice to me and quite friendly so I'm not worried about him. I do my little etiquette for him in the mornings and when I see him so I guess that salves his "Academy" sense.

Wonder how many times a day I look at you — wish I were somewhere and near enough so I could send you small "tokens of love" all the time. Are you going steady with anyone — I'm 5 ft. 10 in., blue eyes (both of them), ruddy to tan complexion, good health, fair disposition, "colleges" graduate and protestant when I go. Are you interested in settling down — will exchange pictures — R.S.V.P.

Guess I'm a little goofy today — it's been a long time since I've seen you and I'm so lonesome for you honey. Whoops, can hear gunfire and "mell the moke" so I'd better finish up and check on things.

Rained like hell this morning but the sun is breaking thru and it's a beautiful sight out. Ideal day to do business with the slant eyes and I hope we run into a slew of them. Old Lou is steaming right along and kicking up a big spray. Guess we were lucky last time — over 200 torpedo planes were looking for us but didn't find us so maybe they will come out again.

Remember — I Love You
Paul

22 Apr. 1944

Hello Darling —

Had a general alarm tonight but it was another short in the circuit. We were sitting around playing cribbage when it let go — boy, oh boy! They sure clear out in a hurry — I was clear down in number one mess hall when the "belay" signal was passed. Can scurry down a scuttle as fast as a prairie dog hits his hole.

One of our fighter pilots was shot down yesterday and our pilot rescued him. We have him aboard here — picked out shell fragments from his arms & legs — other than being sore and stiff he is in good shape. Asked the censor if I could tell you about it and he couldn't see why not as long as I didn't tell where, so here goes.

He and his buddy were strafing the beach when this one got a hit directly in his engine — busted the oil pump so his engine froze on him and he crash landed on the beach. The ceiling was so low he couldn't bail out so he rode her down and hit the beach — the place was full of Japs back in the trees & under brush but they wanted him alive so they didn't fire on him. He managed to inflate his raft and paddle out into the bay — they figured the wind would blow him back but the Lord was on his side and the wind changed, landing him on the opposite tip of the island. He went ashore and a naked native man came out — the pilot made "peace overtures" but the native just grinned and ran back toward the Japs. Said pilot rushed back to his raft and paddled out into the bay, dropped his sea anchor and waited for help. His buddy flew back to pass the word of his being shot down and gave his location. While anchored out there several Zeros attacked him and he was kept busy diving in and out of the water. A pair of our fighters came along and knocked out the enemy planes and our plane rescued said pilot. The only comment he made was "he had tough luck today". This was his second experience being shot down — the other time he crashed and his raft was all shot to hell so he floated two days on some wreckage before being picked up.

The new "abandon ship drill" has me on a raft now — think I'll like it a lot better because I won't have to bail out water all the time.

Saw a good show yesterday and today — "In Old California" and "Sahara". "Sahara" was fair — much like "Immortal Sergeant".

Wonder what the radio is saying these days — especially yesterday and today. Listened to Tokyo Rose a while tonight — she sounds like a man talking falsetto — sure gripes me, the fantastic tales she tells — must hear her tomorrow as I'll know if we are sunk for sure — I might be on my raft right now for all I know.

Nightie, night
All My Love
Paul

24 Apr. 1944

Hello Sweet Girl —

We had an air alarm and it was fun and exciting — several enemy planes were spotted and for a couple of hours it had possibilities but damnit, they never did get in range. Had fun watching the radar screen, the exec explained it all to me and cleared up a lot in my mind as to our battle formations. Maybe tonight they will be a little more venturesome and come in where we can get a shot at them. They liked to come in right after sunset just before it gets pitch dark — come in low, from 10-70 feet above the water where the radar can't spot them, so everyone has to be alert.

Saw a hell of a good show yesterday — "Seven Sweethearts" hit me right and enjoyed it a lot. Today's was Errol Flynn in "Edge of Darkness" — a good show but lighter stuff sets better out here.

Tonight sure had possibilities but only two planes shot down — it's 2300 now and we have secured for now but probably will be yanked out before sunrise. Had both surface and air contacts so they are out here looking for us — everyone is spoiling for a good scrap — the kids on the guns have what it takes and they really turn to when the word is passed.

All my love to you, Darling
Paul

26 Apr. 1944

Hello Darling —

Sure is disappointing operation this time — even the sea is quiet and slick as glass — very humdrum life.

Our watching the sunset these past few days has been interrupted by general quarters but manage to get back topside to see what is going on. A few planes are shot down every day but our fighters do it and we don't get a crack at them. Several sub contacts made each day but don't bother us. Wish they would come out and let us tie into them, but no — nothing does it giff.

Suppose some day they will surprise us and give us a run for our money. They must have something or they wouldn't have started this war.

Don't know how long we'll be here cruising around or where we will go — Towner used to tell us the dope but this new regime won't tell us a damn thing — takes all the fun and excitement out of it.

Washed my hair and "can't do a thing with it" — it's all of a quarter inch long now — becoming a shell back is sure hard on one's coiffure (?) — sure a flock of burr heads around right now.

Am having a hell of a time trying to write and scratch at the same time — prickly heat has got me for sure. Being soaked thru all day sure raises ned with my tender skin, as it were.

Well honey — time for bed — am still getting up early these days — hate to hike down the ladders and passage ways half awake so I'll hit my sack.

All My Love
Paul

27 Apr. 1944

Hellah Pretty One —

Am in much better spirits today — the war looks a little more interesting for the next month or two. They broke down and gave us part of the dope so we have something to look forward to. When you make all kinds of preparation and not knowing what for — it's pure drudgery.

As of today, I'm the new mess treasurer, will give me something to do in my spare time. Damn near was mess caterer but got out of it in good shape.

Twenty less Japs yesterday — our task force shot down five bombers — saw two of them fall myself. Pretty, black smoke & a splash is all there "are" to it. As a whole it's been very dull, but we have had g.q. twice a day in preparation for what ever might come up. Was great to see mountains again — 1600 ft high — no mean hill — hard to believe there is snow on the top, but they say it's true. All we had been seeing was flat islands and small, had almost forgotten there were bigger and better things of terra firma nature.

Wouldn't it be swell if my promotion was waiting for me when we arrive at "- - - -" again? May get a liberty in June & no doubt will see Ade and I'd sure like to wear the maple leaf when I do see him.

It's time for the movie — "Scatter Brain" — so will close for now — all my love and don't worry about me.

Love you good,
Paul

29 Apr. 1944

Darling Girl —

A nice big battle ship brought a little mail out to us today — was nice of her, don't you think?

Your letters sure were welcome — had been a very quiet operation and everyone was bored stiff, but when they sounded mail call — whoops! Only one Jap plane shot down today — none yesterday and five the day before.

MacArthur spoiled the big party we had planned for the operation before this last one — had the Jap fleet located and all set to bottle them up but he "farts" (excuse please) around with his bombers & they sail out pretty as you please & are gone when we get there. We'd have gotten their war ships — he got a few small craft. Don't blab too much about it, will you not?

It's almost 10 o'clock (2200) so I'm going to bed and write again tomorrow. We have two 29 Aprils this time so if you get two dated that way I'm not suffering from operational fatigue. Our task force has been spotted — we intercepted a Jap message, so it may give fire works anytime — tomorrow for sure cause we're going to play a ditty — Down by the Old Mill Stream. [*"Mill" was Paul's code for Truk Island.*]

Nighty Night
Paul

STILL IN THE CAROLINES, the *Louisville* steamed southeast from Truk to lead the bombardment of Satawan Island.

29 Apr. 1944

Hello Honey —

Gosh it was a spectacle this morning, never saw so many planes in all my life and goody — they were mostly ours. One Jap plane must have got lost for he came right over our bow and about a hundred yards up. Tried to bomb the U.S.S. "- - - -" but missed her and got shot down herself. One of ours dropped but all three men were saved. Our planes just got back from a "rescue mission" but one of our subs had already picked them up so no hair raising exploits were forth coming.

Started off stylishly — raining like hell, came down in sheets across the deck and a high wind whipped up huge white caps. The sky was heavily overcast — good day for a murder — looked like the pictures of a storm at sea — huge ships plying thru the waves kicking up a big spray as she cut thru the water.

I had just slipped up to get some breakfast, had taken one bite of waffle, when all the guns let go — really quite exciting. Stayed up on the quarter deck most of the time and watched the shells skipping along the water — hundreds of planes above — some low, others away up in the clouds — all in all it was very fascinating.

We were talking about funny happenings at the table this noon and Murphy told one I thought was funny & cute — typical of an absent minded doctor — seems when Murph was a kid and had to say grace he put out with: "We thank thee dear Father for the good food that you have put before us, Amen." His dad absentmindedly said, "You are welcome."

We just got out of g.q. — probably have a few hours leisure and then we go to work for sure. We are scheduled to bombard and we are first in so maybe we will have some fun — by being lead off men we get a crack at them before their installations & planes are wrecked or they know our intentions.

Yesterday eighty some planes were knocked out, forty plus in the air and 40 on the ground. We lost six but only four killed. Not a bad score for our task force alone.

Love you loads, darling,
Paul

2 May 1944

Hello My Sweet —

Traveled first class on this Cooks Tour yesterday — breakfast in bed and everything, but it was short lived. Had a terrific temperature of 99 so I was placed on the binnacle list. You know me and electric fans — I developed a little sniffle so they said to crap out, take APC and drink a lot of water which I did so I'm all right again. The weather has been nasty, all the ports had to be closed so it was stifling inside — almost every one felt a little lousy. I was afraid of cat fever so I took care of myself and am okay now.

If the war is prolonged and have a chance to stay in the Navy with a good commission I may do it, depends on the economic setup and what happens to medicine & dentistry after the war. Wives will be allowed to go to foreign bases and I will have had my sea duty so we can get pleasant duty either in the States — P.H. — China, etc. You and I could have a big time, see the world and not have to worry about where the next meal is coming from.

Was disappointed in our bombardment Sunday — no opposition at all — we just banged away and wrecked all they had. Can't figure out what is going on — doesn't seem good strategy for them to allow us to go along unmolested as we have more or less. The weather was in our favor but "goodness, gracious" — something has to happen.

All My Love
Paul

3 May 1944

Hello Darling

Six months of sea duty (according to the roster) has passed, maybe by the end of another six months I'll be seeing you. Time really flies but I feel as though I've been out here for years — the only change is in weather, sunset & sun rises with the attendant changes in the color of the water. Otherwise, we travel at the same rate of speed — change course at the same time and do everything as though we were glued together.

We have been trying to figure out what campaign bars & how many stars we are entitled to wear due to these operations but everything has been changed so I don't know what we merit. I know I have the Asiatic-Pacific and American Theater bars — we have been in Jap water and raided some of their "legal" possessions as well as taking the Marshalls so bars may be forth coming from them too.

Lots to look forward to, mail, fresh vegetables, maybe a promotion and a big boom.

All My Love To You Sweet Girl
(Did you hear that — lots of boom)
Paul

4 May 1944

Hello Honey —

What great event took place seven hundred and thirty days ago today? Silly — "we" reported for active duty, salutes and everything — rememberest thou?

This day I did mail one . . . package to you — it's just junk but the best I could do — will do better pretty soon I hope. The ashtray and bracelet (had trouble hanging on to them, everybody wanted them and was offered a good price) for them but they belong to "Dotty B". Hope you like the bracelet & can wear it — it's stainless steel and should stand up okay. The neck chain (woven) was made by the tattooed man of the ship — nice looking kid but all covered with tattoos. If you don't want it — give it to Freddy [*the author*], put a whistle on it instead of the insignia.

They brought mail aboard but hasn't been distributed yet — can hardly wait to get mine — hope there are a lot from you.

It's still hotter than hell & my prickly heat is driving me nuts — sure looks awful but I'm "pure" and it is heat.

Will be here about a week and then bye on a jaunt again — hope it's what it's supposed to be — really be headlines & we ought to have fun.

The lagoon is a busy place & very interesting. The other day a great big sub came along side — sure was thrilling & needless to say, pleased that it was one of our own. Should have seen the kids faces when we sent over ice cream to them. Great Navy, great fellows — none better.

All My Love To You Honey
Paul

5 May 1944

Hello My Darling —

Got a letter from Gregg this evening and he says I have been promoted as of March 1st. He also said he had told you — the big bum. Brown came in from the Island a while ago and said he had been told he too had been promoted but we haven't had official notice of it so I'm still Lt. P. C. as far as I'm concerned or proved otherwise. [*Paul gave no additional identification for "Brown," but a Lieutenant Commander Dwight Irvin Brown (USNR) is one of the seven officers who would later die on the* ***Louisville*** *during Paul's tour of duty.*]

Saw a good show this evening — "Government Girl" — yesterday had "The Sullivans" and the day before, "Mission to Moscow".

The moon is out, nice breeze blowing and a million lights all around us. Lud is playing the a core dean [*accordian*] and the gang is singing — much fun. The Southern Cross is quite plain tonight — feel so smart because I can locate & identify it myself. We are going to miss old "Lud" — he has orders for flight training, supposed to leave in June but the exec said he would be gone before then. Old Lou has business pretty soon so he'll have to clear out or he'll "miss the boat".

May get a "beer" tomorrow believe it or not — have drunk beer in strange places but this will top them all. Bet I fall on my face after one bottle — don't know what a boiler maker would do to me after 4 months lay off.

Sleep good, Honey
Paul

9 May 1944

Hello My Darling —

Had fun Saturday evening, Sunday and Monday morning — believe it or not, I spent a night on the beach — slept in a thatched roofed house too.

To start at the beginning — a party of officers got liberty and went to the officers club at "- - - -", damn near all of us went. It's the first time the fleet was allowed in so we all took advantage of it and there sure was a mob there. All the tables and chairs were taken so about ten of us were sitting on the deck drinking beer & an occasional bourbon and having a big time when I happened to look up and who do you think I saw! Ho, Hum — should wait until a "subsequent" letter before I tell you, but that wouldn't be fair so I better break down and tell before you go nuts — him of all people and one of my good friends — has his own speed boat, plane & jeep — quarters, two Philippino (?) attendants, etc., etc., and he is the new executive officer of the Naval Air Base — just here last Sunday (week ago). Boy, was I set up from then on — the envy of the gang. You probably have read ahead, so I'll now tell you who it is — Wesley J. Wicks, Comdr. U.S.N.R. He was glad to see me and I was to see him — he immediately asked me to spend the night with him so I got permission from Dr. Barber to spend Sunday all day & night, returning to the ship Monday afternoon. Wants me to come as often as I can or want to but I'm not going to abuse the privilege either his or my ship. Am going over with the regular party tomorrow from 4-6 and come back home.

Honey, we did have fun talking over Ann Arbor days, etc., etc. — went all over the islands in his jeep and saw things I never could have otherwise. He has his camera and one of these days I'll have a nice set of pictures for you. Took one of me sitting under a coconut tree with the thatched roof as a background — felt like the King of the Island. [*Incidentally*] while we were sitting there, a coconut dropped and missed me by a foot — am mailing said nut to you. It's quite a nice one but don't know what shape it will be in when it eventually gets to you. It's just as they come from the tree but of course the coat of varnish was added. Just try to visualize sitting under the trees in front of a thatched roofed house — beautiful beach at your feet and the breakers rolling in. We sat out there until midnight — it was so pretty and sure thought of you and longed for you.

His "filipino" boys are gathering shells for you and when I return in the future, you should have some beauties. Honey, the ones I sent you are fizzles as far as the ones I saw over the weekend — they look like rare &

beautiful jewels — nature certainly is a wonderful artist when it comes to colors — in a "month or so" they'll have my collection & I'll send you real beauties.

It's raining to beat hell and I'm about ready to close shop & go topside — have been to the barber shop and had my hair do — gosh it looks terrible! It's just at the "awkward age" and can't comb it or part it — stands up in all directions.

Love You Loads
Paul

THE *GRAF SPEE* (Paul spelled it "Spree" in the following letter) was a German pocket battleship scuttled in the estuary of the Rio de la Plata near Montevideo, Uruguay, in December 1939. Adolf Hitler ordered the ship sunk in order to keep her from falling into British hands.

10 May 1944

Gee Honey —

Seems all I have to allow is — it's so hot my fan has been out of commission since the last boom-boom but now I have a brand new one and am all set for a siege of hot weather. The fellows are sure swell to me — foxy new adjustable fan — a honey of a zipper sea bag — picture of the "Graf Spree" when she was scuttled and a lot of little trinkets too numerous to mention.

It was beautiful coming in from the beach this evening — world of activity but can't say what. Lou is so pretty all dolled up again and I'm sure proud to belong to her — she's quite a gal.

All My Love
Paul (Lt. Comdr. without portfolio)

11 May 1944

Hello Little Darling —

You talked about when we are out to sea slipping thru the water — wondered if we were subdued and all hushed up or just what went on. Will try to explain what giffs it during normal times. In the daytime we have routine "ships work", as it is designated in the vernacular of the sea, which means the various departments carry on i.e., I dentical, Johnson medicines — security division checks & repairs, etc. Late afternoon 1500 until chow we have movies (conditions permitting) and then go eat and mess around. Most everyone is topside slinging bull, singing or just farting (excuse please) around. Of course we are blacked out and absolutely no light showing — the only noise heard, outside of our own making, is that from the blowers or ventilators. When we are in g.q. the men man their stations but the bull still goes on — some sleep, others acey ducey, still others writing letters. The men on the guns of course can't sleep but a lot of bull is slung there, and you can't help but marvel at, and be proud of, their utter lack of fear. Would like a recording of the voices of the big guns when they go on a talking spree — much discussion goes on and it's a wonder they don't come to blows because they get so "het" up. When you go to the news reels don't you get a kick out of the night fighting? Million fireflies winking at you — it's quite a deal.

Best of all, I like to go as far forward as I can on the first deck and just kind of sit and think of you — on moon light nights it's so pretty — lots of stars — batches of clouds — outlines of our neighbors and the sparkling water. As I've often said — it's hard to realize the purpose for which we are out here — seems like a dream, the raids & campaigns we have been on couldn't possibly have happened to me but I guess they did. I imagine from now on the sledding will be a lot tougher and I'll wish a good many times that I were safe home. So far haven't have a certain length of time of this type of duty, so I'm having fun and enjoying every minute of it — Japs or none — haven't been scared yet but ain't saying I won't be fore it's over. I figger there's no use getting scared — I'd look silly out on a raft all by myself trying to get away, and besides, there is too much to see to run and hide — I'm just curious I guess.

Bye "Sweetie Face"
All My Love
Paul

AT LONG LAST, the return address on Paul's May 12, 1944 letter read:

Lt. Comdr. P. C. Bonnette, (DC) USNR
U.S.S. Louisville
%F.P.O.
San Francisco.

12 May 1944

Hello Honey —

The new exec and I are getting along swell. Lately he has been real friendly and I hope he keeps on. I haven't bothered him — kept out of his way but when I did have business or run into him I showed him the customary military courtesies and it's paying dividends. When he asks me to do something, I turn to and get it done stat which seems to please him, at least up until last night.

I was standing on the foc'sle minding my own business, my mind 6 or 8,000 miles away, when he came up and leaned against the life rail and started talking. He seemed in a jolly mood so finally I steered the conversation around to the holdup in our promotions — merely mentioned it didn't make a hell of a lot of difference when we got it but it was only natural to wonder why the other ships were promoting their men on the strength of the list aboard a certain ship. He said if I'd get a copy of the "bull" (as he called it) and our names with file numbers, etc., he couldn't see any reason why the Captain wouldn't act on it, provided it was certified. This morning we're all sitting around wondering if we will be called in for our physical and be allowed to wear the maple leaf. Three hundred bucks a month for you — I'm so happy over it — you earned it during the eleven years of being married to me.

May go to the beach this afternoon — want to see Wes and arrange a small party to visit the native village. They have been moved to a separate island and no one allowed to visit them without permission. Seems when we first took over the enlisted men got to the native gals and became infected with gonorrhea so they are out of bounds now. I've seen quite a few natives in their outrigger canoes paddling around but none close up. Would like to see their native pigs, dogs & chickens — inhabited huts etc.

Wes has two "fat hens" staked out in his patio and every once in a while gets a fresh egg for breakfast.

I haven't been in swimming yet — am scared of fungus infection in my ears — my ears are susceptible to blowing up so I'm watching them very carefully [*Paul made a neat drawing of his face with the eyes watching the ears*]. The water is so inviting and clear — after I've passed my physical, I'll dig out my ear stoppers & take a cautious plunge.

Next letter if all is well I may be Lt. Comdr. — hour later — I am now Lt. Comdr. P. C. Bonnette WOW! Just passed my physical so all that is necessary is the Capt.'s signature and there is no question of his not signing.

Honey — Love You Ever So Much
Paul (Lt. Comdr. with portfolio)

15 May 1944

Hello Mrs. Lieutenant Commander Bonnette —

Really had a big weekend — it all started out innocently — as you know we were called unexpectedly for our physicals — one each physical we took amid much excitement. A recreation party had been planned for the afternoon but a squall came up and the boat sprung a leak so it was cancelled. I had planned to stand the medical watch so Johnson & Barber could go and was all set to write you a nice long letter when everything was called off — that is, the big party.

Foster, Barber & [*Peabo*] wanted to go to the club so I was drafted to go with them — rain & wind notwithstanding — we went, called Wes & he came down so we swilled some beer. When I called Wes he said he was just sending a dispatch out to my ship to have me come in and spend the weekend with him so I asked Barber and he said sure, provided I got the exec's okay. Had a lot of fun drinking beer to my promotion and Wes said if I wanted to use his quarters for a little party Sunday afternoon the place was mine. He said if the gang could get in, he would send us back in his boat. When I got back to the ship I received permission to spend the weekend and, also, permission to have a dozen officers go in Sunday afternoon. I invited the exec but he had the duty, but the Captain might like to go, sez he. Asked the Captain and he was tickled to death to go so I drew up a list of guests — namely Capt. Hurt, Foster, Barber, Peabo, Esch, Grubb, Ludlow, Skelton, Sonderstrom, Padre & myself — oh, yes, Comdr. Swain too — Bowers couldn't go. Well any how, they were all rarin to go and did go — really think they had fun, from the captain on down. They brought 4 cases of iced beer in a g.i. can, swim trunks and a football — you'd have thought they were nuts the way they raced around & let go. They did a little beach combing, touch football, swimming & beer at their leisure.

When you go to the club it's so crowded — the beer is warm and have to rush to get back to the ship — this time they just messed around and had fun. Wes's boat is a speed boat so every one was feeling good as we raced home after the party. Everyone swears it was the most fun they have had since the war — that is when they've been out to sea. The fellows are all swell — picked them so they wouldn't give Wes any trouble and everything turned out swell. It sure didn't hurt me any to have the Captain accept my invitation.

Saturday afternoon you'd have thought I was the Admiral himself — they got out the motor whale boat and I was the lone passenger to the beach so I could have my weekend. Wes and I had a few beers, had dinner and then went to a smoker. Sure enjoyed the matches — Fleet vs. Atoll — naturally I was for the Fleet & Wes the atoll, so we bet 10 cents a match and broke even. Being with Wes, I had a reserved seat with the visiting Admirals, Capts., etc., so I was right in there pitching. You'd have enjoyed the setting — tropics, coconut trees, clouds, stars, even a shower thrown in. The fellows from the fleet were in, dressed in whites and they looked so nice. Sure got a bang out of it and had to pinch myself to see if it really were "poor I". It was hard to realize the planes in the air were bomb-laden and on actual missions — playing for keeps. The air is full of them night and day.

After the smoker we chewed the fat until midnight — slept until 7:30 — had breakfast and I messed around while Wes went to the office. The gang came in at 1400 and left at 1800 after a big time.

All My Love
Paul

PAUL OFTEN MENTIONED the censors and occasionally took a turn "censing" outgoing letters. Sitting at a wooden table, armed with razor blades, censors cut out any reference, no matter how innocent, they felt might in any way be of interest to the enemy. As Paul observed, "The Japs have ways and means of finding out things." While censorship was often enthusiastic, not a single one of Paul's letters shows evidence of the censor's blade.

16 May 1944

Little Honey —

It sounds like we are back in the ship yard. Of all the hammering, riveting and scraping, this is the worst yet. All morning while in the office, they were pounding on the steel deck. Now that I've transferred to my quarters, they too have changed their site of activity and it is again right over my head. Didn't mind it in the yard but out here where it has been so quiet, we really notice it.

Helped censor yesterday just for the hell of it. Ran across a little statement that tickled me — seems he was writing to his wife and about half way down the page, "pardon me, your letter just blew over the side, glad I read it first." Silly, isn't it, but it hit me funny. Some of the letters are kind of pitiful — the spelling terrible but they are all cheerful. Some of the kids are writing to a half dozen girls and of course they are all their "one and only". Some are in a little deeper and are writing to some body else's wife — not platonic either.

It has been, and still is so damned damned hot — sultry and not much breeze. The metal chassis of Lou absorbs the heat and holds it, so when we aren't under way — wow.

Had a little "air scare" yesterday but turned out to be friendly — damnit!

Have I told you about the Officers club — an old Jap building maybe a hundred yards long and fifty-feet wide. One story, screen porch all the way round — the roof is typical of Japanese design (can't spell archytetshure) not much to look at but it's an oasis. The brig is an old Jap radar station — it too is typically Jap.

Your coconut got off in the mail today — don't think you have a bomb on your hands when you first see it. It fell fresh from the tree a week ago

Sunday — don't know how long they keep but it sounds full of milk when you shake it. I traded my Jap helmet for a Jap bayonet and will send to Fred to put with his collection of knives.

All My Love
Paul

THE JAPANESE BAYONET did reach the author. The blademark shows it to be a product of the Nagoya Arsenal near Tokyo that manufactured bayonets from 1923-45. It is a Type 30 bayonet, a standard Japanese military issue, and it is in remarkably good condition.

19 May 1944

Hello Darling —

Thought I'd dash off a few lines to you while I had time. Our time schedule changes at noon — move up a day minus an hour so I'll be all mixed up again. We're changing early so our next operation won't get screwed up.

We're having field day today — that is this morning — this afternoon we have holiday routine because it becomes Saturday at 1200 — no work for me today. Helped censor and ran across some funny ones — one of the colored mess boys became poetic writing to his girl — he says "I fell off a house, I fell out of a tree but never fell so hard as I fell fore thee." The other was "The river is wide I can't step it; I love you & I kain't hep it."

This afternoon is the cruiser party and I'm looking forward to it. Looks like rain but that won't stop us — will go in my shorts and may get rid of the itch. My quarters sure stink — the insulation on my outboard bulkhead was blasted loose during the bombardments and they are just getting around to fixing it. Using some kind of glue — very odoriferous.

Honey girl — it's time for chow so will "belay this communication" eat & get ready for the party.

Love you loads darling,
Paul

"H" Division — Corpsmen and Doctors. Lieutenant Commander Paul Bonnette, standing fourth from right, aboard the USS *Louisville*. The picture is from a book of photographs entitled *Lady Lou*, compiled in 1945 by unidentified members of the crew and dedicated "to those fine, brave shipmates who didn't come back, who gave their lives in carrying out their part in the traditional fighting spirit of the USS *Louisville*."

"For the Body and the Spirit" — Lieutenant Commander Paul Bonnette, second from right. *From* ***Lady Lou***

22 May 1944

Hello My Honey —

Had fun on the cruiser picnic — still like my shipmates best — they all seem to have more fun than the others and they are always up to something. Had a crap game and lost seven dollars, my remaining funds for the month, but am going bye-bye muy pronto so I won't need any money. The U.S.S. "- - - -" furnished a 10-piece swing band so we had swell music without beer. I was hiking down a trail when I heard "Hail to the Victors" so I immediately wheeled around and sure enough there were a couple of Michigan men so I promptly had a short one with them. Imagine hearing the "Victors" out here in a coconut grove — fun. The party broke up about 6 o'clock so we headed for the dock — the other cruisers wobbled on very "sedately" but the "Louisville", nay! Each side of the gangway had a couple of "drowned rats" on it and when a dry member came along he promptly was tossed into the "Blue Pacific". All but Johnson got [*dunked*] and everybody but him had a good time. We sure looked like hell when we boarded Lou but everyone was having a big time and the party was a big success.

Planned on staying aboard yesterday but Foster decided we ought to hitch hike into the beach so he "talked me into it". Seems so funny to hail a boat instead of a cab but that's the way it is done out here.

The water is choppy so by the time you reach shore there isn't a dry stitch on you but you soon dry out. I had some magazines for Wes so we hiked up to his place. He was out flying so didn't get to see him. We were just messing around and no place in particular to go so we meandered around. Went down all the out of the way trails, ran across a couple of native huts, with natives "int", but marked out of bounds — we didn't go into but was interesting as they were less than ten yards away. Farther down we ran across an old Jap brig and it was of real interest. Barbarous looking. Was about 30 feet square and about 8 feet high — made entirely of gosh awful looking barbed wire — interwoven very closely — the walls must have been three feet thick easily of cleverly interlaced barbed wire. Wasn't a possible chance for anythin to escape the enclosure. There wasn't a solid roof over it, just more wire — the poor devils would drown when it rained. The prison was complete — even had cells for solitary confinement and fox holes.

The s.c. cells were just large enough to stand in, couldn't lean against anything, lay down or even sit. The barbed wire we are used to is definitely "femine" [*feminine*] compared to what they use — awful.

We continued our travels but decided to ride — went out to the main drag, flagged a jeep and away we went. Made it to the air strip and watched planes take off — interesting to watch transports come in and go out — always a big hustle, fresh new pilots going in — battle [*scarred*] ones going out. Went by Wes's again but he was still flying — was time for the club to open so we moseyed down that way, stopping now and then to watch a hot ball game. Reached the club by bumming a ride with what turned out to be the bartender — we were still early but we got good service. Foster grabbed a table & two chairs out on the veranda while I went in and got twelve bottles of beer. They only sell 6 to an officer so I drafted one to get my dozen. We sat out on the porch and guzzled beer at our leisure and had fun watching the world go by. The trick is to get there early while the cold beer holds out and tables are available — after that they are at least six deep around the bar and hell to get service.

The officers come in all sizes, shapes, ages and nationalities — an interesting lot and a lot of fun to mingle with. As long as I'm in the service I wouldn't miss this experience of "foreign duty" for anything.

Would hate awfully to be stationed here permanently — that is, without you. If we both could be here it would be wonderful for a term of duty — but to be here alone — too lonesome. I always devote some time just to you and me whenever I hit these places — go out to the ocean side of the island and look out over the ocean and marvel at its beauty wishing for you to be here and enjoying it with me. On one side of the island we have the wide open ocean — the lagoon side holds the fleet and what a fleet! Never tire of just gazing at it and trying to realize I'm an active member of it. The thing that impresses me is at colors — all the ships raise or lower their colors at the same time — just as tho one giant hand manipulated a single line — all act as one. One would think I am proud of "Our Navy".

Wish you could see our boys — stripped to the waist, wringing wet but handling our big ammunition like veterans — good natured cussing and having a big time. It's raining outside so it's sticky as hell and my rash is rearing its ugly head again.

Saw "Gung Ho" the other night. Tonight we have "Madame Curie" — will think of you because I remember you said you saw it and cried.

Bye, bye darling — love you
Paul

23 May 1944

Hello My Sweet —

At Wes's "house" I slept on an iron bed, quite a bit wider than my bunk and was it ever a treat. Could spread out and did same — my bunk aboard ship is swell but too soft and a little narrow. That's a hell of a complaint — bed too soft! My, my these Americans can never be pleased but to me it's a legitimate complaint not to be able to sprawl — makes our shoulders round & don't like that. Golly, what wouldn't I give to be able to stretch out & touch you — to hold and love you — you are such a sweet girl and I miss you so much. There will be a time, little one, so look out.

It's about chow time & I'm starved — had a little diversion today — man overboard, couldn't swim — damned near drowned — two men dived in after him — all safe. Finis.

Remember I love you gooooood.

All My Love
Paul

25 May 1944

My Darling —

Sure a flock of our officers getting orders — five leave next week and Dr. Barber got his orders today pending arrival of his relief. He goes to Treasure Island — you know, out of Frisco aways. I wasn't surprised at all. He was getting to be a pest, especially after not making commander this last time. Some Lt. Comdr. is relieving him so maybe Johnson will be going soon too because that makes three Lt. Comdrs. in the medical dept. To have everyone the same rank wouldn't work out so hot, I'm afraid.

Sure having a time writing — many interruptions and the censors are censoring so I'm hurrying to get this in the mail on account we are going out for a few days. Having a big rehearsal — vocalizing etc., and it will break the monotony of the past few weeks — better put some cotton in my pocket so I won't forget and get caught short.

They are passing out our "shell back" cards and I want to be damn sure I get some so I'm camping on their tail. When I get my big one filled out, I'll mail it to you right away so if it gets damaged on the way I can get another one made up before I leave the ship.

Spend what you want on yourself — all or any part, the rest set aside — the unexpected might happen on this next time out or from now on. If we get shot up or lose "Lou" we'll have to come back to the states. Think our picnic is over — we are crowding them too close and we are just starting — they "ain't saw nothing yet". Think we will be out a long time when we go out this time.

All My Love Honey
Paul

26 May 1944

Hello Darling —

This is more like it — we're on the move and it feels good to be rolling along again.

For a change it's nice and sunny out — what a relief from visibility zero — it's still hot but not that damp, sticky mess we have been in.

Golly sakes, had fun last night. Wes came out for dinner and the movie, had marvelous steaks, french [*fries*], spinach, fresh grapefruit, cherry pie a la mode. The movie was "Riding High" and was filmed in Tucson. Remember the race track east of town? We went out when they were setting up for the picture. I enjoyed it a lot, was in technicolor and awfully pretty.

Am spending Sunday with Wes and the following Sunday he wants me to bring ten or twelve officers for a beer bust, guess I'd better do it for after that there will be a long dry spell. Our Cook's Tour is over — has to be don't you think? If you still say prayers, include Lady Lou in them — some won't be back from the consensus of opinion around these parts.

We're having early chow so bye, bye for now.

Loads Of Love,
Paul

27 May 1944

Good Morning, Honey —

It's either a quarter to five or twenty-five minutes after nine. Had early reveille this morning and then g.q. was belayed due to "inclement" weather. No use going back to bed so I thought I'd talk to you a while. After all it must be at least 1000 where you are "at" and may be getting up. Coffee is on — get up, honey.

Nothing new to report. Had marvelous shooting practice last night — our crews are really on the beam. Hope they remain so for future reference. My observation station was aft this time and I sure fell over a flock of guns getting to my station but made it with the minimum loss of skin and barked shins.

Word was just passed to light ship — opened my port and it's really pretty out. The sun rise really is something. An hour ago it was raining so hard you couldn't see your hand before your face. Now you couldn't ask for anything nicer. That means we will fire again in a little while. Should be back in port this afternoon and may be mail. Hate to think of this next operation and the mail situation. May be out a couple of months so if your mail is irregular, don't worry about it — it will catch up to you.

Think I'll go topside and breathe in a little pure ozone — ere long I'll be in a confined, tiny place so I better stretch while I can.

All My Love,
Paul

29 May 1944

Hello Honey —

Have been hitting the ball in the office this a.m. after a nice afternoon on the beach. Had a few bourbons and beers with Wes and Capt. Michals — a skipper of one of the carriers. Michals is so much like Towner, same personality and very likable. They opened a new officer's club last night so I attended the grand opening with Wes, Capt. Michals & Eddie Peabody (Peabody of banjo fame). Peabody had just flown in with a U.S.O. show — all Navy. He played the banjo — had some card tricks — marvelous singer (John Carr of Metropolitan fame) and music — didn't care so much for Peabody — full comdr. & "all Peabody".

Wes gave me a pinup girl but I'm sending her home to you — the fellows all went nuts over her so I'm having some prints made for them before she leaves for the states. Her name is "Lola" and lives here.

The book *Lady Lou* includes this picture of "Lola." According to Paul, she was a native of Majuro in the Marshall Islands. Apparently this is the same photo he enclosed in his June 10, 1944, letter to Dotty B. "Some gal, isn't she?" he wrote, but, ever the dedicated dentist, he added: "She has an upper left lateral out of line."

Enclosed find some snaps taken on the beach — Wes's house — reef — handmade washing machine, etc. — I'm all teeth, but happy.

The new club is nice — four quonset huts, two end to end with the backs knocked out of course and the other two alongside with the bulkheads cut out, making one large attractive room. Have a nice bar, beer only, cigars, cigarettes (5 cents), gum, etc. — lots of tables and chairs — potted plants, etc. It was Wes's doing and did right smart.

There's a cruiser party this afternoon but don't know whether or not I'll go — one of us has to stay here.

Am learning my way about the islands in good shape. Peabody was to put on several shows & Wes had to be with him so after the 1st performance I left for my ship. The utility boats quit running at 1900 (7) and here it was 2100 — Murph, Grub and I stranded. I got a jeep from the O. D., went down to the dock — even it had been moved and when we found it — no boats. Made some phone calls and a huge speed boat was placed at our disposal and — home. Fun! I couldn't find Wes so did it on my own — felt like a Boy Scout for sure. It's time for chow — the censors are "censing" right after to clear the way for the cruiser party so I'm making this short. If I don't go [*picnicking*] I'll talk to you this afternoon.

All My Love, Honey,
Paul

31 May 1944

Hello Darling —

Sure am having an awful time getting this letter written — Lud is leaving in the morning and he has had his stuff in my room so he is packing and my writing has suffered.

We are busy people these days getting ready to shove off — have really made more preparations this time than ever before. Lou is the hot ship of this operation so we are getting ready for any emergency — will have something to talk about when this one is over.

Admiral Oldendorf is the one aboard us and is the big shot on this business deal so if you run across his name — radio or paper — that's us. We've tested our life belts, guns, rafts and even gas masks so it's going to be something real. Sure hope we get a good crack at them — we have had fun but no real fun.

Wanted to close out May with at least a little note — don't worry about me, honey. I'm not worried at all so don't you be. Everything is under control — everyone is in fine spirits and raring to go — they all "figger" we're out here to do business so let's get at it. I wouldn't swap Lou and my shipmates for any other ship in the fleet — they are 4.0 from the word go. She is maintaining her rep as a happy ship and a go getter — she knows her way around too.

All My Love,
Paul

1 June 1944

Hello Little Honey

There are a million and four jellyfish around the ship right now. There isn't a square foot but what contains a fish or two — sure messy looking things. When you come in contact with them, they sting hell out of you — yes, I'll be careful, honey.

Have seen several good shows. Last night was "His Butler's Sister" — cute, tonight, "Star Spangled Rhythm". The other night the machine broke down so during the lull in the picture the enlisted men started singing and it really was marvelous. We have some fine voices aboard and they led off, kept it low and sang all the old songs so before long everyone joined in. It really was nice — beautiful moonlight — lot of lights in the harbor — quite a deal.

Night before last we had a home talent show aboard from one of the carriers. It really was clever, of course some risque jokes but they were all right. The M. C. was from Bob Crosby's show and the main fellow was Fred Waring's — used to conduct the chorus and was a soloist. He had a marvelous voice, sang "When Irish Eyes Are Smiling" and "Old Man River". The show was held out on the quarter deck, the stage between the two hangars and everyone gathered on "draped" ground — moonlight, music and a lot of laughs deep in the Pacific. Some war, eh?

Am starting my eighth month of sea duty — in a way it seems I've been out here forever. On the other hand seems I've just barely started. Time does fly and will even pick up ere long. When night and day doesn't make any difference and we are in g.q. or alert all the time — that is when it slips by. We'll be into this next mess and out again before we know it. We'll look like hell and pooped out but everyone carries on. Means sleeping in clothes and whenever we can but that's part of it. Sure hope we run into the whole Tojo family.

It's inventory day and they are auditing my books. I'm custodian of several thousand dollars — hope it's all there!

Next day — had fun at Wes's. Wants me to spend Saturday night & Sunday with him so guess I will. Big gang of big shots coming in for the smoker and should be interesting. Will definitely be my last crack at terra firma so I'd better take advantage of it.

Had a nice morning of extracting teeth — had some dandies. Now it's field day to get ready for Captains's Inspection.

They are building an air scoop in my room — should cool things off considerably — can't wait to get underway in order to try it out.

Still Love You Loads and Loads
Paul

5 June 1944

Hello Little Sweetheart —

I don't feel very healthy but the mail closes for a couple of days so thought I'd better drop you a few lines. Had a big time over the weekend but will save it for my next letter.

Have added a homey touch to my room — procured a native mat and placed it in front of my bunk so when I hit the deck, it's a lot more comfortable.

Word was just passed that outgoing mail had to be in the P.O. by 1100 so I'd better get hot & finish this. Don't worry about me, I'll be all right. Lady Lou will bring us thru in good shape.

Take care honey and remember I love you good.

Paul

ON JUNE 6, the *Louisville* left Majuro for the short run to Roi in Kwajalein Atoll, staging site for the Marianas campaign.

6 June 1944

Hello My Darling —

I feel so much more better than I did yesterday — a couple of alarms and a good night's sleep fixed me up.

Am so glad my little package arrived — not much in it but it was from out here. I have another just about ready — mail may go out tomorrow so you at least will have a letter. The red sticks are a form of coral — when you see it alive it's really beautiful — it's the tail end process and I guess exfoliated — the whole mass wiggles and crawls off. The rattan or what have you is native grass, don't know how they color it. The shells are polished by being buried with crabs in them — ants eat the insides out and polish them at the same time. All the natives do is to dig them up again, wash them up and there you are. The ones I'm sending you this time are prettier & the string can be torn down & remade into an attractive bracelet — necklace or even buttons.

The clipping you sent me of Okla.'s Admiral Mitscher — I met him the other night with Wes at the smoker.

So you like being Mrs. Doctor Lieutenant Commander Paul C. Bonnette. I'm glad you are Mrs. D L C P C Bonnette — would have no other share the title with me.

It's about time for me to collect mess bills so will close for now — maybe can write later this evening.

All My Love
Paul

PAUL'S NEWS of the "invasion" in the following letter refers, of course, to the June 6 Allied invasion of Normandy, France. The final Allied campaign of the European Theater of Operations, D-Day led to the eventual surrender of Germany in May 1945.

6 June 1944

Little Honey —

Just had a wicked set to in 4-handed cribbage — we won the cokes but the games wound up two & two. A little poker session just started so I thought I'd pack your little box and it might get out tomorrow.

I started getting fat so I took myself in hand and took some setting up exercises — when I took my physical I weighed 179 — a lb. heavier than when I entered the "noivey".

News of the invasion just came over the air. That should be a big whing ding.

Had an awfully nice time Saturday evening. I was late getting to the beach and missed Wes and Capt. Michals on the first go around but joined them later. They waited for me until five o'clock and then went on to the carrier party. I got to his quarters a quarter past but word had been left to make myself at home and they'd be back at 7:30. I drank a few beers and read until they came in. They had a good load on but had to go on to the atoll commanders quarters. Had a few drinks there, met a lot of admirals, captains & commanders. Spent an hour or so there & then went home. Wes & Capt. (M) passed out — that is stretched out & promptly fell asleep. I was wide awake, it had quit raining so I took some beer & my ciggies and sat on the beach a couple of hours.

Were your ears ringing Saturday night? They should have been for I sure was concentrating on you. It was so pretty out, the skies were overcast so the moon would give an indirect lighting affect for the most part, but would occasionally break out in all its glory. The sound of the ocean pounding the reefs — sparkling breakers — planes overhead — the fleet standing in — velly pletty. Got up at 6:30 — Wes had to go to work by 7 so we had breakfast and then I jumped into my shorts and "played" on the beach. Wes came back about 10:30 for a beer — needed it bad, had a few and went back to work. He finished about noon so we decided to have some more beer and talk over old times. Were joined by Comdr. Potter from Detroit so the bull really flew until the man delivered a case of Schenleys to Wes. We killed a quart and called it quits for the weekend — goody! It will be a long time before we'll be back together so we did it up brown. He gave me a quart for after this next big deal — said we might need it. Can't tell you the set up, but from all indications, the Cook's tour is over.

Sometime when you are in a mailing mood, send me some pajamas size D — if they say a D is too large, tell them that is what I insist on. The two pairs I started with have been reduced to one — laundry is tougher than hell on clothes — two of my khaki shirts gave up also, so a couple of size 15 collar & 34 sleeve would be swell. There is a shortage of shirts out here so I've been sort of handicapped.

All My Love To You, Honey
Paul

8 June 1944

My Own Darling —

It's so pretty out, the moon and sky are gorgeous — the water so calm it shines like a mirror, reflecting "everything" on it. It's one of the prettiest nights I've seen — everyone else seems to feel the same way for they were all out on deck to drink it in. The mail definitely closes tomorrow and life belts and knives will be the uniform of the day so we're all getting a last letter off.

For some of us out here it can easily be "a last letter" off — sure hope "Lucky Lady Lou" runs true to form on this operation. Not trying to scare you honey but I want to explain once more the allotment deal. If anything happens to me and I'm reported missing, it will run a year, then if I'm not found and am reported "lost in action" you get a six months base (250) pay gratuity and the insurance starts. It isn't nice to talk about but anything can happen and I want you to know what you are entitled to.

Now for the less serious side of the big deal.

Remember I once told you about being Grand Central Station? That was small peanuts — today looked like farmers day at the State Fair — sure was a bee hive of activity but can't tell you about it, will save it for when this is over. Tomorrow will be still worse, closing day but it's sure exciting and fun.

We are the big shots this time so we will get our crack at the limelight.

Lou looked so trim and pretty tonight in the moonlight — her "vocal cords" look ready for grand opera — hope her voice doesn't change when she is called on to perform.

Gee, honey, I wish I could tell you what's going on — mighty gripping

Lt. Comdr. P.C. Bonnette (MC) USNR
U.S.S. Louisville
F.P.O.
San Francisco
AIR MAIL
UNITED STATES OF AMERICA
JUN 8 A.M. 1944 NAVY
Mrs. Paul C. Bonnette
1700 NW 17
Oklahoma City (2)
Oklahoma
PASSED BY NAVAL CENSOR

and exciting. Wouldn't miss it for the world, so different than anything so far — tell we're really doing something for the cause this time.

Remember darling, "if" — I was thinking of you and still loved you with all my heart, you're swell.

Bye honey, all my love,
Paul

Poor Devils on the Beach

ON JUNE 10, 1944, *Lady Lou* led the way out of Roi anchorage. She spent the next two months with the U.S. Fifth Fleet in the Marianas as part of OPERATION FORAGER's goal of securing Saipan, nearby Tinian, and Guam. Taking the Marianas would help secure the growing American supply lines and would bring the Japanese home islands within range of mighty U.S. bombers.

The fleet, made up of 535 vessels including 15 carriers, 7 battleships, 21 cruisers, and troop transports packed with nearly 130,000 soldiers and Marines, was not unchallenged. Japan mustered its dwindling sea and naval air resources only to be devastated in the three-day Battle of the Philippine Sea, the greatest carrier battle of the war. On June 19 alone, the Japanese lost two carriers and over 300 aircraft in what would be remembered by U.S. Navy fliers as "The Great Marianas Turkey Shoot."

Following bombardment from air and sea, 20,000 Marines went ashore on Saipan on June 15, 1944. The fighting would rage for over three weeks. Admiral Jesse Oldendorf claimed that as lead bombardment unit, the *Louisville* set an all-time gunnery record by firing steadily night and day — pausing only to replenish ammunition and for a burial at sea — for the first eleven days of the Saipan operation.

In the pre-dawn hours of June 16, Japanese defenders launched a fanatic assault to drive the Marines into the sea. The attack was finally stopped at sunrise by Marine tanks and, according to historian Morison, "the Japanese withdrew under a blanket of gunfire from cruiser *Louisville* and destroyers *Phelps* and *Monssen,* leaving about 700 dead on the battlefield."

Tinian fell in a week after thunderous bombardment from battleships, cruisers, and destroyers. On July 31, the *Louisville* joined battleships *Tennessee* and *California* and cruisers *Montpelier* and *Birmingham* in firing over 600 tons of shells to support the Marines' final push.

"The Tinian operation," said Fleet Commander Admiral Raymond Spruance, "was probably the most brilliantly conceived and executed amphibious operation of World War II."

SeaBees went immediately to work, turning the 60-square-mile island into a mammoth air base and setting the stage for Tinian's most enduring claim to fame. At 2:45 a.m. on August 6, 1945, a B-29 named "Enola Gay" took off from Tinian and flew 1,700 miles to drop a uranium bomb named "Little Boy" on the Japanese city of Hiroshima.

As mopping up continued on Tinian, 100 miles to the south Guam was invaded and, like Saipan, Guam became a week's-long bloodbath.

Lady Lou finally left the Marianas, having fired 24,948 rounds of ammunition, on August 9 to spend a week at Eniwetok in the Marshalls. On August 19, she steamed south toward Espiritu Santo in the New Hebrides Islands to prepare for the invasion of Peleliu.

Peleliu was the final stepping stone to the Philippines, but its place in military history is controversial. Some strategists urged bypassing the small spot of coral and limestone. Others insisted that even with the lessening threat of Japanese air power, Peleliu's major air field could not be ignored. While the planners debated, the invasion force set sail so the Army, Navy, and Marines got a green light for D-day, September 15.

Commanders knew it would be tough, but many fully expected to have the island secured within a week. In fact, the last organized resistance would not be rooted out of the caves and deep, linked passageways for over two months in a cave-to-cave campaign that claimed the lives of 10,000 Japanese and nearly 2,000 Americans.

The *Louisville* left the Palau Islands on September 25 and spent the next two weeks at Hollandia, New Guinea, and in Manus in the nearby Admiralty Islands.

10 June 1944

My Darling —

Started off rather poorly. Overslept and of all times I had to pick the day of the big conference. The wardroom had to be cleared by 0800 and I came to at 0745 so I jumped into my clothes, no shave, bath or even a face wash and managed to grab a bite to eat. Went on down for sick call, did a few extractions and then started my boy on field day. Went back to my room thinking I might just as well write a couple of letters before cleaning up.

They gave us the dope today and it's gigantic — it sure makes it a lot easier, eases the tension to know what & how we are going to do it.

To continue with the perfect day after yesterday — I finally got shaved, cleaned up, listened in on the conference and then got word I could go over to the island if I had "official business". Grub, Padre, Johnson & I got a crack at it — the Padre just had to see the chaplain, I needed some unheard of dental instruments, Johnson medical supplies & [*Grubb*] had to contact the supply officer. The exec said "not to bring any junk" back — just stay out of trouble so away we went. Can't tell you the name of the islands but they were of special interest to us because they were our second targets [*the small connected islands of Roi and Namur*] when we first came out. They took an unmerciful beating and they looked it — several Jap block houses & Pill boxes remained so we crawled over, through, around & what have you around them. They are a masterpiece of construction, three to four feet thick — solid concrete with a dense matting of inch & a half steel rods interwoven in the concrete — thick steel doors and sliding windows. They took innumerable hits but still stand! Shells are still laying around — unexploded ones. The houses and pill boxes had been banked with many feet of sand so they cushioned the shells with the result a lot didn't explode. No, I didn't bring any back with me — "too heavy" to carry. The stench of death and blood is still in the air — especially when you go by newly turned ground around the air strip or other construction. You never know when you will stumble over the remains of a dead Jap. Sure glad I'm aboard a ship and a combat ship at that — we can take care of ourselves and "we got variety".

Went by the American cemetery — we have one all right but not as large as one would expect after such an operation. It's neatly kept up — the markers are half round and painted white instead of white crosses. The Japs are buried in several places on the islands — big ditches ten feet deep are dug by bulldozers and the bodies dumped in so they are covered with about four feet of dirt — one woman is buried with them — rather unpleasant isn't it.

We toured the entire Islands, walked some & rode some, wound up at the Officers Club & then headed for home. It's a neat club, quite pretty inside and made out of quonset huts. Each officer was allowed one beer & one coca cola — I took beer — we have cokes aboard ship. I'm [*sending*] you the coke chit, so if you ever are out this way you can have a "coca cola" on me.

Talked with the dentist. Sure wouldn't swap places with him — foot motor, bucket for a cuspidor — very primitive.

Time out for beddy bed — company dropped in so we had a couple hours of music and bull slinging — I'll finish this in the a.m. Good night, Sweet.

Good morning — it's a "beautiful morning" in the Pacific — feel like a million. Answered sick call, bathed, shaved, dolled up in a clean uniform, slung a little bull and then went to church. Services out here still impress me and I sure hate to miss them, wonder if we'll have them next Sunday.

Perhaps it's the simplicity of the whole thing — the officers all in freshly [*laundered khakis*], enlisted men in dungeres (?) — no worries about who is the best dressed or what the Smiths might be thinking of you. Our choir still consists of one fellow with a swell tenor voice and music furnished by an accordion, violin, and a guitar. When the ship lists to port, we list with it — when she goes starboard — we go starboard — something like watching a tennis match — back & forth. We sing our hymns, have a scripture reading, solo, short sermon, hymn, silent prayer, hymn, benediction & it's over. The Padre did real well — mentioned how plans for this operation had been completed & now embarked on. He had a simple plan for the "spiritual operation" consisting of two simple points, Confidence in God and Prayer. It was nicely done, only wish he had closed with the song "Eternal Father, Strong to Save" — it's a beauty.

Thanks again for the pictures — I've almost worn them out looking at them — you're such a sweet kid & I love you.

Still having silly rains, one side of the ship is wet — the other dry & sunny.

Enclosed find a picture of Lola — some gal isn't she? Now I know what the smaller strand of shells are for. Notice "she has an upper left lateral out of line" — I did.

Sweet girl — don't know when you'll get this letter — everything is under control, everyone on their toes and raring to go — it won't be long now.

All my love to my one & only —
that's you honey.
Paul

12 June 1944

Hello Little Girl —

Sure feels good to be under way — nice breeze blowing and the water is so pretty. Last night we sat out on the foc'sle and argued what colors were in the sunset. The sky was robin egg blue and was it something. The sun rise was beautiful too, the air so clean and fresh — made you feel like a new man after being in g.q. an hour or so. Breakfast wasn't served until 0715 so Comdr. Bowers & I played cribbage from 0500 to 0715. He beat the socks off me but I'll get him in the morning.

Have seen some good shows — particularly enjoyed Henry Fonda & B. Stanwyck in "You Belong to Me". Also saw Frank Sinatra in "Higher & Higher" — didn't care for his acting. You should have heard the gang when he let loose on one of his swoon songs.

Not much fun so far but as the Monkey said when he got his tail caught in the lawn mower — "Won't be long now!"

All My Love,
Paul

13 June 1944

Little Darling —

This letter may be written on the installment plan — we don't know what's up, may have to rush for our battle stations any minute — that isn't conducive to coherent letter writing, but at least I'm thinking of you.

We're off for B. stations — by pro tem.

Back again for a little while, hope until at least 0300 — start our little business deal then. Had some interesting goings on today — broke the monotony of the past few days. Sure is hot when we are in g.q. All ventilation is cut off as well as the fresh water — I sweat like a nigger any how so you can imagine what I look like after a short time below deck. My heat rash is under control as of now but I'm afraid these next sixty days will bring it on again. We're in for a rugged time but as long as we are making "history", we should worry — nez pas?

Ate baked or something spare ribs & sauer kraut this noon — really stowed it away — it really was good. Yesterday I actually ate an omelet and it was delicious. The eggs had been beat up and then grated or cut up cheese added & then cooked. If you never have tried it, mix up a batch & see if it doesn't tickle your palate. With the omelet we had fried ham, cabbage salad & toast — oh yes, mixed fruit, too, not bad for war, I'd say. The food [*continues*] to be A-1 — it's hard not to take second helpings but I must watch my waist line — good eats and no exercise sure is hard on the tummy.

Can hardly wait for morning — it's just a few hours until reveille — then breakfast, then g.q., then - - - - - -!!! ??? - - - - - - - fun, I hope. I have my dark glasses and cotton handy so I can view the scenery but I'll be careful.

All my love to you honey,
Paul

THE CASUALTY in Paul's June 14 letter was not a victim of enemy fire. The sailor was accidentally crushed under one of the *Louisville's* gun mounts.

14 June 1944

Hello Honey —

Guess it was a busy night but I sure didn't know anything about it until this morning. Went outside before breakfast — the sky was all lighted up by star shells and off to our port some Jap ships were aflame. Watched them go under — as long as they were Japs, it was a beautiful sight. It's now 0830 and have been topside most of the time watching the bombardment — still get a kick out of it — it's a different target than any we have had before. Several Jap ships in the harbor — several have been sunk so all you can see is the super structure sticking out of the water. Sounds like we are having a "thunder storm" and it's raining debris.

Had one casualty so far, poor devil, watched him die. My battle station got the word so we went out after him and took him to sick bay where he passed out. Horrible death — body completely crushed — face was black as a nigger's, rather his entire head from the neck up. Just last week I was an observer with him during firing practice — now he is ready for burial at sea. It's really tough and I feel badly over his going out — before I get back I'll no doubt see a lot of it, but don't think I'll ever get used to it.

Lady Lou is doing a swell job of firing — she is some ship — the fellows are the damndest gang I ever saw. The repair parties and those not on guns, telephones and or essential posts are laying around asleep, reading, playing acey-ducey or just "spectating" as I've been doing. Get a kick out of the Japs firing at our planes — so far haven't come within a mile of them.

There's a temporary lull in the activities so we can air out the place and get a drink — in a few minutes we start up again on new tactics so I must go topside and watch. They sighted a submarine a few thousand yards out so want to see what happens to it. This little show has possibilities — with the exception of the one casualty, it's been a swell performance. Was fun watching a loose mine floating around in the water — a destroyer is after it to neutralize it — hope it isn't magnetized.

Sweet girl — I'll be careful — I'll stand behind a fat man — must go see what's going on.

All my love dearest, and don't "fret" about me.
Paul

THE "SPECIALISTS" in Paul's June 15th letter are probably Navy "frogmen" — Underwater Demolition Teams. During the pre-invasion bombardment, UDT units scouted the most suitable channels to Saipan's beaches and blew up obstacles that might prevent boats from reaching shore. The *Louisville* eased in close enough to cover UDT teams with automatic weapons fire.

15 June 1944

My Darling — Hello

Am a weary chick but we're still going strong — was up at 0200 this morning and have the medical watch tonight so it's going to be a long day, me thinks.

Haven't had anything to do but "spectate" and it was a good show — suffered my first casualty — a fellow standing at my side took a dip of snuff and some blew into my eye, but that is the hazard of war.

Started some beautiful fires again this morning and several very fine explosions. Was fun watching the air strike just previous to the landing of the troops — really quite spectacular. The Navy however has developed a set of "specialists" that really out dare fliers, para-troopers or what have you — they are unsung heroes but what a job they do.

Had a little thrill before lunch. I was up in sky control with Art Esch & Peabo, having a fine time watching the Americans land and the gun fire when r-r-rat at tat-tat the Japs let go at us. I know now what it feels like to be shot at and have bullets splash around you. It was machine gun fire and nasty stuff — not as much fun as the big stuff.

No coconut trees around here but lots of sugar cane — looks like what I'd imagine the Hawaiian Islands look like from the little glimpse I had of them a long time ago. Really quite pretty & a shame to bang hell out of them but I must say we are careful — can see several beautiful missions and we are leaving them alone even though they are in the target area.

Am enclosing a clipping from our news digest — it was my first burial at sea and it really is quite impressive. When the bugle sounded taps over him last night as he slid into the water just at sunset — honey, it kind of gets you. I deleted his name — doesn't mean anything to you and it would be awful if by some act of fate his name got to his folks before they were officially notified. I'll always remember that ceremony not only for the burial of one of my shipmates, but the setting of the whole thing — we paused briefly but you could hear and see the big guns still going at it and more gold stars being run up.

Will write again tomorrow. Remember, honey, you are my one and only and all my love is yours.

Bye,
Paul

15 June 1944

Hello Sweet —

Must ask you to excuse the pencil again — it's just too damn hot for a pen — the paper gets wet from perspiration and then is a mess.

Am afraid we are in for a tough night — several groups of enemy planes are messing around and the shore battery is firing at us. All we need is a submarine and then we'd be getting it from all sides. Our big guns are doing the talking now and as usual is jarring hell out of us.

This afternoon after I finished writing to you, Foster & I sat out on the well deck eating ice cream and watching the bombardment — some war. They fired on us again but missed us again, goody! Glad I had the ice cream — just as we were ready to eat dinner g.q. went off for an air raid and we are still chewing the fat with them. Don't know when it will be over but Lou is still riding high wide and handsome. The sky is too dark to see now but a while ago it looked like it had black measles or full of blackheads from the anti aircraft we threw up. They pick the damndest times to come over — right at dinner time — nasty little devils.

Did I say it was hot? It's terrible. No ventilation and everyone is sweating streams, especially the ammunition passers — they are earning their money these days.

Pearl Harbor couldn't have looked worse on Dec. 7 than this island does now — sh-h-h — lot of Jap ships and most of them burning — must have had huge cargoes of fuel. Saw my first Jap flags flying — they were on the masts of some of the ships — now I feel we are actually fighting Japs and not an imaginary enemy.

Sweet, it's so hot, am going topside to take a gander to see what's going on — just thought you might be interested in what's happening and that we are on the job.

Still love you and am thinking of you in spite of frequent interruptions.

All my love, honey,
Paul

16 June 1944

Hello Little One —

Thought I'd check in with you tonight to let you know all is well and we're going strong. Had a breather today and looks like a quiet night tonight so I'm going to catch me some sleep.

We were in and out of g.q. so much the past couple of days & nights we're about g.q.'ed out. We fired all night last night and are about to resume firing for an all night session again tonight but I'll get to "sleep" on account I had the watch last night. Am so used to the guns by now I could lay up against it and not be bothered. We ran out of ammunition this morning so we had a breather while we took on more, saw some interesting sights but can't tell you about them until this is over. Spent the entire day watching activities thru field glasses — what sights I saw! The Japs have five less ships as of this morning — sh-h-h — that is on our side of the island. Started some beautiful fires and they are still burning tonight. One must be an ammunition dump for it's still going in all directions and can hear the exploding shells — quite spectacular. Have been watching the bombardment ever since after dinner — it's really pretty — flashes of the guns & then watch the tracers streak out across the sky & then the explosion. Star shells illuminate the terrain — that in itself is quite a deal but the pay off was just a few minutes ago when a ship scored a hit on the grand daddy of them all. Must have been millions of gallons of high octane gas — the storage was behind a hill in a ravine. When the hit occurred, there was a pink flash, then a huge ball of red flame came up from behind the hill, looking just like a rapidly raising sun — so solly, velly pletty, please.

The Jap fleet is on the way out to get us but damn it I'm afraid we are not going to be in on the intercepting party. Our reserve power is going out to meet them — we are too busy right here. We expect to have our hands full the next few days — whoops! Wish you could have heard that — shook the ship so something big must have gone up — wasn't us for we still are afloat. Am going to get in bed and cover up my head. I's tarred and tomorrow is supposed to be a hotsy totsy day — want to be able to spectate but good.

All my love to you. Wish you could see all this — better than movies, that's for sure.

All My Love,
Paul

17 June 1944

Hello Honey —

If I remember correctly, last night when I wrote you, I made the statement I was going to bed and get a good night's sleep. Well, I did for an hour and fifteen minutes, just nicely asleep when bong, bong g.q. sounded and away we went. Nothing happened so we finally got back to bed — thought maybe our guns would keep me awake but hell no, went right off to sleep. Everything has been knocked loose in my room so I don't have to worry about anything falling in my mouth. You have no idea what these big guns do to one's fixtures — all my lights are always knocked out, my ventilator comes down and other numerous objects banged up. That is the disadvantage of being right under a turret but mighty handy if a bomb should drop on the deck.

Went to sleep again but set my alarm for 0400 so I could bathe and shave before g.q. — got that nicely done, had some coffee and sat out on the deck to watch the show & wait for reveille to sound. Got so engrossed in a Jap tank counter attack I didn't notice the time until reveille did sound and it was 0700 — here I spent three hours spectating when I could have been sleeping — when I spectate, I spectate. They didn't have g.q. at all. Sat out all day and had a big time — we were close enough in so I could watch the actual fighting between the Marines and Japs — watch the men come in — tanks firing — Japs blown out of buildings — divc bombers come in — ground strafing and all the tactics of war. It was better than any movie & was the real McCoy.

The evening started out like a dime thriller. We bombarded & fought off an actual aerial attack all at the same time — used all the guns we had and some of us even "pooped" to help out. Most spectacular & awesome thing I've ever seen. Now I'd like to have a submarine fire a torpedo at us and then I think I will have run the gauntlet.

I guess the Japs didn't mind us being in their front yard but when we came up on the porch "they resented". It isn't near as Cook's Tourish but still plenty of fun and plenty of excitement — still would like to be a director on one of the guns instead of a spectator.

All My Love
Binocular Paul

19 June 1944

Dear Honey

We, meaning Lady Lou, really has her work cut out for her and is doing a magnificent job of it. She is in a ticklish spot but so far it hasn't even phased her — she is a noble gal and I'm might proud of her. Sure would feel awfully bad if anything were to happen to her.

We have been under aerial attack several times now and it still is the most thrilling and exciting. Don't know how to describe the curtain of fire unless I liken it to one of those fountains we usually set off on the 4th of July. They dropped several this morning and one is laying a few hundred yards from us on the beach — a big 52 painted on its tail but is Jap. Always wanted to see a dog fight, now I've seen several & it's a lot like those P 38s that used to chase tails but when you see tracer bullets coming out you realize it's for keeps. Lots of interesting sights — this morning saw several hundred native prisoners all corralled in a little sandy cove and guarded by Marines. Men, women & children — the Marines must have ordered a bath for them because they were all scrubbing themselves. The natives in the Marshalls hadn't had soap in over two years and were suffering from filth sores so perhaps the Japs had deprived these natives of soap also and they welcomed the chance to clean up.

Our Marines are the damndest guys — you should watch them "working". Watched them clean out a nest of Japs yesterday — followed it from the very beginning through to the finis. We were only about a thousand yards from them & with 7 power glasses it was just like watching a play. It's a lot like hunting rabbits — the climax came when they tossed a couple of grenades into the shack — the shack disappeared and most of the Japs, but a few lived to run — a little ways — then ping — so solly bly bly Jap.

We chased out several bunches ourselves — one in particular was inter esting because it was in a cane field and we could see what was going on. There was a gun emplacement in a stone block house. We blasted it to pieces with our big guns and then sprayed the bushes with our lighter guns — you should have seen them get in gear and head for the trees — no honey, they didn't quite make it.

It's kind of exciting when you see a flash on the beach in Jap territory. You don't know whether they are shooting at you or the Marines. We don't lose any time training our guns on it and "neutralizing" it.

You know we have been busy when we have run out of ammunition three times and are out again — lot of lead has been tossed these past few days. A little old destroyer was going at it hot & heavy the other day — it was so fast & furious they had to play a steady stream of water on the gun barrels to keep them cool.

I think I know one kid that is glad we are busy playing war. He's a kid not over a minute past the legal age — tiny and looks like a cherub for sure. Apparently his job in "peace time" is silver ware, for three times a day every day we have been out to sea, he has sat out in front of my office with mountains of knives, forks & spoons around him — gazing off into space & mechanically wiping silver ware at a w.p.a. worker's speed. He is comical to watch — oblivious to anyone around him — just gazing or singing and embarked on an apparently endless job.

Enjoyed an hour's nap — now I'm going to take a shower & clean up — starting a little earlier today because yesterday several waves of enemy planes came over just as I hit the shower — didn't scrub too carefully.

Am having a lot of fun but miss you terribly — thought I'd get used to being away from you but it's just the opposite. After this operation I'll be ready for a breather — so will the other thousand or so. Would it be something if they sent us to the states for a rest come September? We certainly have earned a decent liberty — haven't had one since we left the states & have been in all the actions so far — believe we rate a rest.

All My Love
Paul

20 June 1944

Hello Darling —

Really was scared this morning, thought sure I was headed for a general court martial. I was sleeping away peacefully when all of a sudden the bugler sounded "Secure From General Quarters" — looked at my watch and it was 0500 — My God! Had I slept thru g.q.? Was scared stiff but soon found out they were securing from the condition set up for the night. Boy! Was I relieved, turned over and slept until 0700 — a real treat.

Seems so quiet and peaceful out there — haven't heard a gun or an alarm all day — we had some "shopping" to do so we withdrew from the scene of activities and used up some "C" coupons. We are headed back now and it won't be long now before the old familiar sounds of guns will fill the air & we will have to make up for lost time. By being away today we missed at least one good air attack but will be on hand for tomorrow morning's little set to. Big things are going on out here — suspect the radio has given most of it to you by now.

What's new at home? How are you making out with your gas coupons — ration stamps etc.? It's going to be hard to adjust myself to rationing and 21-cent cigarettes when I get home. Don't believe I ever have tasted any better meats than I have out here and cigarettes only five cents a pack. Sure would like to send you a case of ciggies but am afraid Uncle Sam would raise an eyebrow.

You don't know it but you stand with me each day up in Sky Control and watch the battle. It's the damndest show I've ever seen — more thrilling than "Hellzapoppin" — it's popping all right.

Honey girl — sure love you and miss you terribly.

All my love
Paul

22 June 1944

Hello Honey —

Didn't write yesterday — everything was quiet and we were taking on ammunition — it's ticklish work because we are where it's hot & heavy. Visited the ship and met the doctor, inspected sick bay etc. He is from Boston, a two striper and his first time out and in the battle area to boot. He was scared stiff, poor devil. Wonder how long he'll last before he cracks up. He offered us a drink (Johnson & I) but we politely refused — aren't I getting good.

Had an air raid this morning at 0100 — g.q. sounded and away we went — thought it was the "sun rise usual" but them came early — no damage done but was glad we weren't tied up to the ammunition ship just the same.

Lots of debris floating by — mines, oil drums, crates and a few dead Japs — they don't look so pretty with their shaved heads.

We laid down one of the prettiest and most intense barrages of the "season" this morning, sure was pretty, but awful too. Lou is a hot mamma and really going to town — the Japs are calling her Dynamite & she is to them.

Sure feels good to be back "working" — never a dull moment and the time flies. Tojo isn't doing right by his little yellow men — evidently Tokyo doesn't know what is going on for a Jap plane blithely set down on the air strip & when he stepped out of his plane, the big bad Marines grabbed him up — bet his face was red — that's for sure.

All My Love
Paul

23 June 1944

Hello Darling —

The screen is clear — should go to bed and catch a little sleep while there are no enemy planes around. Yesterday evening, midnight, early morning and at noon today they pestered us but our luck held. Had four close ones though — three bombs and a sixteen inch shell chased everyone to cover but they missed the ship and their explosion merely shook us up. Last night the "- - - -" in the berth next to us stopped a torpedo and is now limping for home.

We are firing star shells now to light up the terrain for the land forces — aids them but sure makes us a good target.

Sure enjoyed the foc'sle last night & tonight — a cool breeze is blowing, in fact a jacket felt good. Inside the ship it's hotter than hell due to all ports being closed. Last night we cut didos — slashed thru the water — zig zagging and turning — the ship would lean away over and the waves wash the decks — really great sport and thrilling — far better than riding in a car or plane. There is something about it that sure gets you.

Our spotting planes came back all shot up again today — they sure have been doing a swell job of directing our fire. The boogers skim right over the heads of the Japs to see what they have & then send in the word & we blast hell out of them.

There are quite a few water buffalo on the island and they were half crazy at the firing at first but now they calmly chew their cuds & pay no attention.

The island really is pretty — wouldn't mind visiting it in peace time. The mountains [*the highest "mountain" on Tinian is 690 feet*] are a relief after the atolls we have been messing around with.

Still love you good & have a "yen" to see you.

Good night, all my love
Paul

24 June 1944
Time "2010"

My Honey —

Am wondering if you have been away from the "Noivy" long enough to have forgotten Navy jargon. I try not to use it but sometimes it just slips out. I'm not trying to be salty but an eyebrow is raised if we say rope for line, wall for bulkhead, etc.

Very quiet today up until about one hour ago. This morning did routine bombardment, this afternoon sunbathed & watched the battle. Tonight we were having our nightly bull session & enjoying the breeze on the foc'sle. You have your arm chair generals at home and we have foc'sle admirals out here. We were "winning the war" very handily when all of a sudden Bong! Bong! and away we went — enemy aircraft! Went to my battle station, checked on my boys and reported, then went topside to see what giffs. Saw a nice show — apparently they went after us so our duty was to lay down a smoke screen — we did & honey that's for sure. It's the first real one I'd seen & they are really something. Watched them drop their bombs and then return anti-aircraft fire — it's really something to see — sure wish you could be here to watch it. It's kind of confusing and thrilling because you can't see the planes & you don't know whether they are coming toward you or going away. The only thing you are sure of is when they are hit and crash — then scratch one, two or whatever number it might be — fun.

Just realized why it has been so miserable out here — we have been going thru the doldrums again — just went through them awhile back on our other "locations" and now we hit them again here.

The monsoon or rainy season starts July 1st and should be cooler, in fact it's raining a little now with much thunder and honest to gosh lightning. Sure hope these steel ships with their towering masts are lightning proof — I'm scared of it — don't mind a bomb or shell but lightning — ouch!

Had fun watching the flying fish this evening before the air raid. They are quite a fish and interesting to watch them take off and then crash land. They sure hit the water at the end of their flight but seem to enjoy it.

It's also interesting to watch the debris float by — see almost everything. Saw a truly hideous Jap come by — he was all bloated — still had a life jacket on so must have been on one of the ships.

Believe the outstanding sight was a bloated hand and half an arm — it came floating by by itself in a mess of cane — the body must have been covered up for an arm couldn't float by itself — here we go again 2050.

Hello Honey [*Paul often wrote "Hello Honey" in quavering letters*] 2228 Yi-i what a show! Wow! Whoopee! The all high so far and the stage was all set for all hell to break out again but we shooed them off and it's all quiet on the western front again.

Sure wish I had the power for description — help me remember the night of June 24th. The Japs came over high and dropped nine flares all in a straight row — suspended by parachutes so they came down awful slow — burned for such a long time and bright! Looked like huge flood lights and what I mean is they flooded the area with light. The stage was all set for a torpedo run but we ran them off at least temporarily — they'll probably be back again tonight. Nature was on their side to boot — huge black clouds, lots of them — rain, wind and intense lightning — what a night. You can imagine the effect the flares had when they were way up in the clouds, the clouds plus white smoke screen, black smoke screens, anti aircraft fire with their mixture of white and red tracers, artillery fire & exploding shells and on top of that — amber colored stars fired by Japs and white ones by us plus burning buildings, fuel storages and ammunition dumps. We expected the shock of a torpedo any second but Lady Lou is still queen of the water. Whew! Tomorrow is Sunday — wonder if we will observe "holiday routine" — be sure and read next week's installment — do bad old Japs come back & does Lou rise up in arms?

All My Love
Paul

26 June 1944

Hello My Darling

Today is going to be a scorcher — I'm wringing wet already and all I've done is eat breakfast and whip Comdr Bowers in cribbage — yes, we got started early on our daily routine.

Our guns are hungry again so we are feeding them this morning — they sure have gone thru a lot of vittles these past ten days.

We spent the night away from the noise of battle but could see the flashes on the horizon — very pretty.

It's time for sick call so I will turn to & get it over with.

Sweetie pie — love you good and am always thinking of you — wish you could have been here last night for the nightly meeting of the Grand Order of Bull Slingers — subject was "Pets Aboard Ship" — the grand prize went to Gunner Gibbons with his seven cats and their private custom built hammocks — can't you just see them rocking back & forth in their beddy beds?

All my love
Paul

27 June 1944

Hello Honey —

Don't get scared when you look at the picture of the four of us — we really don't look that bad actually. We had had some tough days and nights but no liberty parties. we were "safe" at the battle front. Murph, Grubb & Johnson wanted pictures of their mustaches, wanted me in it so we had one made. The kid tilted the camera up so Murph and I got the benefit of it — especially his neck.

We have had a lot of fun with the picture [*amongst*] the four of us. Murph's "longnecker" or Zombie, I'm The Octogenarian or Old Ancient, Johnson is Hose-Nose & Grubb is Pin-up or Frannie Grubble. What you see in the background — they are life rafts — I'm standing by A-2 which is mine. Ain't they pretty? Twenty two men and two officers are assigned to each one — none but the severely wounded ride, the rest just hang on to the ropes along the sides. Liable to get soaked if we ever have to use them.

The other picture was made shortly after we hit what must have been a powder cache because it gave a big "woof" and didn't last long. It looked like a giant toad stool when it went up, awfully dense smoke, looked like dirty sheep's wool. The explosion occurred quite a ways inland beyond the air strip.

There is an air strip in the valley just behind the dark ridge — if you look closely you can see Jap gun emplacements, revetments & oil tanks — we are in pretty close now but we get in a lot closer a lot of times.

Actually watched a lot of honest to God fighting on that strip you see and we had a good spray of machine gun bullets handed us.

See the plane in the sky & the burst of anti aircraft fire ahead of it? Our plane & a feeble Jap effort to down it.

Aren't the clouds & water pretty — try eliminating the strip of land and extend the clouds to the horizon & you get an idea what it looks like when we are at sea — entirely hemmed in by clouds plus the beautiful colors of sunset or sunrise.

We have had an awfully quiet two or three days — haven't fired a shot — haven't been shot at or a damn thing — mighty monotonous but it's just the lull before the storm — bigger & better things are in store for us. Lot of debris still floats by but haven't seen any more Japs — guess they've all sunk.

We had our nightly bull session on the foc'sle but nothing of interest —

no one could get steamed up, guess it's been too quiet. The nights when g.q. is a constant threat is when we really get going — we know we can't go to bed so we are wide awake & the tall stories fly.

All my love
Paul

THE *LOUISVILLE'S* SPOTTER PLANES were bi-planes with two wings, one over and one under the fuselage. That explains the plane in Paul's June 29 letter getting its "lower wing" shot off.

29 June 1944

Dear Member, "Lonesome Heart Club"

How are you? I am fine. Do you hear the guns? I hear the guns, and they are very noisy. Do you enjoy the war? I do not enjoy the war.

Well, Honey, guess I'm nuts — we're having quite a day out here — guess the Japs are mad at us for they are firing back quite stylishly. They shot the lower wing off our plane this morning but missed the pilot & observer — both "returned safely." They evidently found the range finally but then they have had enough practice the last couple of weeks.

Where does the time go? Here it is Thursday again — just had one a day or two ago. Time sure flies when we have a business deal on.

The nights are getting beautiful but a bit tricky — a half moon and do we ever shine out — seems brighter out here guess it's because there is no smoke or dust (except in certain locales) to dim it out. The battle was fun to watch in the moonlight — star shells, flares, guns, bombs, etc., all added their bits of color. Had an attempted air raid but three of them were shot down so the rest left.

Watching one get his — about three bursts of anti-aircraft, one of which scored a hit — a shot of orange flame, then he glided like a comet for some distance, then a huge burst of flame as he exploded and then the long journey straight down to the crash & another burst of flame. Finis — yellow belly — so solly.

We've been going at it hot & heavy all morning with good results on our side — think we have the best team — we are nearing a record — think it will be in the bag by night time — hope Lou gets her due credit.

Can't seem to get in gear for letter writing. The guns & jar "lulled me to sleep" — I just finished a nap — put my room back together and now it's falling apart again.

Think I'll cotton my ears up and go take a look — if we're not too busy tonight will drop you another note.

Darling girl — love you loads
Paul

1 July 1944

Hello Dorothy Darling —

Missed writing yesterday on account I was up to my neck in mess treasuring — next to you I think I'm the world's worst bookkeeper. When I had the job forced on me I warned them they would have a mess on their hands — sure tried hard but they finally balanced. Missed last night's aerial show and today's fun but the books are all squared away and I can [*breathe*] for another month — I'd be a dollar over, then seventeen under, then over, etc., etc., — counted cash over & over again until I see it in my sleep. Have close to $5000 in my safe — will get rid of half of it tomorrow & have to hold the rest until next month.

The chief censors at some distribution point have been recensoring mail — mail from service personnel back to the states. One of our higher officers had his recensored but nothing deleted. Have any of mine been opened? [*There was no indication of this.*] Officers were the big offenders — aboard ship here we try to be extra careful not to divulge any military secrets as to where we are, number of casualties, plans concerning present or future operations etc. About all that is left to talk about are things in a general way — fires — smoke — and boom boom. Don't believe I've ever mentioned dates, operations or names of ships — feel that my nose is clean so I'm not worried.

The mess bill went up to $30 a month and we easily slough off twenty a month so it costs 50-60 bucks a month to get by. The favorite sport is to roll dice to see who buys the root beers, cokes or ice cream. At chow we usually roll for the ice cream if it isn't on the menu. Seven to fourteen roll so when you get stuck you're not killed unless it hits regularly. Last month's bills were high due to new shoulder marks & gold braid — cigars, etc. I passed cigars, as is the custom, to the entire wardroom, both ours & warrant officers plus "H" division. The promotion was worth it and there won't be another for at least two more years.

You once asked if you should send Wes some magazines or something — it isn't necessary for they are getting them now & I supplied him with things from our Ship's Service so we are pretty well squared up. Sent him four really good chicken dinners the last night I was with him — he and his gang were too busy to eat when chow was served — I got back to the ship before second chow so I had them fix up four nice plates & sent them over. For once the chicken was good — fryers and cooked just right — know it tasted good to them.

Quite an unusual night out earlier this evening — the sunset gave up — the sky & water really look ominous. Thick haze of smoke & dust — a terrific barrage was being laid down — hard to believe people were killing themselves or each other just a short ways away and we had just gotten up from a white table cloth & a delicious dinner and setting out on deck killing time & looking on. Kids boxing — swapping lies — listening to the accordion or what have you. We have our rough times but nothing compared to the poor devils on the beach.

Love
Paul

2 July 1944

Hello My Darling —

Worked like hell this morning — got my books all squared away, wrote up a couple of cases I had in sick bay, got out my Form K and then loafed around on the foc'sle in my shorts — drank root beer and grape and watched the battle. Still hard to believe they are going at it hot and heavy — don't see how the Japs stand up under it but they do somehow — they're not humans at all.

Have read several books — one was a lulu, perhaps you've read it —

"The Strange Woman" — she was the world's meanest woman, that's for sure. Have "Tortilla Flat" on my desk — think I'll read it tonight.

All My Love
Paul

3 July 1944

Hello Sweet Girl —

Just finished a swell shower — wet myself good all over, then turned the water off and soaped myself with cashmere Bouquet soap until I looked as though I were ready for a bubble dance — rinsed myself and then repeated the soaping — gee, it was swell — am so refreshed and actually smell good for a change — won't last long, but good while it does.

Our work schedule has been shot today so I slung bull this morning & cleaned up my room. It really looks nifty & it's nice and cool — have my wind scoop out and the fan going so it really is comfortable. We've been underway all day — not going anyplace but just moving — a big air raid was due and still is so we still are on the alert. Maybe before the night is over we'll have some fun — it's been too quiet so something is bound to pop — that's another reason I thought I'd write while I had time.

Saw a cute show this afternoon — "Princess O' Rourke" — it was swell and gave everyone a lift. That's a novel way to fight a war — sody water & pitcher shows — bet no one else had them — that's why Lou is such a swell ship. She has developed arteriosclerosis & arthritis during the bombardment but she broke and has set a new record for bombardment in any one operation. Can't tell you how, when or where, but the old gal did and we are mighty proud of her. She is so pretty in the moonlight — never get tired of looking back at her & admiring her. There isn't a cruiser out here — even the new ones — that can touch her as to her graceful lines.

It's a beautiful sight to see ships passing each other — especially war ships — they are so trim — everything lashed down & the decks cleared for action — the gentle dipping & rolling as they glide thru the blue water — cutting the water forward and leaving a foaming wake aft — honey, guess I love the sea and am not disappointed. It is so colorful and peaceful looking — but "they ain't nothing to the peace & quiet out here" — always the menace of bombs, torpedoes & shells — it's swell and I'm thrilled every minute. A thrilling sight is to have another ship come along side for one purpose or another — the waves & spray they kick up as they approach — the activity of tossing and securing lines — transferring passengers or cargo while underway — get a big bang out of it. Everybody rallies topside and gathers along the life lines — it's like a bunch of busy bodies hanging over the back fence and swapping gossip. Everyone is brown and on the smaller ships every one seems to be trying to outdo the other in growing whiskers — sure have seen some beauties.

Another day has passed and no mail — guess I'll write to my congressman and see what it giffs.

Love you ever so much & take care of yourself.

All my love
Paul

5 July 1944

Hello Dorothy Darling —

Can you imagine a moon big and bright enough to cause a reflection in the clouds? Think God worked overtime to bring about the beauty of tonight — and just a few hundred yards away wholesale slaughter is going on.

Watched our line advance today, won't be long now — time out, air alarm!

Much later — a belated 4th of July but "shore was purty" — search lights — flares — star shells — bombs — artillery — everything but cold beer. The smoke screens were something to see in the moonlight — looked like huge fuzzy [*caterpillar*] worms.

As I started to say earlier, watched our lines advance today and won't be long now before the Japs will have to jump off the cliff into the ocean or get killed. They are in the well known tight between a rock & hard place — anyone but a Jap would have surrendered long ago.

Lady Lou's luck still holds — she had one of her planes shot down & joined Davey Jones locker but the pilot & gunner were saved. Was interesting to watch the rescue — our boys get the job done, that's for sure.

I'm eating fruit cake & debating whether or not to ring for a root beer — guess I won't because I ate two dishes of chocolate ice cream this evening and must pay attention to my figure. Hell of a war, never felt better or looked better in my life. We've been too busy to worry but I suppose there will be a let down and find we really are pooped.

Gee, Honey, wish you were here — it's so pretty out — just cruising around in the moonlight — not always on a straight line but doing a little dance routine to "Drums Of War". During the alert a quartette of enlisted men really did some nice harmonizing — others rolled up in their blankets sound asleep topside — after all they were mostly mess cooks and their day's work was over.

Will be a month Friday since we've had mail — tain't right.

All My Love To You Honey
Paul

8 July 1944

Hello Honey —

Still no mail. the days are very quiet although the boys on the beach are still having quite a time — the nips just won't give up so you can't say they don't have guts.

Am getting a cute pot belly — in fact everyone is — no exercise and too hot for individual workouts. Have cut out butter and take only one small helping of food in an effort to retain my youthful figure, but without much results.

We did our usual tonight — watched the sunset and told lies. The Gunner is still winner and was wound up tonight.

Last night's and tonight's colors were various shades of blue, white & gray — the sky was baby blue & the water dark blue — really was nice. The star shells looked like xmas greeting cards — all quiet & peaceful on the surface, but far from it actually.

We had two alarms last night but turned over and went back to sleep. It was only enemy planes and as yet they haven't given me an anti-aircraft gun so nuts to them.

All My Love
Paul

9 July 1944

Hello Darling —

Went to church this morning and it wound up all right but started out terribly. The chaplain was from the famous St. Marks Parish in the Bowery, NY — not much to look at and prayed & read the Scripture in a fast drone — you know, no inflection and leaving a sentence on the up beat. When he got to his sermon, he settled down and was really good. Spoke on hypocrisy — the usual meaning of pretense, being better than you really are, etc., etc. In seafaring men it's hypocrisy in reverse — the tendency of pretending we are tougher than we really are — useless & needless profanity — obscene stories — carousals, etc. He spoke a lot of truth — some of the enlisted men really are terrible — that's for sure. It's going to be tough on the "working girls" when this crew gets on the beach again — almost seven months now that they have been restrained — some are really hellers.

More Japs floated by today — these were more stylish — they were lashed to canvas stretchers and came by in style — dead but good.

The dusk still majors in blue — a beautiful blue — numerous showers all around us — can count them and steam around them. It's like that cartoon of the one ray of sunshine shining down on the U.S.S. "- - - -" only this is a shower on a lone ship, the others in sunshine.

The same old wail — no mail, looks like at least ten days before we can hope for any unless a miracle happens.

All My Love
Paul

10 July 1944

Hello Sweet Girl —

The gunner is still wound up — used to have a rabbit that could whip his tom cat! Also had a duck that took him three weeks to get sobered up — "I don't believe it."

Had quite a procession of dead Japs float by today — nine of them & they sure were hideous looking. They were still in uniform, they were so bloated they looked like balloons & as ugly as apes. We were downwind of the island and got full benefit of the stench.

Had company — the gunner just left. He came in for my well written westerns that I had finished. He told a few "lies" and just left. He's a good egg and a lot of fun.

The captain and I had a nice visit this afternoon while watching the Japs float by. He is awfully nice & very pleasant but hard to get acquainted with. He was in good spirits and I popped a proposition to him and he okayed it. I'll really have some fun on our next bombardment — hope it's soon — whoops!

Had a good day in the office — worked like hell all morning — have already done as much this month so far as I did all of last or the month before. Had a sweet impaction and it really clicked — the patient is swell and got a lot of nice publicity on it.

My heat is rearing its ugly head again. When I put in much time in the office it sure breaks out on me. It's so hot & stuffy and I get wringing wet.

We have run out of starch so they are using corn starch in our laundry — sure stinks — bring on the deodo.

We rec'd a half bag of mail today — nary a letter for poor I, but very few did get one so I don't feel too bad.

A bloody chapter closed yesterday but still a lot of [*mopping*] up to do — there'll be snipers for months to come. It's so pretty out here it's hard to believe all that blood shed has gone on right under our noses. One of the Jap generals tried to commit hari kiri or mati hari or something, but his knife must have slipped so his adjutant had to finish him off — nice people.

Oodles of love
Paul

THE "BLOODY CHAPTER" Paul referred to was Saipan, where the Army and Marines lost 3,426 killed or missing in action and the Japanese dead numbered some 24,000.

The loss of Saipan was announced in Japan on July 18, at which time General Tojo and his cabinet resigned.

12 July 1944

Hello Honey —

Put in a good day at the office again this morning and then this afternoon had a "Happy Hour". It was like a planned picnic — rained of course most of the time but we had our show. Had ten swell boxing matches — music by the Louisville Hot Shots — quartet of negro singers — burlesque wrestling match and a solo by our very fine tenor. It was a lot of fun and the afternoon passed quickly. We have some really good fighters and one of these days when the fleet is all together and they have the tournament to pick all Navy fighters — we will have some damn good men.

The Top of the Mark, Frisco — has been out of bounds but understand they got squared away again. Believe it was because they sold liquor to "young" service men.

How is your supply of chewing gum — need some? Bought a couple cartons of Spearmint today and will send it to you. Are hot tamales still rationed? I've had a terrific yen for some lately — if some time you run across some in tins and you have time — please send me some. Wouldn't trust a glass jar — things have a tendency to become "misshapen" enroute out here.

Japs floated by, by the dozens today. Saw one woman and a youngster. They sure look awful — arms and legs missing, some decapitated — others, clothes blown to shreds & what have you. Taint purty, McGee, and don't smell so good — they're not violets by a long shot.

Still quiet out here. Must mention the sky as usual — no sun set tonight but very pretty — the sky was overcast, that water was slate gray and awfully calm. Looked like a plate of "uneasy jello" if you know what I mean.

As ever
Paul

16 July 1944

Hello Little Darling —

Have you seen any good news reels recently? The official photographer was aboard the other day and said he got a lot of beautiful shots of us bombarding and also got some stills of us while the shells were dropping all around us — just happened to be watching us and had his camera trained on us (lots of us-es) when they hit — there were lots of them and say the pictures should be swell. I'm hoping to get some of them so I can prove we were in action.

Quite a lot of stories are coming out of "- - - -" these days, by fellows who were there. The natives sure must have caught hell from the Japs. They had been intimidated by them and warned if the Americans should come and they fell into our hands, they would be tortured & then killed. In the closing days of the battle this officer watched a native family do away with themselves — couldn't get them to prevent it. The father, mother and five children — the father took the children, one under each arm, waded out into the ocean & drowned then — drowned all five, his wife and then himself. I call that tragic and damn the Japs.

After we captured a few natives, fed & given them medical aid they were isolated or sent back & the word passed how kindly they had been treated so the wave of suicides has abated. Another cute story — a Jap admiral ordered a suicide counter attack then he and four aides returned to their cave where the admiral beheaded his aides & then committed whatever you call it — harem scarem or something. Nize pipels! Countless stories but can't tell you all — perhaps it might be interesting to mention the bad time the women are having. They all seem to be pregnant — have a suckling babe already and the constant bombardment, bombing and artillery fire brings on premature births etc., so the medics are delivering babies constantly.

A Jap prisoner upon questioning what they feared or hated most on these invasions replied — #1 naval gun fire, #2 bombs and #3 artillery fire. They could never tell from what direction or when a naval shell would come in so they could defend themselves or return fire and knock out the guns. Guess the Navy isn't washed up after all.

Have seen a lot of souvenirs recently — have had a lot of visitors — come out to bathe, get a square meal & auction off trophies. I haven't bought any so far — prices are terrific: $500 to $2000 for swords — $100 for flags, etc. Jap teeth sell for a dollar a piece, they knock them out with rifle butts! One of our "nice" American Marines dug up a bunch of Japs after they were buried and stripped them of belts, buttons, etc. — nice going, ugh! I lost my appetite for souvenirs after hearing that. Any I get will be gathered by yours truly & know the history.

One more tale — seems the Japs don't like us (meaning us Americans)

— we chased a bunch up into the hills and into their caves, then dug in to wait for them to come out. The Japs would yell down to the Marines in perfectly good English — "Come out of your holes, you American Bastards." They probably were graduates of our best American universities — nez pas?

Kind of keep the stories quiet. Yes?

All My Love
Paul

MANY SAIPAN AND TINIAN civilians killed themselves rather than be captured by Americans. Despite loudspeaker pleas from Marines, whole families not only drowned, as Paul related, but flung themselves off cliffs onto jagged coral. Sites of these tragedies are still designated as "suicide cliffs."

18 July 1944

Hello Honey —

Feel meaner than hell tonight — disgusted with the war and things in general — damn! Still no mail and there is no excuse for it. Just damn poor management some place. Everyone is getting mean and something is going to pop if they don't get squared away in short order.

All our June mail is held up and we have had only two less than half filled bags of July mail for the entire ship — sad state of affairs. After all the big promises of quick mail service on this operation — crap! They know where we are and [*could*] be here several months. It isn't as though we were chasing the Jap fleet & hard to keep up with. We haven't had a new shipment of magazines since March — those we have, have been read by so many they are limp as rags. Wish the guy that distributes the mail had to be confined to a 600 X 68 space for six months and then have his mail held up. Honey, I'm in one of those moods where I could really go to town on the "- - - -" that's causing this hold up. Jeepers!

Lot more stories came out today — Japs really are fanatics. They're more like animals or monsters. Sure would like to know the working of their minds, especially the military leaders. Can you imagine the fanatical zeal to behead your own soldiers and then commit suicide? That's what one Jap officer did to his detachment when they were cornered on the beach — he ordered them to kneel down and he went along and whacked their heads off with his saber! Don't imagine he cut his own off but fell on his sword in the approved manner. They have actual photographs of their committing heri kiri (?), throat slitting and strangling — I'm trying to get some for my art collection.

An unusual sun set tonight — beautiful shade of red — slivers of clouds — everything caught the reflection — even the water, looking like we were sailing thru sparkling Burgundy — very unusual.

Love You Little One
Paul

20 July 1944

Hello Darling —

WE GOT MAIL FINALLY — WHOOPEE!

It's quite a nice world after all and all is forgiven.

Saw some thrilling dive bombing this a.m. — beautiful and fearful at the same time. Our boys come straight down out of the clouds on to their target, release their bombs & then zoom over our ship — barrel rolling and kicking up their heels like a bunch of young colts. Very satisfactory performance.

Sure a shame to destroy such pretty country — fields of beautiful greens — lots of trees and quite a city. Wouldn't want to live there right now for they're sure catching hell. There's a huge sugar cane mill & distillery standing on the beach — they haven't fired on it yet but I want to be present when they do — should make heap big fireworks. Don't need binoculars we're close enough to see "plenty well."

Lou has gargled & has her tonsils in perfect shape — she is doing a swell job of "orating".

Love You
Paul

20 July 1944

Hello My Darling —

It's a little early to go to bed — I want to open my port and am afraid some one will barge in and turn my lights on — that's "bad" out here so will wait until I'm reasonably sure I won't have visitors.

I got heat [*rash*] this time — drives you nuts. Everyone seems to have it so one no longer feels self conscious when you "scratches and squirms".

They issued an order — enlisted men not on watch can go about without shirts — very revealing as to tatoos (?). Some are keeping score of the ships they've been on — others, various duties and still others just "pitchers". The one that made that necklace for you has a "beautiful rose" [*tattooed*] on each breast, another fellow has suckling pigs on that same location — funny and disgusting too.

See my time & paper is running out on me so will crawl into my sack — may have an interesting day tomorrow — hope I hope.

Love you little one. As usual was thinking about you so thought I'd say hello and good night.

Night Honey
Paul

22 July 1944

Hello My Sweet —

Don't know how far along I'll get with this letter — we're pretty "busy" and the ship shakes and shudders a lot when she speaks to the Japs. Nothing spectacular going on just the methodical destruction of Japs and their installations. The big guns blast the gun emplacements, then the smaller ones lay down a terrific barrage all thru the area to take care of any fleeing Japs. It's sure merciless but that is what it takes — they'd do it to us and do do it so we're even. It's quite interesting to watch thru glasses although we are just a few hundred yards out — "there you see it, now you don't" is the way it goes.

Felt like hell yesterday but okay today. Had a sore throat — ached in all my joints — took A.P.C.s and soda — am a well man today. We have had a lot of guests from the beach and believe they brought a mild epidemic with them as we were all well until shortly after their arrival.

Still hotter than hell out here — flies! Beautiful, fat, blue green bloat flies — they are so fat and lazy, when they light on you, you have to actually move them by brute force. You can imagine what the beach is like if we have them out here. Still think I'm in the right branch of the service.

Sounds like they have something cornered so will go investigate.

Love You Darling
Paul

AFTER FOUR DAYS of bombardment, the amphibious landing on Tinian took place July 24. The *Louisville* lost a pilot and observer when their spotter plane was downed by anti-aircraft fire only 600 yards from the ship.

24 July 1944

Hello Darling —

Today my dental office is being used as a morgue. We lost two this morning — burial at sea tonight at sunset. It's tough going — the pilot just reported to us a short time ago — a hell of a nice chap — just this morning we were beefing about breakfast and I was examining his leather napkin ring — a couple of hours later he checked out. His rear gunner also went out — just last Thursday he finished showing me all about the machine gun and the radio in the plane — so it's one plane lost, no survivors.

It was God awful this a.m. but exciting and mighty thrilling — war really is terrible and no fooling. Believe it is getting more intense and deadly as the days go on — these birds at home that think the Japs are a push over and the war is about over should just "drop in sometime", they'd soon change their minds. We really had a ring side seat — the landing craft passed right under our nose — what a sight to see them steaming in — all sizes, shapes and color — they were so close you could toss ciggies at them. I got a bang out of watching them thru glasses and sort of looking over their expressions, that is, on their faces — some were tense, others nonchalantly smoking — others grinning and having a good time. They were all seasoned Marines and a mighty tough looking outfit. They without a doubt are the world's greatest fighting outfit and I take my hat off to them as a fighting unit.

Sure got a thrill out of the way our flags were flying — seemed as though they whipped in the breeze with a little more pride, spirit and what have you. You'd have to see the "drama" to appreciate what I'm trying to say. It was early, the sun was up but was obscured by the smoke and dust of battle. It was like an Oklahoma duster aboard ship. You have heard a number of carpenters all hammering at the same time — multiply that by several thousand and you have an idea what the theme sounded like. The background was the woof, woof of bombs and muffled roar of cannon — was awful — couldn't hear yourself or anyone else talk. Then the waves of landing parties going into that awful hell — their guns blazing and the Stars & Stripes standing straight out in the breeze — made your blood really tingle. When the landing crafts near the beach, the barrage lets up and as the air clears you can see them scramble. Sure isn't pretty to see Jap shells fall amongst them — now you see them, now you don't! How those damn Japs live thru the intense shelling they receive — I certainly can't understand it, but they do and give us hell in return. Lou's luck is still holding out — was demonstrated this morning again. We'd been in a certain area for several days shooting point blank range and nothing happened. Today several others went in and were standing off quite aways but got hell blasted out of them & resulting in a lot of casualties — lot of gold stars will be hung up somewhere. In just a little while we are going in to knock out the guns that did all the damage — should be exciting and hope our luck is still riding high. The firing is still pretty intense so we can tell my writing — guess I should have waited until later to write but expect we'll still be busy so "figgered" now was as good as any.

For a breath of air in the wardroom we leave a couple of ports open, the ones farthest away from the turrets. The blast still is sufficient to knock your glasses off or the pipe out of your mouth unless you're all set for it. The mess attendants have a devil of a time setting the table — the flash comes in — looks like flame and the blast blows the table cloth off. I eat facing the ports but am getting used to it and have quit "crawling under the table".

Honey, we're going in now, will close for now — am thinking of you always — I'll be alright — I'm in fine fettle so must go see what's going on —

All My Love
Paul

Much later — mission completed and the "goose hangs high" — no runs, no hits, no errors, so all's well on Lady Lou — she did her job and didn't get a scratch.

A magnificent sunset tonight — seemed as tho nature tried to make up for the day's turmoil — we slipped the two bodies into the sea from the starboard side — the water was deep blue — after the services, walked over to the port side and the water was golden — really gorgeous.

What ho tomorrow — won't know until it rolls around so guess I'll hit my sack — 0330 comes awful sudden. Can hear the "carpenters" but we're not carpenting ourselves.

Love you honey
Paul

26 July 1944

Hello My Pet —

Seems funny to have it so quiet — gets on your nerves. We had a picture show, then I ate a dish of chocolate ice cream — took a nap and bathed. In the morning tho, I really turned out a lot of dentistry — same this morning. The same picture is showing this p.m. so think I'll take a sun bath and try to get rid of my rash. Everyone has it now and it's really rough — drives you nuts.

Right now I feel I could sleep a year especially if I had a double bed and could sprawl. Sleeping in one position seven months finally gets tiresome. We have been on dehydrated this & that for some time now — our fresh stuff gave out. After all we have been out fifty days and that's a long time in the tropics. No relief in sight but this is "wah" so can't complain.

May drop you a note this evening when it cools off — I'm in my "set ins" now but the good old sweat is rolling and my rash rashing — miserable!

Love you sweetie pie —

All My Love
Paul

27 July 1944

Hello Sweet Girl —

Had damage control problems this morning & worked at dentistry afterwards. Had a good lunch of navy beans (you know, the white ones, not baked) fried sausage, string "beans", ice tea and apricot tarts. Just hit the spot & I'm velly contented. This afternoon we have a smoker planned but the weather is running true to form & it's raining — may clear up, hope so.

Our evening meals aren't so hot lately due to lack of fresh food stuff but at that they are superior to K rations. Hominy grits, rice, spinach & asparagus are plentiful — I don't like any of them as of now but dare say I'll be eating them with gusto ere long. Our meats are still delicious so I'll make out.

Bet we have a "field day" ere long - 5000 bags of mail hit the beach this morning! The Lou should have her share for we have been without so long — whoopee! — back letters — papers — magazines & DEODO!

Pure — dat I am — fifty two days on the water wagon — have turned down drinks a lot of times during that time. Only last night I was asked in for a few short ones but declined. Ain't ya proud of me? Several have it aboard — regular Navy, academy at that, but this little reserve is keeping his shirt tail clean.

I posted your clippings and every one got a bang out of them — especially the mail & beer ones. The dumb clucks at home that are afraid having beer aboard would ruin our morale and lessen our efficiency as fighters. If we were allowed two bottles of beer just before dinner it would work wonders. There would actually be less trouble when they hit the beach too — the way it is now they are starved for it and go hog wild when it is obtainable. They should just spend one week below decks and they'd clamor for beer too — our boys have been at it seven months, in the tropics under hazardous conditions and for the majority of them it's their first time away from home. We have the most loyal group of boys in the world — they're swell. Do you realize we haven't been in friendly waters since we left the states? We're making them friendly and it's been a lot of fun and exciting — that's why it burns you up to have the old Fuds at home tell us what is best for us out here. Guess I'm steamed up but believe rightfully so — can get along without the drinks — don't miss them at all, but let us have the pleasure of turning them down or having one if we want it.

It's about time for the smoker so will go out and see what it giffs — "will call you back and talk to you later."

Hello "Baby" — saw a good smoker, won a dish of chocolate ice cream from Foster, took a nap, bathed, laid out a clean uniform — now I'm all set for my spinach or what have you.

It's getting near chow time so think I'll don my pretties — have my foundation garments on — and head for the wardroom & the nightly session of the foc'slers.

All My Love
Paul

28 July 1944

Hello Darling —

Quite a stiff breeze is blowing & the sea is a little rough so we are pitching & rolling quite a bit — hope you don't get seasick reading this.

We are sending a boat in for mail tomorrow, haven't had any for three days now, but with over 5,000 bags on the beach we should have a large amount — that is if they have it sorted. The men that have to do with the sorting must have been former W.P.A. charter members. If I don't write tomorrow it will be because I'm busy getting caught up on my back mail and must ask to be excused pleeze.

It's very quiet out here for us — the situation seems to be well in hand so it's very dull and monotenous (?) — Missie Lou gave them a lot of sass all morning so it was "very noisy" but not exciting. They dropped a beautiful pattern the entire length of the ship but they were all a little short so our luck held through today again.

It's interesting to see the shells land in the water (satisfying too) — you can't help but wonder if the next salvo will score a hit on you or if your own guns will blast them out of commission before they can correct their range & fire again.

We rescued two Army fliers this a.m. but their plane sunk — their chief concern was whether we could pick them up before they were washed ashore into the nest of Japs that were waiting for them — we did. One was so concerned over his cap — the plane had turned over, so in the process of extricating himself his cap came off — he saw it floating away from him — he sez to himself — By God, They're hard to get — better to get it — and he did. He was wearing it very jauntily when they pulled him out of the water. I didn't get to see the actual crash but watched them thru my glasses until we came alongside them. Guess funny things go thru their minds — worrying about drifting into the hands of the Japs and then taking time out to save a 15 cent baseball cap.

Had sub contacts last night but a few depth charges either sunk them or dispersed them — any ho — no more troubs and makes for a [*monotonous*] existence.

Take care of yourself honey — love you

Paul

30 July 1944

Hello My Darling —

Some of the men are "bitching" about the food so I'm buying some field rations and letting them have it — no ice tea, lemonade (synthetic) coffee, chocolate milk or a damn thing but warm water. That is what the men on the beach have to eat for weeks at a time — we still have it awfully good but naturally our choice is getting limited due to being out so far and for so long. Great life but everybody really is happy — just have to beef about something.

There must be well over 10,000 bags of mail on the beach but not a drop for CA 28 — it's all old mail but ours still is fouled up someplace. If we don't hurry and get it — it will be another long stretch before it can catch up with us.

Saw my first water spouts yesterday — looked like a cyclone, you know — the funnel shaped clouds and then as it got near the water rose to meet it — looked like a fountain, very interesting.

Seems we are in the area where typhoons are prevalent — may have some exciting times due to nature. There's a storm in the air — huge swells are coming in and it looks "fitten for a moider". As usual we sat on the foc'sle and swapped lies until dark — I have a favorite spot to wind up with. You know, away up in the bow — the very tip of the ship where the anchors are. It's so pleasant and cool there — the wind whips thru your clothes — no forward sensation at all just up and down with a gentle roll.

You can see the length of the ship — her super structure against the clouds — very beautiful.

It's getting about bedtime and still have my mess books to balance — I'm 5 bucks over — guess that's better than being short.

Comdr. Bowers just invited me over "to his house" to play poker, but as usual decline — still am not interested in learning the game.

No news — very dull even tho a flock of ten Japs tried to steal one of our big sea planes last night — they didn't get the job done, bang, bang — so solly.

Have got to quit — have thirty-some odd papers to sign — forgot I'm on the Rating Board — they just laid the forms on my desk so will have to "turn to".

All my love to you honey
Paul

31 July 1944

Hello My Sweet —

Didn't do so hot sleeping last night — was wide awake and when I did fall asleep Bong Bong Bong and we had to hit the deck again — just secured from firing a few minutes ago. Lou has her eagle eye sharpened and did a swell job — they sang her praises over the radio — you know, beach to ship — not "universal hookup" — we're really hot on these surprise calls — saw a beautiful air strike — they are always thrilling to watch.

My quarters are a mess again — I'm right under one of the turrets and when we fire everything comes down. Light fixtures completely broken off — medicine cabinet knocked off — even my "roof" leaks now. My "colored attendant" and I finally got it squared away and am waiting for the ship fitters to come in and weld, bolt and glue me together again.

Must shave & get ready for chow — could even eat spinach — I'm that hungry.

All My Love, Darling
Paul

PAUL'S COMMENT ABOUT "our new secret weapon" in the next letter may refer to what was possibly the first wartime use of napalm, the jelly-like gasoline mixture that increased dramatically the effectiveness of flame throwers.

1 August 1944

Hello Honey Girl —

Really feel sea going these past few days — the Pacific is antipacific for sure — it's like riding a bucking bronco. Tonight it is kicking up stylishly — just came in from the foc'sle — there hasn't been a sunset the past few nights but pretty anyway in a different sort of way. It's more like the paintings one usually sees of ocean scenes — white caps & ships covered with spray. It comes across in sheets — very damp to say the least — the moon is out and gives enough illumination to show up our neighbors — all in all — beautiful.

Watched an exciting battle yesterday — our Marines & tanks versus holed up Japs — really was something. Can't help but feel just a little sorry for the devils — they sure bit off more than they could chew when they picked on the U.S. Can't give you the details but it was terrible — they're hidden in caves and have to be smoked & burned out — saw flame throwers at work — it's a godawful weapon. Also saw what must have been our new secret weapon — that it's effective is putting it mild — has unlimited possibilities, particularly later on.

Finally got my wardroom books squared away — am all set for another 30 days — goody.

Think I'll sleep with my "side boards" up tonight — roughest weather we have had since we've been afloat — whoopee! Will sleep fast tonight so I can look for mail tomorrow. Be good to yourself.

Love You
Paul

"At Sea"
2 August 1944

Hello My Own Darling —

You can chalk up last night and today as time to be remembered — my poor legs are about pooped out from bracing against the roll. It's the worst binge I've ever been on. We go down, then way up — then to one side — then the other and wind up with a barrel roll or what have you. Had a hell of a time taking a shower but came thru in one piece — dropped my cake of soap and almost didn't get it picked up again. No Mal de Mer yet for yours truly but there are several "green faces" around. Our whale boat went after mail this a.m. and hasn't returned yet — may not make it. Wish I could describe the sensation & what it really looks like to see the huge swells come in. To say the sea is uneasy is a gross misnomer — has ants in its pants or something. Must be a terrible storm somewhere — it isn't a quiet summer day here.

News must be scarce out here because the kids in their letters home are telling what a "wonderful" dentist they have aboard — will have to check and see if my corpsman is filling & extracting teeth.

Am about to read Berlin Hotel — just finished The Moon & Six Pence. Saw a good show this afternoon — Spencer Tracy in "Edison, The Man" — really enjoyed it. Tracy is a marvelous actor in my book.

Must quit rambling and get going — chow time and "anchors aweigh."

Bye sweet — love you, ain't no word for it.

All my love
Paul

ON AUGUST 3, 1944, the *Louisville* took up her position off the coast of Guam. A U.S. possession since 1898, the undefended island was invaded by the Japanese on December 10, 1941. On July 21, 1944, 55,000 American troops stormed ashore. Guam was secured on August 10 at a cost of nearly 18,000 Japanese and 7,000 U.S. casualties.

3 August 1944

Darling —

Tonight, or rather this evening, was one of those "painfully beautiful" sunsets — not a gorgeous riot of color but a study in black, white, purple and blue — all sober colors except for a chunk of sky that looked like taffeta — a watery colored strip of not-too-vivid reds, greens, browns, etc. Towards the sunset, the water was deep purple — the island appeared a black black — a narrow strip of blue sky with white & dark gray cumulus clouds hanging low over the island. The sun went down as a huge golden ball, as it receded, the blacks, grays & purple deepened — finally as it disappeared there was a lone pink cloud left in the narrow strip of sky — pretty soon a single white strip of white cloud appeared just below the pink & then out pops a solitary twinkling star just at the tip of the white cloud. Then the dying reflection of the sun caused the taffeta effect to fill in the space between land and the clouds — as that faded out and everything grew darker — star shells, our white ones and Jap orange ones, sprung into being. You can imagine what they looked like in that dark background. "Local" bits of color were added by the red tracer shells that would shoot across the heavens and land with a burst of light.

That was the picture looking West — back over your shoulder you had a gorgeous full moon — believe it or not it came out balanced on a fluffy white spike of a cloud — a lone cloud in that part of the sky — the sky was blue and the water a definite dark purple — what do you imagine the "path of the moon" did to the picture — I'd say just topped it off and made it an "Oscar". No fooling honey, it was something to see. Would like to have been off little ways so I could have seen Lady Lou riding the soft waves.

Sweet girl, the really beautiful sights I have seen out here more than make up for the horrible ones — doesn't seem possible that actual pathos is all about us — the heart breaks & sufferings of the innocent natives — I really feel sorry for them.

Three hours & 15 minutes later — the Flag Secy. just left — he wanted to read me the official war diary & criticize it — very boring on account of I saw the actual doings and he doesn't write worth a damn.

Love You Good Little One
Paul

4 August 1944

Hello Honey —

Spent a couple of hours in fairy land again tonight — it isn't right I should be seeing all these beautiful sights and you not by my warm side. I miss you most these beautiful moonlight nights. We were driven off the foc'sle this evening and are standing by to fire the main battery any minute so it's just as well you "ain't" here.

Felt so sorry for a little pooch yesterday — he had to be left behind — he'd swim part way out to the boat & then be shooed back, finally after the boat was loaded and shoved off he stood on the beach awhile wagging his tail, finally saw it was useless & gave up — climbed back up the cliff and sat forlornly at the mouth of the cave that had been "their" home for some time. While the loading was going on he was so frisky — scampering up & down the little beach — then he must have realized he was to be left behind & tried to swim out to them — if I'd have been in that whale boat I believe I'd have weakened & smuggled him in — was kind of bad leaving him but there were circumstances that wouldn't allow it.

Glad I made it to the bottom of the page — the tempo of the guns is stepping up so will call it done — talk to you tomorrow.

Love you honey
Paul

5 Aug. 1944

Hello Darling —

The boys didn't need any urging to lay to when the word was passed to haul in the motor whale boat when they saw those bags of mail. So far I've received two letters.

We're going to have a bond drive aboard ship — I'm going to make a bond allotment for the duration of my sea duty so when they show up each month you'll know there is no mistake. I have two hundred dollars on the books now — I don't want any more because I'm liable to slough it off if we should hit a liberty port. One hundred of that is for an unexpected trip home — I'm determined not to write a check — the other hundred is for gifts & a liberty if & when.

Money on the books is lost if the ship goes down — we're moving in all the time and the "business deals" are of greater magnitude as we move along. I feel I have at least ten more months of sea duty so from now until xmas I'm buying a $75 bond each month and if it works out will step it up to a $100 bond for the remainder of the time. It will cut me to a gnats eye lash but I'd rather skimp out here where it can be done without too much trouble and have a damn good nest egg for whatever is ahead of us. If we don't need the cash we can let them ride to maturity and then do something worthwhile with it.

Remember I'd planned on a tailor made uniform when I made Lt. Comdr.? I've moved that up to when I make full commander if I'm in that long — with scrambled eggs on one's cap — one must have a "hand made" suit.

Damnit — the pest from next door has spent the last hour here and now my trend of thought is all shot.

Any ho — guess what I'm trying to say is I'm being a good boy and saving my money so you and I can do things together. You will have had a rest and may be can put up with me for another eleven years or so.

All My Love
Paul

7 August 1944

Hello Darling —

We're going alongside a destroyer now to pick up more mail, supposed to be 86 bags — no doubt will be papers & magazines because we didn't get any in the other night's thirty-four. Gee, it's a thrill to go alongside another ship, especially to pick up mail and in a rough sea to boot. It's even more thrilling than the time a "converted ship" came up along side to pick up orders & a passenger. The other ship was an underwater demolition craft loaded to the gills with TNT & other explosives — they had to keep a certain distance away due to the danger of setting it off by friction — it was dark as hell and a heavy sea — was glad when they completed their business with us and shoved off again. Those boys should have double pay.

I'm not going to answer all your letters tonight — "god ah cold in de hade and my right eye is bleeding" — look like I've been on a big binge.

Dotty B (second from right) and family members show trinkets from Paul most likely sent in May 1944 from the Marshall Islands. From left: Dotty B's brother, Fred Lankard, and his wife Dorothy (“Freddy” Lankard's parents), Dotty B and her sister, Mary Sue Stetler. The picture was taken in Dotty B's Oklahoma City apartment in August 1944, probably by Mary Sue's husband, Bob Stetler.

These fans get me down but they are a necessary evil out here. It got my frontal sinus and I had the damndest tooth ache in my edentulous upper and partial lower. Really ached & still is tender — better go to a dentical parlor.

My dieting apparently is helping my waistline — weighed this morning and tipped the scales at 177 — want to hit 175 and then keep it that way. Haven't eaten butter for so long I hardly know what it tastes like and have cut out seconds for a couple of months — yust won dainty helping is all I allow myself.

All my love
Paul

P.S. Two torpedoes missed us last nite! Goody!

IN ONE OF HER LETTERS, Dorothy had obviously mentioned going to a bootlegger to buy liquor. Oklahoma was a "dry" state until 1959, so before that time bootleggers were the common source for liquor. In most communities the bootleggers' identities were common knowledge. Liquor purchases, even home delivery, were routine matters.

The *Louisville* left Guam on August 9 and arrived at Eniwetok on the 12th.

10 Aug. 1944
Thursday 1850
At Sea

Hello My Pet —

Seems in one of your letters you suggested I put the day on my letters so you would know when it was written — that doesn't help any on account the day and calendar dates are the same as home only we hurried up twenty four hours. What messes me all up is the extra hours we have lost — it's seven hours from here to the coast and two more to Oklahoma, making a difference of nine hours disregarding the whole day. It is seven o'clock or 1900 right now out here, Thursday, August 10th, 1944 — at home it really is 2 a.m. Thursday, August 10 the same year, therefore we are seventeen hours ahead of you — sabe? Tomorrow we gain, not lose, an hour so you will be sixteen behind.

My letter writing sure has been all shot to hell — can't seem to get in gear — guess it's the letdown after the strenuous times we have had the past two months. We counted up our score the other night — assaults, bombardments, raids & carrier task forces — we have been on fifteen — not bad for a land lubber. I could count only thirteen — had completely forgotten two good ones. I couldn't pronounce the names so I sort of scratched them off. Lou has been a busy gal and a good one too — has a "splendid" record.

Would like to have gone to the bootleggers with you — do they have any variety? I have 1/5 Schenley's and probably will tap it either Saturday evening or Sunday. Wish we were going to be at Wes's but no — I'm going to lay in the water all day in an effort to clear my rash. Haven't slept for three nights & it's driving me crazy — sure miserable stuff.

Night Darling
All My Love
Paul

THE FOLLOWING LETTER is dated 10 August, although the sequence of events and its number in Paul's August series indicate he made a mistake when he dated it.

The *Louisville* returned to Eniwetok on August 12. Paul describes the atoll as once being covered with vegetation but now looking like "a dressed chicken."

10 August 1944

Dearest Honey —

Quite a thrill to steam into port — we led the procession — quite a picture to see them steaming along one square behind the other — like playing follow the leader. It was cute the way they all blew out their tubes (make smoke) all in succession — it's keeping up with the Joneses. The water was so blue and clear — can't you just see those ships plowing thru — flags flying — sheet of spray off each side of the bow — mighty thrilling.

The atolls look like a dressed chicken with a few pin feathers — once was a lush growth of palm trees & other growths — now barren of all signs of vegetation — nothing but tents and implements of war. Would be awful to have duty there — ugh!

Looks like Coney Island tonight — wish you could see it — sure would like to have a picture of the scene for it's really something.

Tomorrow there should be a beer party — think I'll go in with the "first wave" and come back after they have secured the club.

Saw a cute show tonight — don't know the name of it but Jinx Falkenburg & Buddy Rogers played in it — was light & airy, good entertainment.

Honey it's bed time so will call it quits for tonight — will give you a detailed account of my touching terra [*firma*] again — seventy five days is quite a spell.

All my love
Paul

14 August 1944

Good Evening Mrs. Bonnette

Had fun last night & this morning but felt diseased all day — there was an epidemic aboard ship but believe it's under control now.

For a while it didn't look as though we would make it to the beach — in fact I had given it up and was taking a nap when the exec came busting in all excited and said we were leaving for the beach and beer in five minutes — I was dressed and ready with four minutes and forty eight seconds to spare. Got out to the quarter deck & there was the Admiral's barge waiting for us — there were six of us and away we went — off in a cloud of spray — fun.

The beach looked like Coney Island on a busy day — thousands & thousands of sailors lined the dock & beach — there were so many small craft of all descriptions we had a hell of a time getting to the dock and finally had to transfer to a shallow water boat in mid ocean. Finally effected a landing — fought our way through the mob and reached officers country. It was all fenced in so we wouldn't fall out, I guess.

Sure were a lot of good natured drunks — every one benign and glad to see everyone — much back slapping and more blah blah. Most of them were in shorts — it was funny to watch them try to get into their pants — it's real sandy, try & try to balance on one leg & over they'd go — everyone seemed to be falling on their faces — no one cared, they were "relaxing". We behaved like little gentlemen — we had our troubs when we got back aboard — there were several "open houses" — finally closed down at 0530. It was quite a deal — lot of fun and no one hurt.

Tonight we had new boiled potatoes or boiled new potatoes — cabbage, slaw & fresh uncooked carrots — boy oh boy! Did it ever taste good. We've been on dehydrated foods for so long anything fresh really hit the spot. The world looks rosie right now — if I could only see my little girl I'd be awfully happy.

Ordered some grays today — khakis we can't get out here anymore so I bought two pants & four shirts — it will be a change anyhow & as long as we don't have to wear blouses it won't be so bad. When I get all dolled up I'll have my picture made & will "remit" one to you.

The new medical officer seems to be a nice fellow — ugly as sin — tall & skinny — some where in his thirties — had eighteen months of destroyer duty — has done no surgery and is a seven day adventist! No smokie, no drinkie — no nothing but I think he is going to be okay. He is a relief after Barber — Barber was highly excitable, nervous & always stuttering and jabbering — sort of got on your nerves.

Quite a thrilling sight out here in the lagoon at night — early evening it looks like a million or so fire flies winking — very picture skew [*picturesque*].

They had a swim call this afternoon & it's fun to watch — the kids swim like fish and dive off from all parts & heights of the ship — no one has hit bottom as yet. I don't care for the swim in this location — we're out quite a ways and all the waste from the other ships floats by — not very inviting looking.

All my love
Paul

IN WRITING ABOUT GUAM (his code for Guam was "Wrigley"), Paul mentioned a "bright spot" for which he feels the *Louisville's* participants should receive the Navy Cross. The ship's history reads: "When the island of Tinian had been secured, the ship moved south to assist in bringing the assault on Guam to an earlier close, and on the first day there, the *Louisville* successfully made a daring rescue on enemy-held coastline of four natives who were sought by the Japs." An enclosure in Paul's September 6 letter will cover the August 3 event in detail.

20 August 1944

Hello Darling —

Won't mind tomorrow's initiation — I'll be a spectator — goody. I still have a shore spot on my heinie and don't believe it could go thru another clubbing.

A lot of wild tales came out of Wrigley and were they ever glad to see us. Some of our mess attendants used to live there and were allowed to visit their folks. Must have been a real thrill for them and everybody was hale and hearty believe it or not. Some were less fortunate — allowed only three cups of rice per month for the entire family! Can't tell you about the experience we had — hope to some day — it really was a bright spot and the kids actually involved should get the Navy Cross. If they were Army they'd get several medals & 30 days leave at least.

Hello Honey, this is several hours later. I've had chow, have seen a good movie, am going to the smoker, then act as a judge in the Royal Court — dish out penalties, eat, meet with the foc'slers to watch the sunset — maybe write another letter or read and then if I have time, will go to bed. Isn't it a hard life? It's a Cook's Tour for sure today.

The morale of the crew is picking up again now that we are under way. It always has been good but during the lull they were very quiet. Seems when we head out they really come to — just wonder what they will do when peace comes and no excitement just around the corner — some sure will get restless.

My heat rash is driving me nuts again — it's terrible — I look as tho I have tertiary syphilis, german measles, hives and "rash" all at one time —

it itches, burns and my skin seems to crawl. When I say I's got the misery, I mean misery! It's supposed to be spring where we're going — sure hope it's cooler and I get some relief.

Think I'll go topside & get a little sun — may give me some relief. I actually hurt.

All my love
Paul

23 August 1944

My Darling —

Having a mighty rough sea — several cases of Mal de Mer but I'm still riding high — guess I'll knock on wood.

May get to touch terra firma tomorrow. I have several cracked dentures aboard so I have an official excuse to go ashore. Dr. Zinke and I are going over if all is well. He seems to be a good egg.

Enclosed find a picture of a good Jap — ain't he purty? He's pretty ripe — note the bulge at his throat, arms & shoulders. The white is where his hide has exfoliated — isn't the water crappy looking — if he'd have hit the Lou believe he'd have popped!

My poor little room is inundated again — will rust thru one of these days then I'll have a basement. Sure noisy out — tons of water crashing against the bulkhead — shakes the whole ship. The "forecastle" gang couldn't meet tonight — went out to check on it but the wind damn near blew me off before I got there and the spray completely covers it so I retreated.

Love you loads & am thinking about you as usual.

All my love
Paul

THE *LOUISVILLE* ARRIVED at Espiritu Santo on August 24. The New Hebrides island, southeast across the Coral Sea from New Guinea, was never occupied by the Japanese and the U.S. established a base there early in 1942, which would account for Paul's comment that his location was "untouched by bomb or shell fire."

25 August 1944

Darling Girl —

We hit port yesterday morning and what a beautiful spot! At last I feel like a sailor, a world traveler and my sea duty is a success. All the previous islands had been bombarded all to hell but these are untouched by bomb or shell fire. Huge coconut plantations, the trees set out in perfectly straight rows and thousands of them. Really a sight and thrilled to death — beautiful, lush green grass and a sight for sore eyes.

I didn't go ashore today but will tomorrow — have a "dinner date" — guess with whom — Roundsley and Dickey from Tucson! Dickey was out to see me yesterday but I was on the beach. Roundsley was out this a.m. & caught me so I have permission to go ashore tomorrow. Will get a chance to get into the jungles — see the "tree climbing" fish etc — stuff we have read about. Saw a few silly looking flies yesterday — cross between a mosquito & a fly — dumb looking. There is a cute little settlement on one end of the island — white houses & red roofs — can't you just see them against a background of green green and I do mean green! There is a "toy" mission there and they say it really is something to see — real ancient and crude I guess — hope to see it tomorrow.

The natives sit on the ground & eat with their fingers entirely — good thing Emily Post isn't out here. There are 28 dental officers out here — saw two I knew and will see some more tomorrow — one was a kid from Sulphur, Okla — used to send me patients. The other is Rose from Minnesota — also saw a couple of corpsmen I used to know — really glad to see all of them. I was well treated — had several cases, cracked plates etc., I wanted to get fixed — needed x-ray film & stones — got them. Visited the hospital — really nice, all in quonset huts — green, green grass & huge coconut trees. The grass is like a mat — don't believe they have to cut it — I go for that!

The weather is delightful here — supposed to be winter time — tsk tsk — about 90-100 degrees! Looking down from the Officers Club (Fleet) the harbor is so pretty — blue water with "much activity" — surrounded by dense green growths of various sorts. Over the settlement the British flag and the French flag flies — kind of thrilling, but best of all the good old Stars & Stripes.

The Fleet Officers Club is really nice — set on a hill — nice building — patios with tables & chairs — tennis court & swimming — everything clean as only the Navy knows how to do it — shines so it hurts your eyes. Drinks really delicious, good grades of whiskey — rum & gin — Pabst beer — cokes — ginger ale — soda etc and served with ice "int". What a treat after warm beer & sitting on the deck.

Saw some nurses! Didn't know whether to tip my hat, curtsy or what — first woman we'd seen since January — I still love my little girl in Okla.

It's really amazing what has been done to this base — am anxious to explore tomorrow.

Didn't buy you a grass skirt — do you want one? Not very pretty — $3 and full of lice! Am afraid the lice wouldn't be compatible with your roaches.

All my love
Paul

27 Aug. 1944

Hello My Honey —

Bet tomorrow will be a lovely day — almost everyone is "diseased" today, had a final fling last night. Back out to sea for our health now, but we had fun — but good.

We didn't get into the jungle or go exploring this time but understand we are coming back and have been promised a trip to some islands that the military hadn't touched and is out of bounds except on official business. Will get to see the "bushmen" in their native haunts and witness a sing-sing.

We look so pretty — have our sides freshly painted and they start the superstructure tomorrow — nothing like being dressed up when we promoted a "business deal" — must stand out in the moonlight. She's still my pet and am proud to be aboard her — every place we go everyone speaks so highly of her — she is a good wan and looked so pretty sitting out there in the bay.

The gun boss (Bowers) just stuck his nose in to see if I had recovered — everyone seems to be perking up.

Had my office painted today — tomorrow my quarters get a new paint job — I'll be the envy of the wardroom.

All my love
Paul

THE NEW COUNTRY that Paul wrote "Bud" would enjoy in the next letter refers to the Solomon Islands, some 500 miles northwest of Espiritu Santo. "Bud" Solomon was a boyhood friend of Paul's. The *Louisville* would spend the next week in the Guadalcanal area preparing for the bombardment of Peleliu.

29 August 1944

Hello Darling —

Here we have been steaming along the past couple of days and making as much noise as tho we were in the yard — a campaign of paint chipping, hammering, riveting and what have you. Was supposed to have had my room chipped today but they did Zinke's so I'll get mine tomorrow.

Seeing some new country — "Bud" would enjoy it. May get a few beers — sounds good on account it's awfully hot here. Tonight at chow there wasn't a dry stitch on anyone and the sweat — it's no longer perspiration — actually dripped off one's nose — sad state of affairs & I'm glad my Deodo arrived. Guess I told you it was winter where we just left so I guess we notice the "change in weather" — must be at least one degree, but it did seem cooler.

Just finished reading "I Was Hitler's Doctor" — quite a book — he's a mess.

It's past bed time but it's so hot & tonight I won't get to open my port so that means sleeping under a fan and "sinus" tomorrow.

Supposed to be an erupting volcano around here so will go topside and look for it — cool off and crawl into my sack — have to hit the deck early tomorrow — g.q.

All my love
Paul

PAUL REFERRED to his location in his September 2 letter as "quite a historic area." He also says: "if one could see the bottom of the bay here it really would be something." Guadalcanal was a brutal battleground in late 1942, and the waters between Guadalcanal and the Florida Islands to the north had become known as "Ironbottom Sound," after all the ships that had sunk there.

2 Sept. 1944

Honey Girl —

We are in an even prettier spot now — simply gorgeous — beautiful flowers, green grass, bananas — coconuts, grass, chickens, dogs, ducks and natives galore. Quite a historic area and can't believe I'm actually here — if one could see the bottom of the bay here it really would be something.

Am taking a trip around the islands tomorrow — will see some more famous spots.

All my love, Sweet
Paul

PAUL'S SEPTEMBER 4 LETTER describes an incident that had taken place in the Brass Hat Bar, located at Espiritu Santo. Sitting at a table of strangers, he made a comment referring to first lady Eleanor Roosevelt, then becomes alarmed that an Army colonel at his table may be a relative of hers.

4 Sept. 1944

Hello Darling —

Did my first "bitching" the other day — won my point so far, don't know how long it will last. We are getting nine new officers aboard, so immediately a move to renovate rooms was instituted. My single room was on the list due to R.H.I.P. (rank has its privileges) — all was well until some others started raising hell and got away with it — I hadn't said a damn word so they came in, measured the space above my bunk and were going to install another bunk eighteen inches over my head! That meant when my roommate crawled into his sack the bottom would be less than a foot from my nose — I didn't relish the idea of having his you know what in my face all night so I objected. My room if you remember has a high ventilator in it and breaks up my overhead until it gives very little clearance — in other words, my room was never intended for anything other than a single room. Several rooms have ample space for from 4 to 8 additional bunks — but no, it would be "inconvenient" to them, so-o-o-o it was belayed but my little room was still on the spot. I still wasn't going to say anything but when one of the chiefs who had to do the work said it was a damn shame and wasn't practical, I got mad and went to the 1st Lieut and asked him if he was still going thru with tearing up my room. He said yes because Dr. Zinke wouldn't give up his room or allow a bunk to be put in and said that they could squeeze one into mine because on destroyers they didn't even have that much room & got by with it.

That really made me mad so I requested permission to see the Exec & "for why". Told him [*the first lieutenant*] I hated to bitch and it was the first one, but I had one coming and he'd play hell wrecking my room until the others had been fixed up and if then they still needed my room — okay. Gave me a chance to air myself according to regulations so I did — net result, still have my room — no changes made — didn't have to see the exec and everybody is happy (fingers crossed). The 1st Lt. was nice about it and said he didn't blame me and my room shouldn't be touched, that he'd see the Exec and have it belayed. It's a great life — if they ever get me in the regular Navy they'll have to give me a senior commission — these kids that are Lt. Comdrs. now would ordinarily be Ensigns — result, some get mighty rank conscious. So much for that — nobody hurt — great life and the Navy is swell — still love it but would like to kick some "- - - -" and straighten a few out.

The censors are censing so will slip this in the mail — will get a chance to write again tomorrow I'm sure. In closing have a Life's Embarrassing Moment to relate. I was sitting in the Brass Hat Bar having a beer in my own quiet way — a Naval Captain, Army Colonel & an Army General came in and sat at my table. After while conversation loosened up and they were commenting on the "LADIES" sign over one of the doors. Everyone made their guess — me with my big mouth pipes up with: "Maybe they expect Eleanor" — The Naval Captain smiled politely — the colonel showed his teeth fleetingly and the general damned near died laughing. I thought something was wrong and got to thinking the colonel's face was mighty familiar — jeepers! Could it have been? I asked some of the fellows who it was and sure enough it was one of the family! I went to the head on the double and didn't return.

That leads up to another pretty good story but will save it for tomorrow or for when time hangs heavy at sea.

All my love
Paul

6 Sept. 1944

Hello Darling —

Yesterday afternoon heard a commotion outside my port, so I investigated to see what it was all about. A fuzzie-wuzzie in a native canoe was selling sea shells and our boys were giving him a bad time. The natives are quite clever, have a convenient dumbness and it's quite comical to watch and listen to them. The kids lowered a bucket with money in it and just about the time the native would reach for it, they'd jerk it out of his reach. Finally he got the bucket containing the coins — then the bickering started — finally our smart [*alecks*] got five shells for $2.50! They tried to get them for a penny a piece but the native "couldn't understand" and when asked if he understood English the answer was "no" — he understood all right when they said 5 for $2.50 so he promptly counted out five small shells in the bucket, of course first taking out the coins, and waved the bucket off with a big grin. Expected him to be upset any minute because the canoes are mighty tricky to start with and he had the bucket clasped between his knees, manipulating a paddle with one hand and picking out shells with the other — during which time the kids were yanking on the rope to which the bucket was tied. You probably have read descriptions of the natives — the part that fascinates me is their hair. It's real fuzzy and has a peculiar color — have never seen any color just like it — reddish coco — rusty or something and most of them have a long comb enmeshed in it some way and extends over the left eye — quite rakish, don't you know.

My favorite story that has come out of these parts is — when the Americans first landed here and much bartering was going on, a group of Marines ran across some natives with war clubs so they decided to buy some. They were arguing amongst themselves how they should go about gypping them out of the clubs when one of the natives spoke up, "Ah say, Ole Chaps — cut the B - - - S - - -, they sell for" so & so, whatever amount it was. It tickled hell out of me — don't doubt but what it's true for after all they have English Missionaries & teachers here.

The canoes are dugouts — sure would like to have one but don't worry I won't send you one even tho you and I would look awfully good in one on Uncle John's Creek. The natives sure handle them skillfully — four pile into one, have a little sail rigged and it's quite a picture as they skim thru the — guess it's over the — water. They paddle in perfect unison and without a splash.

Seems you asked what the "platforms" were on one of the canoes of which I sent one each picture — they, my girl, are outriggers and help keep the canoe from capsizing. The boogers go away out in the ocean in those tiny craft.

In some of the pictures I have sent you you will note feathers in their hair — that denotes their standing in the tribe — said standing is determined by the number of dead pigs they have. Seems their God is very fond of pork so they have regular pig killing ceremonies called sing-sings during which time they go thru a regular ritual. Start at sun down, dance all night and then in the morning the pig killing takes place. Beautiful feathered costumes are worn and from all reports it's quite a sight.

On with the pig killing — they have a bamboo cage in which the owner of the pig and his guests stand — the pig is stretched on bamboo poles and brought in by natives — head of said pig is thrust through an apeture — appeture (?) anyhow, an opening in the cage. The guest is handed a "pig stick" (knobbed club) and he delivers the first blow — one across the snoot & crushes it. Then the stick is handed to the owner and he clubs the pig to death. The head is then cut off and placed aside for ten days — not to be touched by anyone — the remainder of the pig is cut up — hide, bristles and all — some eaten then & there and some given away. All work is done by the women — good idea — nicht wahr? Don't know what part they give to their God, but the idea is the one that gives him the most pork and thus appeases his appetite is assured of a place in heaven. What with ration points we'd have a hell of a time getting anywhere.

Guess I've told you how pretty the view was from the club, the bay seemed so tiny after being on the ocean all those months. Our next Beer Stop was even prettier and had a much more exciting history. The club was located on quite a steep hill, in order to reach it you climbed a winding set of steps — most of which were rough hewn out of the hill. Quite a climb up — especially when you were dry, but coming back — nothing to it — just fall out. The site formerly belonged to the Bishop but when the Japs came, they ran him off and used it as headquarters. Of course we changed it but the view remains the same. They have a large main room, and one smaller one set aside for Lt. Comdrs. & above — it is called the Brass Hat Bar — fun.

The head is located at one end of the club and over looks one of the prettiest scenes I've ever seen. The Bay is at your feet on either side — that is a sight in itself but the payoff is the native village. It looks like a park, beautiful wild flowers — little plots of green grass smooth as a carpet, tropical trees, native huts with natives int and a natural rock garden fed by a tiny stream from a higher peak. Chickens and ducks overrun the place — no fooling it is pretty as a picture. It's all cut up — that is everything on a different plane — sort of terraced like and on the hill side where the stream is the grass is like a curtain — mighty, mighty pretty. Numerous pathways run thru the area and every so often there is a little arbor covered with dense vines and heavily flowered. The scene is so captivating the Padre got so interested he forgot where he was and got his feet in a certain drain and didn't notice it until he was soaked to the knees.

All my love
Paul

OF ALL PAUL'S enclosures to Dotty B, the only one to survive with the letters is in the September 6 letter. It is a copy of the August 4, 1944

USS *Louisville* "Daily Press News." On one side of the single pinkish legal-size sheet is a crude line drawing by "DEC Texas" showing the profile of a *Louisville* whale boat in the water. Tops of heads are shown, each one identified as a participant in the rescue mission. On the other side of the sheet is that issue's single typewritten story, which is reproduced below. The story's first reference to an island location has been inked out, although a second reference to Guam is not. Paul mentioned this August 3 event in his August 20 letter, saying he felt the participants should be awarded the Navy Cross.

> LOUISVILLE SENDS RESCUE BOAT TO JAP HELD BEACH
>
> In answer to a signal for help, yesterday afternoon the Lady Lou steamed close to the Jap held north eastern tip of [*island name inked out*] to effect the rescue of Felix Q. Mauta, seaman second class, U.S. Navy (Insular Service, Guam) and three pro American natives. A boat was put over the side as the Louisville stood out 1000 yards from shore within easy range of shore guns. The rescue party in charge of Ensign J. A. Rehberg consisted of: Koopman, Cox., Cox of Boat; Johnson, S1c. Bow Hook; Baird, F2c., Engineer; Ward, Bm1c., Asst' to Boat Officer; Norkus, Sm1c., Flag Signalman; Egan, PhM 3c, H. Div. corpsman; Willey, Pfc., 5th Div. Rifleman and Golden, Corp., 5th Div. Rifleman.
>
> All the ship's AA batteries were trained on the north end of the island and the ships plane with Ensign A. L. Sheiner at the controls and E. C. Shelton, ARM2c as radioman hovered about keeping a sharp watch, as the boat made for the beach to carry out the rescue in true Frank Merriwell fashion.
>
> Ensign Rehberg reported that as they came to within twenty five yards of the beach, they sighted Mauta, whose knowledge of signaling probably saved his life, and three other men, Jesus Cruz, his son Peter Cruz and Norberto Miguzman. He called to the men and they swam out to the boat and were brought back to the ship.
>
> Mauta was a member of the crew of a Y. P. Boat which was scuttled when the Japs invaded Guam in December 1941. He reached the beach and disguised himself as a native. He was picked up by the Japanese authorities and sent to a concentra-

tion camp. He remained there three weeks and was then put to work on an air field for which he received one yen per day. While working for the Japs he said he was able to wreck five (5) trucks. He also gave aid to American sailors who were hiding in the hills. Later he was permitted to go home to his ranch.

Twenty eight days ago, Japanese authorities sent out word for all men to report to headquarters. Mauta and a group of pro American natives and their families went into hiding on the northern section of the island. Here they lived, constantly hunted by the Japs. Their food supply was barely enough to keep them alive, the main diet being rice and fruit.

Yesterday Mauta attracted the attention of the Louisville and explained with signal flags, who he was and asked for a boat.

All the men were fed and clothed and given medical aid when they came aboard. They will be turned over to Naval Intelligence for further questioning.

Mauta told of the hardships and suffering of the natives of the island, the scarcity of food and the constant danger to life. He also spoke of the Jap propaganda which spread the story that Australia and Honolulu were in Jap's hands and the people in the United States were starving.

The "Louisville Expedition" will be remembered as one of the thrilling feats of this war. The men of the party with traditional courage and bravery of the U.S. Navy faced the danger of enemy guns in a truly heroic manner. We all salute them.

THE *LOUISVILLE* headed northwest in early September 1944 to bombard the island of Peleliu. They arrived September 12.

8 Sept. 1944

Hello Honey —

Made a mistake this a.m. — we turned our clocks back an hour and I did all right with my wrist watch but neglected to correct my alarm clock — the result was that I got up at 0245 instead of 0345 and that made today a long day. Will do better tonight — we changed another hour so I set my alarm first.

Yesterday morning a beautiful sunrise greeted us after securing from g.q. — this morning a heavy sea — overcast sky and a drizzling rain. Felt good to stand out on the well deck with the wind lashing your clothes and with salt spray and rain in your face. It's so much more fun steaming along than setting dead in the water.

Nothing new to allow — routine drills etc. Very necessary but boresome.

Bought some gray trousers & shirts and they say I look good in them — at least it's a change and they feel cooler. Got them the other day off a supply ship — am not going to stock up on them — just a couple of outfits, no blouses, shirts without ties, sleeves rolled or down — we try to be as comfortable as we can be but it's still hot. When we go ashore the uniform is the same — no formality at all — if it's a beach party — swim trunks is the uniform of the day.

All my love
Paul

10 Sept. 1944

Hello Dorothy Darling —

They are doing an emergency appendectomy below. Had planned on assisting this one but we have an official photographer aboard this trip and he wants to take pictures of it so I'm staying out. Someone would be sure to pipe up with a lot of blah, blah about wanting to get in the picture, so nutz to them. The photographic officer is a nice looking chap — full commander — Annapolis etc. — he looked the various ships over and picked the Lou. Speaks well for her and may be indicative of us playing a leading role again — sure hope so, never a dull moment.

The patient (appendix) is from another ship and was transferred to us while underway. I always get a thrill out of watching them throw the lines, rig the stretcher and away they go — wonder what the patient thinks, suspended between two ships and the waves leaping up at him. Believe I'd choose another time to have an attack — no, guess not, might be fun.

I'm a disillusioned boy — my waist line has gone down a good two inches — I can stand erect again and feel like a million dollars — last time I weighed I was 176 — tonight I weighed and it was 180! Take consolation in the fact I was fully dressed this time — last time I was scantily dressed due to being caught short when g.q. sounded and had on tennis shoes and the rest of my gear over my arm. Oh, well — my figger is getting good and if I can only keep it that way for the duration of my cruise I'll be a happy boy.

Speaking of g.q. — do you know what the bugle says? Can't give the sound effect but the words are: "General Quarters! General Quarters! Jesus Christ!!! Hurry Up!" When mail call sounds it is: "I got a letter, I got a letter — You get a G.D. Postal!" Antiaircraft goes like this: "Airplanes! Airplanes! Go Get Em! Go Get em! Ta Te Da." Movies is: "Let's Go To The Movies-s-s!" This one I haven't heard yet but the bugle says: "Let's Go Ashore! Let's Go Ashore! Who's Got The Price Of A Two-Bit Whore!" That's a hell of a naughty one to wind up on but I think they are cute — wish I could set the words to music but dat I can't — you've heard enough bugles to get "an idea of the mountains."

A bugle always gets me — when we were sitting in the bay you could hear the notes floating across the water at all times of the day from the various ships. Can't say very much about what went on while we were in but you can imagine the bee hive of activity. It really was a deal and we were having an awe inspiring and fear instilling parade right now. It's a beautiful sight to us but for prying eyes — a headache I'm sure.

The gunner has his orders and we're giving him a rough time — he has only been at sea twenty-seven years so we call him "short termer", does he rave! He said the other day he wanted his picture made with me before (Jeepers! — was halfway to my battle station then — someone clanged a gong outside my door!) he is detached. He's a swell person and I know I'll miss him — the lug. This noon we were sitting on one of the guns watching a "- - - -" come alongside — hotter than hell and had our shirts unbuttoned away down. The gunner's hairy chest was exposed — one of the fellows came along, stopped in front of him and said, "Jesus Christ! Gunner, why don't you take that fur coat off!" You should have heard the exchange of insults — it was really side splitting. We have so much fun out here — everyone is over their little peeves, it's the monotony of sitting that gets them. If we were idle in a port where you could go to town or something like that instead of getting off for two hours to lap up drinks & then have to report back — that's deadly.

The other day when I hiked up to the native village — as I passed by some of the huts I was greeted by several "el laas" — they were saying "hello" — was cute, their musical el laa. Later on my way back I ran into three little boys on their way down to the dock — they were "clothed" by the Navy — one had a USN bath towel around his middle, one had a pair of dungarees hacked off above the knees and the other a pair of [*khakis*] treated the same way. Wondered if they wore any other "garments" under the lava lava — soon found out — an old timer was walking along the beach, decided he had to go so opened his wraparound (lava-lava) and proceeded to urinate without missing a step — two handy gadgets I'd say. They are all great pipe smokers — carry their pipes — all straight stems, in the center of their mouth and very solomenly (?) puff away, never touched their hands to it.

The islands are mighty pretty but awfully hot, damp and sultry. The clouds are low and hang over the mountains, great patches of mist hang in the valleys — mighty unhealthy and the natives back in sure look it — lots of T.B.

Had an interesting dental case — sailor of course. Was perfectly well when he left the ship to go drink beer on the beach — came back not feeling well and glands swollen in his neck. New medico checked him saw a sore on his tongue & touched it up with silver nitrate. Patient became worse — they diagnosed it as trench mouth & called me. They hadn't questioned the kid at all as to onset, duration, etc. Upon questioning him he was all right when he left the ship, drank a few beers and then ate coconuts. There was my clue — so ran it down and sure enough they dug into it with their teeth — bruised the gums and tongue — used a dirty sheath knife — dirty hands — south sea island — result, a virulent infection. Took three days to clear him up but he is well as ever and thinks the dentist is all right. Still don't know what it was other than a damned serious proposition — he swelled up like a poisoned pup — couldn't swallow — temperature and very painful. I'd never seen anything like it and no one else had — sulfa drugs did no good and all other medications failed so I used a dye [*probably Gentian Violet, a potassium permanganate solution that is no longer in general use*] and presto — hale & hearty — fun, now.

Since the pest left have had a medical [*confrere*] and customers for my lending library so I give up — have to hit the deck at 0345 so it looks like it's my sack for me.

Am sure I'll have time to write tomorrow, in the mean time — I still love you.

"as ever"
Paul

EARLY ON TUESDAY MORNING, September 12, the *Louisville* took part in the preinvasion bombardment of Pelcliu, southernmost of the Palau Islands some 650 miles north of New Guinea and 400 miles east of the Philippines. As flagship for Rear Admiral Jesse B. Oldendorf, the *Louisville* headed a fire support group of five battleships, five heavy cruisers, three light cruisers, and 14 destroyers.

0450
12 Sept. 1944

Hello Darling —

Hold your hats, here we go again — we're all at our stations awaiting the opening whistle — won't be long now.

Have run my "cotton exchange" so everyone in this area is all set for the blast of guns and what have you.

Always kind of exciting these first zero hours on a new operation — all kinds of reprisals, new weapons and other threats against us. We have been promised a surprise — love surprises — "present day" — wanna open it, whoops!

It's old territory here but we are on a different mission this time so we ought to have a lot of fun. Wonder what the big surprise is — probably "nobody home" sign out, but I think it will be a little more entertaining than that. All kinds of possibilities so anything [*can*] happen.

I have my binoculars handy so I'm all set to see what they shoot, but good — fifteen more minutes and #1 will be on its way. Everyone is feeling fine — feel like they are on the beam and all set for whatever they throw back at us. More fun than waiting for the opening whistle of a Michigan-Ohio State game.

Ten minutes — time is running out — my sterilizer is singing a burbling song — instruments and dressings all laid out so all I have to do is hang out the "Open for business" sign, but sure hope I don't have any — it ain't for cash.

#2 plane was just catapulted — seven minutes to go — the readiness horn, "stand by", just sounded so will get my shirt on, grab my hat and take my box seat. Word just passed "secure all ventilation, cut the fresh water", so it won't be long now — for what? That's the question.

Sweet girl — don't worry about me — wish you could hear the scientific thunder that just started — we're next — so here goes.

All my love little darling — love you with all my heart —

Boom
Paul

13 Sept. 1944

Dear Honey —

Today is some kind of anniversary — eight months ago today we left for parts unknown — we're still going and for parts still unknown. Great life so guess we'll celebrate again today — nothing beats a good display of fireworks.

Yesterday was uneventful but very, very noisy — there it goes again — General Quarters, General Quarters, J.C., run like hell! What a life.

Had breakfast early this a.m. — hit the deck at 0330 — ate — did my chores and now talking to you. It's an easy life but what ungodly hours. No opposition yesterday — a little return fire but nothing to write home about. Looks wicked for the poor Marines but they will handle it when the time comes. Fired almost the entire day — my poor room is a shambles again — put it back the best I could but what's the use — will fall apart again today and many more times before we are through.

The "Pest" fell apart yesterday — he collapsed due to operational fatigue — he has been going at it hard ever since we came out and it finally got him yesterday. Will be some more crap out if we don't get a little rest — none in sight. The M.O. talked to the "- - - -" but no luck, he said we are the "- - - - group" and no rest in sight. Oh, well — I only have eight more months so to hell with them — as Foster says, "You asked for sea duty and brother you're getting it!" He says it's the toughest he has put in in all his eleven years — the old timers say it's a bit rugged, I don't know so can't crab too much.

There isn't any news — dressed up in my new shirt the other day — I bought some new shoes too — Florsheim Navy shoe — you know, the Fleet's In kind, they sure are comfortable and my feet feel real stylish. A supply ship came along so we had a chance to buy a few necessities.

It's about time to start firing so guess I'll go topside and watch — will be careful so don't worry — Foster and I have changed our routine a little — we drink grape instead of eating ice cream while "observing" — the last plane just took off so here we go —

All my love
Paul

14 Sept. 1944

Hello Darling —

Another day another dollar. Just came from topside and a breath of fresh air. It's really pretty out in spite of the ungodly hour — the moon just came out — a million stars in a black sky — the path of the moon causes a beautiful phosphorescent glow — the flash of guns on the horizon reminds you of ambitious fire flies.

It's a marvel to me how they can keep the ships in formation all night and arrive back at a certain point at a definite time. Of course there are a few "ties" but that is to be expected in any large business deal.

Had a little more fun yesterday. We got chased off the topside no less than six times but only one Purple Heart was awarded. Three hits but no damage other than one slightly wounded — our luck still holds but can't say as much for some of the others.

Saw a spectacular explosion yesterday afternoon — a plane just unloaded her load of bombs — either one exploded under her tail or was set off by gun fire — anyhow it blew the tail off and half of one wing — the rest of the plane plummeted to earth and ended in a huge explosion and burned. It happened so fast the pilot never knew what happened — hate to see them go out like that.

One of our planes came in with huge holes in two of her wings — a foot over and the pilot would have been blown out of the cockpit. He brought her in safely — we had our rescue squad out in the whale boat but he made a spectacular landing — the plane will fly again and so will he.

The island isn't pretty like it used to be. When we first arrived it was like a picture — one dense growth of trees & underbrush — couldn't see thru it for hell or high water — now it's blasted away and wow! What it had concealed — a lot of work ahead of us yet — wonder what today will bring forth — getting trickier by the hour and they are up to their old tricks of laying low and then letting go. We got sprayed a lot yesterday — funny to see the kids scramble — dive through the hatches like rabbits into their holes — weird music, combination of "Flight of the Bumble Bee" and then the "kerchuck" of a frog diving into the water.

The planes are off — must go topside and start a new day — should be a little excitement today but am waiting for manana — whoops! I'll be careful and play rabbit with the boys. Love you honey and will spectate for both of us.

All my love
Paul (The Rabbit)

ONCE THE CONCEALING FOLIAGE had been blasted away, as Paul observed, the American forces found that Peleliu was honeycombed with pillboxes and hundreds of caves.

15 Sept. 1944

Darling —

I missed getting out my early morning communique this a.m. but I was too busy and it was too noisy — what a day!

Sure would like to see some clippings of this date — it was awful and I'd like to see what the papers say about it. Honey, it's unbelievable — one can't describe it — you have to actually see it and then you wonder if you aren't having a nightmare or something.

What are these Japs made of — surely not flesh and blood — they're not even of the animal kingdom or they'd crack up during one of these bombardments.

The morning broke and gave promise of a beautiful day — that is under ordinary circumstances. Nice sunrise, no breeze at all and the ocean as smooth as a mill pond, but big things had been planned. By so and so o'clock the sun was blotted out and the island was invisible due to the pall of smoke and flame over it. The smoke and dust went straight up and clung over the land — no breeze at all — even our flags hung limp as we went in so you can imagine what a calm there was.

But they don't show any news reels of what happened the next few hours. The Japs had a field day — like a page out of Terror Stories or Weird Stories. We were within a couple thousand yards of the beach where the landing took place and closer than that this afternoon for the other waves. I was up in the superstructure watching thru glasses so it was like having them right in my lap — it was awful.

Saw the dead piled up — wounded lying around the men and equipment blown up — the Japs aren't whipped yet and they get tougher as we get closer to their homeland. There is no question as to the final outcome but it isn't just around the corner unless some miracle happens.

War is the most devastating thing in the world — merciless, cruel and most fearful thing imaginable. I can't believe such things are actually happening and I'm out here in it — it's so heartless — don't think I'll ever go hunting again — wish you could get a chance to see the official movies of one of these deals — Buck Rogers come to life in all his fantasies — Wow!

Will write tomorrow — am still going around in circles — am having lots of company & the topic of discussion is the day's happenings — guess I wasn't seeing things.

I'm swell honey — feel fine & spectating "good".

All my love
Paul

16 Sept. 1944

Dearest Honey —

Feel like a banker today — at least am keeping banker's hours. Didn't have to get up until 0445 — had a stylish breakfast of baked beans, bacon, muffins, toast, pineapple juice and coffee — went out on deck and watched the fireworks. Didn't have g.q. this morning — we are standing by for called fire and "fired all morning". Ran out of big ammunition so it's safe to straighten up my room — had it done, took an hour's nap, showered, shampooed my hair, read your August letters and here I am in my skivvies and attempting a conversation with you.

The little yellow bellies are still giving us trouble — they still have mortars and keep on firing back at us — how they manage to live thru an invasion, I sure don't know. They must be so deep in the ground and full of "sacki" they just don't feel anything. It shakes us out here on board ship and whips your clothes around — can imagine what it does to them when the shells and bombs land on top of them.

No excitement today, routine shooting and being shot at — will be glad when we move on.

Love you sweet girl.

All my love
Paul

17 Sept. 1944

Hello Honey —

It isn't quite chow time — have been to church so I thought maybe I'd write a few lines. We didn't have music this morning other than that furnished by the near-by machinegun fire, bombs and shells. Seems funny to be in church and have all that destruction and killing going on so near.

Can't think of a thing to write about. Wood smoke and powder smoke wafting in thru my port — the wood smoke smells good. The parade of bodies has started — cows and pigs thrown in for variety — great world.

Love you sweet heart — take care of yourself.

All my love
Paul

18 Sept. 1944

Good Morning Honey —

Yesterday was a beautiful day — about the hottest day we have had — not a breath of air stirring and the water was like glass — have an idea what the Ancient Mariner meant now. Last night was especially pretty, not a cloud in the sky except those along the horizon — looked like banks of snow. The water was so blue and calm so the clouds were perfectly reflected — looked like a fairyland. Hundreds of flying fish were up and at them — have been disillusioned — flying fish don't play, when they fly they mean it — they are escaping from danger. They get their propulsion from their tail — it remains in the water and whips back and forth at a high rate of speed — the only time they are clear of the water is when they are blown out or washed up on deck. They would leave a perfect pattern on the glazed surface — looking like someone had been practicing penmanship with a giant pen — perfectly [*symmetrical*] in every detail.

Feel so sorry for the poor birds and fish out here. The fish are killed by concussion and the birds don't have a "home to go to anymore" — many, many of them float by — the fish of all varieties — odd shapes, sizes and all kinds of markings. The birds I'm disappointed in — haven't seen a brightly colored one yet. Have seen giant bats — about the size of our buzzards at home — dem I don't like!

As the Japs say — "we are poor jungle fighters" — we just tear the jungle down — guess they object or question as to the fairness of it. That is why I feel sorry for our feathered friends — when we get thru blasting there isn't a tree or anything left standing — you have to actually see it to believe what happens — whole mountains are blown away — concrete block houses pulverized — nothing left but dust and a few skeletons of buildings. A bomb or shell will go thru the roof — can see where it entered and then the concussion blows the walls out and leaves only the bare framework. Watched a huge tower topple yesterday — really was one grand crash and a beautiful cloud of dust.

You didn't happen to hear a broadcast by way of Frisco Saturday night about 2200. It was a direct broadcast from one of the warships out here to the states — originated at noon yesterday (Sunday). They of course left out the part I was interested in hearing or "not hearing". Tokyo or Tokyho — how in hell do they spell it — anyhow "Rose" has us wiped out. We were "repulsed at the water's edge" with the loss of 3500 lives. That's really tuff and feel so sorry.

All my love
Paul

21 Sept. 1944

Hello Honey —

Must be summer time down here — thought we had had hot weather but it has been nothing compared to what we are having now. The thermometer goes over the top in the wardroom so you can imagine what it is like when we close the ports for "darken ship" at our night meal. There hasn't been a breath of air during the day but last night a breeze came up to make the foc'sle a comfortable place. But to counteract that, we had "Flash Red" the past couple of nights so we have to rush for our battle stations and get all sweat thru again — we are the well known "drips" for sure.

Last night was a beautiful night for an air raid — sky overcast, low hung clouds and an "uncertain light". You could see the shadow of the planes and see their exhausts — quite thrilling and a few "tense moments". Nothing like a few enemy planes to keep the morale up. Wish you could see the men at their guns on these occasions — they're swell and the best in the world.

Still can't believe there is an actual war going on at our feet — we sit so comfortably — calmly would be more appropriate — we still have heat to contend with, while just a short ways away the air is filled with tracers and explosions. The tracers look like roman candles — every "- - - -" one is a tracer and is red so you can trace it to its target. Looks like a dotted line — can you imagine thousands of them? Throw in a lot of star shells and flares and you get a mighty pretty pyrotechnical display. We're being jarred quite a bit right now, so please excuse the flourishes of my writing. Where these little B's come from and how they continue to live thru all this, is beyond me — they ain't human!

We had a couple of beautiful dusks recently — one night the water was so calm and the sky so full of bright stars, they were reflected in the water so clearly you hardly knew which was actually the sky and which the water — was really out of this world. My friend Venus is unusually bright out here and really did her stuff night before last. I always go topside each evening just to look at her, she is so bright and friendly — does you good just to gaze at her. This particular night she was the only one out — sea calm and clear — she was so bright she made a regular path in the water. That was swell but all of a sudden "something" happened — the ships all started moving around causing undulations in the water and then Venus's reflection really went to town — seemed to be alive.

Murphy is very solicitious (?) of my well being. I went to bed early — was sound asleep in no time and finally woke up due to being uncomfortably hot — the monkey had slipped into my room and returned my bath robe he had borrowed previously. Instead of hanging it up, he carefully covered me with it so I wouldn't catch cold. I got him next morning — he is one of these birds (know a little girl bird who has the same failing) that likes to sleep in the morning. He is the world's worst for getting up — his legs are rubber, etc., etc., even at a decent hour but these g.q. hours are really hard on him. I usually set my alarm three quarters of an hour early so I'll be awake for g.q. — revenge is sweet — I "stole" into his room, carefully picked him up and set him in the corner — don't think he knows yet how he got there for sure, but I haven't been covered recently. We still have fun — still some damn fools around.

All my love
Paul

PAUL SAYS the *Louisville* went on a "special mission" on September 22. That was to deliver what the ship's sketchy history describes as a "diversionary bombardment on Arakabesan Island," a small island near Palau's main island of Babelthuap.

23 September 1944

Hello Darling —

Life goes on as usual out here — had a little fun yesterday but no one hurt. Went on a special mission which had possibilities — did our little job and are now again on routine duties. The little B's are really stubborn but the outcome is inevitable.

Heat is still the favorite topic of discussion. It has been terrific — you can fry eggs on the decks and bulkheads. You know how the steering wheel or window ledge on the car gets — that's the way it is out here — then when darken ship is in effect it gets stifling. I had taken a nap but the sweat trickling into my ears kept annoying me so I got up and thought I'd go on a letter splurge — no could do. Thought maybe I was the only one having trouble writing letters but everyone is bogged down — it's a sad state of affairs and I sure don't know what to do about it.

We have been cautioned again about being careful what we say so I guess that helps put a damper on writing. The Japs have ways and means of finding out things — they knew all about our last deal and told us about it before time so there you are.

The gunner is still going strong — the heat gets him too — said he got out a fresh shirt, hung it over a chair while he went out to get a drink of water — when he got back his shirt had already started sweating!

Whoopee! My laundry just got back — I was getting short — was reduced to my romantic skivvies — fastened with a safety pin and reach below my knees — very stylish and most becoming.

Think I'll put it away and check to be sure my new shirts & p.j.s came back — I keep them in my safe between times.

All my love
Paul

P.S. Bong — WOW!

25 Sept. 1944

Hello Sweet One —

It was so nice on the foc'sle tonight, we're creating a breeze and it's actually cool for a change. It's been so hot we have had to keep the hose turned on the sides and deck on the ship in an attempt to cool things off. The Padre, Foster, Zinke & I had a bull session — the gunner is sick and couldn't attend. Quite a bit of sickness aboard, mostly cat fever, nothing serious. It's been so terrifically hot — get wringing wet and then stand under a fan or blowers, it's no wonder everybody isn't down. I'm knocking on wood because I feel in the pink — my ears haven't bothered me at all but once in a while my right frontal sinus kicks up.

We have so damn much gold braid aboard now we're top heavy. We're big shots now for sure so we ought to have fun on this next deal — we have done all right to date so we're going up the ladder.

Sure glad I raised hell about my room when I did — a lot of changes had to be made — so far I'm still entrenched in my fox hole and hope to remain so but one never knows.

All my love
Paul

26 Sept. 1944

Hello Honey —

My room is nice and cool today — have my wind scoop out and it really is scooping in good old sea air. With my fan going too — I'm very comfortable for a change. You asked me how I'm doing with the heat rash. "I'm" is no more — it's all rash so nothing more to worry about. There is a lot of ring worm and impetigo but have escaped so far — hope I don't get caught with it.

Saw a fair show this afternoon — "Reveille With Beverly" starring Anne Miller. When she put on her dance it brought the house down — after all the kids have been out eight and a half months and they are getting nervous.

Think I'll go help Murphy censor — a lot to be censored so all help is appreciated.

Bye honey
All my love
Paul

THE *LOUISVILLE* ARRIVED at Hollandia on New Guinea's northwest coast on September 27, 1944.

“Dugout Doug” and the “he” in quotation marks in Paul’s September 27 letter are references to General Douglas MacArthur, whose headquarters was in Australia. “Harry’s Boys,” the ones Paul doesn’t trust, is the U.S. Army. The name probably came from Paul’s friend, Dr. Harry Ford, who was in the Army in England.

27 Sept. 1944

Hello Darling —

We are in a beautiful scenic spot — quite a thrill to enter the lagoon. We have mountains on three sides of us. This afternoon when we first entered they looked purple with low hanging fleecy white clouds blanking out the peaks. Lush vegetation covers them.

It’s a bee hive of activity right now — much gold braid & may get to see “Dugout Doug” — dat I would like, just for the hell of it. May do business with him and have a chance to form my own opinion of him.

It’s been very quiet — a few sub contacts but nothing happened. Just routine stuff.

They put my quarters back together again today — will last a few weeks and then go all to hell again when they start firing.

Hours later — had interruptions, ate dinner and saw a cute show, Henry Aldrich in something, didn’t get the title. It was a crowd pleaser and the kids whooped and hollered.

It’s a beautiful, lonesome night — hazy half moon — no black out and it sure feels good for a change. We sure didn’t look like a warship during the show & just before — radio over the ships loud speakers — kids lined the catapults — had chairs & benches out on deck — was more like a “moonlight cruise” they have on the Lakes. Lots of real honest to gosh lightning over the mountains — heat lightning I guess. Anyhow it wasn’t man-made. It’s so quiet & nice — feeling of security but still there are thousands of Japs in the neighborhood — hope they really are “neutralized”. Hope “he” knows what he is doing — I don’t trust “Harry’s Boys.”

All my love
Paul

THE *LOUISVILLE* MADE the short run from Hollandia to Manus in the Admiralties, and arrived there September 30.

30 Sept. 1944

Hello Darling —

We got sneaked up on yesterday — 116 bags of mail came aboard — was all second class stuff and I received June & July papers so now I'm getting caught up. Everything was beat up pretty bad and wet but I dehydrated them and made out all right. No recent mail but may get some this afternoon when we hit port. I'd "admire" to have some mail & a cold beer. The sea is mighty rough today — we are pitching and rolling to a fare-thee-well. Fell out of my office several times until finally my operating light blew out so I came up, got my wardroom roster prepared and all set to collect bills tomorrow.

Damned near got drowned a while ago. Had my port open — we heeled over and a huge wave met us — result, one damp room.

Next week you should receive three $25 bonds — the first in the series — three each month for nine months. When I find out what my next duty is, may extend the program.

Have a good supply of magazines again — picked up all Colliers, Liberties, Americans, etc., so I'll be all set for this next operation. Am reading "Lilly Crackell" by Caroline Slade & enjoying it a lot. Reminds me of the River Bottom gang in Okla. City.

Did you read where Italy is "demanding" equal rights and being restored to pre-war status? Got awfully burned over it — they probably will get all they ask for.

Guess I'll try to shave & get ready for lunch — may cut my throat but will try to synchronize (?) with the ship. Am looking forward to new scenery & want to be ready to go in with the first wave.

All my love to you honey girl
Paul

1 Oct. 1944

Hello Darling —

Had fun last night. We're in a beautiful harbor — an officers boat made the officers club last night — open from 1900 to 2300 on Saturday night. Remember we are a day ahead of you folks. Hadn't planned on going in but had the duty today so they talked me into it. It was a beautiful night — bright moon and the water was like glass so I weakened and went. We were issued quinine and had to take it before leaving the ship — holds true only at night. Beautiful spot — looked like Coney Island — millions of lights. The Club is about a hundred yards long with a smaller room about fifty yards long built on a tangent at each end for Brass Hats & private parties. Cost a dollar to join and 2.00 to 5.00 for chits — beer is two for a quarter (ice cold) and high balls 25 cents.

Never saw so many drunks in all my life but I guess the fellows have earned it — it had been a tough month for everybody and "everybody" is in — a magnificent sight on the water.

Service was good — had table service and plenty of bar tenders. The bar runs the entire length of the building and the place was packed. Outside the building they have a huge beer garden and an orchestra shell with a band playing — very gala and a typical Saturday night. Lots & lots of fun and met some old friends.

Saw a screwy show tonight — Veronica Lake in "I Married A Witch". I enjoyed it but we got a "Red Flash" and had to man our stations for a short time. Boy, oh Boy! If they ever dropped a torpedo or bomb in there — Wow!

All my love
Paul

4 Oct. 1944

Little Honey —

Honey, I don't know what I'd do if I was stuck on a base like this — go nuts for sure. It's hot, muddy, swarms of mosquitoes & other insects, stinks from rotting vegetation, food is terrible, live in a quonset hut with only one army cot in it, do their own laundry, can't stray away from camp because of Japs still around. They go to work at 0600 and quit at 1515. He is senior man in the fleet Dental Clinic and has to take care of all personnel from the ships that don't have dentists. He has four dentists with them — the equipment is excellent but Oh! the surroundings — rains all the time & that means lot of good old sticky & stinky mud — terrible. I'm having the three over for dinner Thursday night and they are tickled to death at the prospect of getting away from powdered eggs & other dehydrated "crap".

They all were advised to let nature take its course and not ask for sea duty and look what they got! Believe you me when my turn comes up again for duty outside the continental U.S. I'll again ask for a combat ship — they get around and you have "fun" — they're no more dangerous than other ships and are built to take care of themselves. A tender, repair ship, transport, etc., just hangs around and it's pure drudgery — but a combat ship — Whoops! When my turn comes up again I may be too senior for another cruiser so I'll request a battleship.

I'm not very happy or glamorous boy these days — impetigo finally got me! My hands are covered with it so I had to knock off dentistry for a while. If I can keep it from spreading to my face I'll be a happy boy. It's sure nasty stuff and is treated with silver nitrate — it turns black so you can imagine how it looks on a person. It isn't painful but it itches — that plus heat rash gives misery.

Still have my single room — Zinke got stuck with a roommate (tee hee) — my turn may come yet but I believe the influx of new men is over. Will hold a field day in my quarters tomorrow so I'll be all slick & clean when my "dinner guests" arrive.

Art Esch just came in for his exercise — I had a chinning bar welded to my overhead and have quite a gym class now. It's the only chance we have to exercise so the fellows utilize it. Had a room full of company last night — not the gym class but bull slingers — so I didn't get to write — I like to have them in but my letters suffer.

We are having a Louisville party Sunday & Monday nights — I went over yesterday and made arrangements for the Club — bet there will be some glorious hangovers afterwards. Had only four beers yesterday, no schnapps at all — just wasn't in the mood.

They have an awfully nice, neat and well kept cemetery here — went over and looked it over — didn't see any names I knew — was mostly Army, thought a familiar name would loom up — makes you realize the war is for keeps.

It's almost lunch time so will clean up, put my shirts & trousers on and eat — I'm starved — should weigh a ton but I'm trim. This leaving the table while still hungry is good for the "figger" but oh my!

Love you Loads
Paul

5 Oct. 1944

Hello Darling —

Not much to allow today but thought I'd send a few words along — won't have time later in the day due to my having company. Have my quarters all squared away and look real cozy. Handed in my mess books for audit — so have nothing on my mind except thinking about my girl, wishing it were you I'm having as a guest.

I have the Medical Watch today — had it last Sunday with only one case — a kid got his eye split open and I sewed him up in elegant shape.

Saw a good show last night — "Destination Tokyo" — enjoyed it a lot. It was a nice night out so I drug out a soft chair and watched the blinkers, lights on the beach and planes coming in for a landing. They are the first planes with their running lights on since we left the states — can't understand why ships have to be blacked out while the beach is ablaze with lights. You clean up for dinner but with the ports closed you are a mess in just a few minutes.

Having rice and curry for lunch today — I hate the damn stuff so guess I'll get a couple of candy bars and call it quits.

Bragged too soon about my mess books — blankey blank. In making out the roster I counted 74 members when it was only 69 — so damn many are leaving and coming & I don't get the word until everything is typed up nice & neat. It has no bearing on the past month's transactions, only in figuring the mess share for this month and I hadn't as yet charged the new members so it doesn't really make any difference. I'm going to stay with this job until I turn in one with out error — woe is me! Sure glad my cash always balances — have gotten so I can keep that squared away. This month will be a headache on account of so many new men — some of our staff members are on temporary detached duty so they'll have to be prorated — hate to think what that entails. Must clean up my books so will not start another page but will write after my dinner party.

Paul (Book-keeper Extraordinary)

6 Oct. 1944

Hello Honey —

Didn't do so good with my dinner party last night so I know what the young bride feels like after her first party — I do mean "dinner party". Here I worked my fingers to the bone — had nice breaded veal cutlets, creamed asparagus on toast, pickled beets, hot rolls, butter, iced tea, iced coffee, chocolate ice cream and oh yes — extra good vegetable soup. Had the places all set, my room squared away and me in an extra starched pair of trousers & my new shirt — felt in such a festive mood — boo hoo — "I could just cry and go home to mother." What would do in a case like that? Goodness! Forgot to tell you what the trouble was — THE GUESTS DIDN'T SHOW UP! At the last minute, the boat schedule was changed and everything was a mess — they were to have caught the 1600 boat but it didn't show up until 1730 so I guess they just gave up. Will go over today and see if they are still waiting on the dock or went home.

Love you little girl — take care of yourself and I'll write as often as I can before the snow falls.

All my love
Paul

9 October 1944

Little Sweetheart —

Gee honey — I'm hungry for a sight of you — it's just as well I'm out here right now — you sure couldn't like me. I'm the world's most miserable and repulsive looking individual. I'd have to stand away off and wave at you. I have called it quits on everything and have confined myself to my quarters — had rubber sheeting put on my bed & pillow and am going to smear my entire body in ointment until I get rid of the damned infection.

It's a combination fungus, impetigo and heat. Has started on my face now — just so it doesn't get into my eyes and ears — Wow! It itches to beat hell and my arm pits are raw — thought everything was under control but this a.m. it broke out with renewed vigor — my waist line is raw — back and shoulders raw and is starting on my legs — pretty soon there won't be a square inch of me left. Have had my fill of the tropics — I haven't been completely dry for months so I guess I'm just rotting away but good.

I've been so careful too — wash my hands a million times a day — haven't gone swimming or a damned thing. The water is loaded with fungus infection so I guess the salt spray is sufficient to infect one. There's quite a bit aboard so I'm not suffering alone. So much for my misery — I'll live thru it and perhaps my hide will be tougher after this siege.

Wonder just how the election will turn out — in ordinary times I'd almost go for Dewey but right now I prefer F.D.R. Got quite a bit of dope on "Tom" from one of the fellows aboard who hails from N.Y. — according to him, Dewey's skirts aren't so clean either — so, what have you. I wouldn't be a politician for love nor money — it's the world's lousiest set up, that's for sure.

Lots & lots of war correspondents out here — wonder what for? Must be a convention of some kind. They were having a private party at the club last night — they were in one wing and us in the other. We had a lot of fun — no hangovers today but had to pour three into sick bay. We picked up two strangers that were passed out on the dock. They were there when we first arrived and were still there when we were ready to leave so the Exec told me to load them up & put 'em in sick bay. They slept it off and went back to their own ships this a.m. — no charges referred.

Think I'll call it quits for now and scratch awhile — I've kept from touching myself so I wouldn't contaminate the paper but I feel the urge to dig in with both hands. Don't worry about me — I'll be pure when I get out of this area and it won't be long now.

Paul (itchy bitchy)

PAUL DIDN'T DO a bad writing job considering his hands were "swathed in bandages." The lines are just a bit farther apart and the script is not as smooth as usual.

10 Oct. 1944

Hello Honey —

It's a little difficult to write due to my hands being swathed in bandages but I'll do my best.

This afternoon I'll go over to Club "75" — a club just for cruisers — supposed to be real nice and not crowded. It's much closer too so maybe I can look half way decent when I get there. Could go for a few cold beers, then a good dinner, movies and then my sack — sounds like an interesting day doesn't it?

The other night when we returned from our party, the mess boys dropped two of our silver trays overboard — cost $45 a piece. We called out our divers and recovered them.

The "- - - -" next door is raising hell and getting so I'm getting disgusted — sure glad I'm not connected with him or serving under him — would give fireworks and to my detriment. Such is life and so it varies.

All my love
Paul

PAUL'S LETTERS had been crisp and clean until the past few, which are badly smudged at the creases and corner, probably from being folded and sealed with bandaged, ointment-covered hands.

10 Oct. 1944

My Darling —

I don't know what is in the air but the wardroom is filled with censors. Maybe my last word out for a while so I'm saying, "Hi Keed". Love you above all else, so if anything happens to me — forget me and start all over — thems orders.

The Padre and I saw a beautiful sunset tonight — I've never seen one just like it, such a pacific one. Wish you could have seen it. The Padre is one swell person, we get along swell.

Wish I could remember everything that goes on — the conversations, impressions, comparisons of duties, thrills, confidences by younger members, the future and "what giffs it". With my bandaged hands and thinking ninety to nothing I'm having an awful time.

As of now, I have all clippings sent me and will try to preserve them. The ones rec'd today were most interesting but they failed in a lot of respects. The headlines for instance — re-read one of my letters, think I referred to Buck Rogers — the fantasy and utter inhumanness of destructive weapons — honey, it's unbelievable unless you have seen it. Ours is an unspectacular war but God! it's grim — talked with a fellow that was thru the Atlantic war — the war there is up and above board — here it's no holds barred.

This letter is very, very poor — just want to be certain of a possible last word. We're heading toward the rising Sun by way of "- - - -" and honey — tell you something, have loved but one girl — you are the unfortunate one. Love you loads.

Paul (plain)

11 Oct. 1944

Good Morning Darling —

We are still around so here goes another small letter. Last night everything was in an uproar and it's a mad house today. Looks like Grand Central Station and a big convention.

Had fun at the "75" Club yesterday — quite a nice layout and a lot more convenient. We went over in a motor launch and it's the first time I set out clean and arrived clean — felt like a human being in spite of my skin quivering with itch.

The club is two huts long with a screened in porch along the seaward side. It is set close to the beach in a coconut tree grove & quite pretty — a nice view of neighboring islands. A lot of fuzzie wuzzies around — I think they are cute and very friendly — get a kick out of their rusty hair and orange-to-red teeth — give a startling effect.

Am looking forward to the coming events — I'll be careful and watch good — should be most interesting.

Little girl — I love you and will be thinking of you — don't worry about me, everything is under control — we're all rarin' to go and Lou is straining at her anchor chain — CA 28 will see us thru.

All my love
Paul (Cruiser-kid)

ON OCTOBER 12, with Admiral Oldendorf on her flag bridge, the *Louisville* set sail at the head of a bombardment and fire support group. Their destination was Leyte Gulf, in the Philippine Islands.

A Happy, Lucky, Shooting Ship

OCTOBER 1944 BROUGHT the long-awaited invasion of the Philippine Islands. One of the war's most historic photos is of General Douglas MacArthur, Supreme Allied Commander-Southwest Pacific Area, wading ashore nearly three years after he was forced to flee the islands. Paul was not impressed with the photo op, calling MacArthur a "damned publicity hound."

October also brought what has been called the greatest battle in the history of naval warfare. Involving nearly 300 ships and almost 200,000 men, the October 23-25 Battle of Leyte Gulf was comprised of several naval actions played out over a wide area.

The *Louisville's* bombardment and support group was in Leyte

Gulf protecting the 6th Army forces that were pouring supplies onto the beach and moving inland. These fire support ships were ordered to face Japanese Vice Admiral Shogi Nishimura as he steamed into Leyte Gulf through Surigao Strait.

The resulting Battle of Surigao Strait was lopsided, but it remains unique because it was, in all likelihood, the final battle in which massive warships slugged it out toe-to-toe.

By 1944, air power had changed the traditional format of fleets blazing away at each other. Most of the famed naval encounters of World War II — such as the Battle of Midway — found surface ships defending their aircraft carriers from attacking planes while sending their own planes far over the horizon to strike at the enemy carriers.

But this was not the case in the Battle of Surigao Strait the night of October 24-25. American carriers were busy elsewhere and the Japanese, despite the relatively few planes that continued to harass the *Louisville*, no longer had the numbers of aircraft or experienced pilots to make their air arm a decisive factor.

Air power disrupts naval formations, and its absence at Surigao Strait set the stage for another historical aspect of the pending fight. A classic, but rarely achieved tactic is called "Cross the 'T.'" As vessels of one force approach in single file, vessels of the other force form a straight battle line and move across the opponent's path. The force crossing the "T" is in position to deliver withering broadside fire against approaching ships that can use only their forward guns.

The USS *Louisville* would lead the battle line that crossed Admiral Nishimura's "T."

Nishimura and his fellow Japanese admirals entered the Battle of Leyte Gulf lacking ships, planes, manpower, firepower, technology, and seamanship. When the battle was over, the Japanese Navy was no longer an effective fighting force.

However, the Japanese were still more than willing to fight and die during the Battle of Leyte Gulf. They introduced the U.S. Navy to a desperate, terrifying element, the kamikaze corps — or, as Paul describes them, "suicide crash dives."

Man of War, a book compiled by members of the *Louisville* crew, described the first such attack on the *Louisville*:

> He drove through the mists of darkness like a projectile.

> Every man felt the plane was directed at him as he froze in position waiting for the crash. Then suddenly it was over. The Jap had missed the ship by inches. As he plunged into the water on the starboard side of the boat deck shrapnel flew back aboard ship, killing one of our men. That was our first Kamikaze. It has caused our first action death aboard the Louisville.

This was not *Lady Lou's* last kamikaze attack, nor was it her last death.

November provided little excitement except a quick raid on Luzon and a typhoon that finally turned Paul green and sent him to his bunk. The *Louisville* repaired her storm damage and took on supplies and ammunition at Ulithi Atoll, then headed for New Guinea and several weeks of shuttling between Hollandia and the nearby Admiralty Islands.

13 Oct. 1944

Hello Darling —

Feels good to be under way again. This time next week we won't be steaming along peacefully without a "worry" in the world — gold stars will have a field day — should be rugged.

Saw three Red Cross girls at Club 75 the last day — saw a nurse once before so our record of not seeing a woman is broken. These weren't so hot — still love my own little girl back home. Some of the gals have quite a racket out here — charge $50-25 for "it" and they are cleaning up. On "- - - -" Island one gal cleaned up $17,000 in four months — when they have had enough they get pregnant & go home — about the only way they can be relieved. Better not say too much about it — let them have their fun (?).

Think I have my impetigo under control — only a few new spots have broken out — I can lower my arms with some degree of comfort now — they have been so raw — especially in the arm pits.

Sure a lot of changes aboard ship — got in a flock of "Trade School" boys class of '45 — some look to be about thirteen years old — awfully cute and eyes a-gog — they really will bug out next week — great life.

All my love
Paul

14 Oct. 1944

My Darling —

Still battling impetigo but am gaining on it — for good measure I have thrown in a little ring-worm to "round" it out. Now if I become a leper or develop elephantiasis, I will have run the gauntlet of common tropical skin diseases.

Had a busy day yesterday sewing buttons and belt loops — finished with my trousers but when I was ready to hang them up — I found I was firmly attached to them — no I wasn't in them and didn't get hurt. Mom's kit she gave me when I went "down to the sea" sure has come in handy — the laundry is awfully hard on buttons and I'm getting quite adept at replacing them. Now don't get any ideas, young lady.

Hate to think about my poor little room next week — they finished tightening all bolts and nuts so for the next three days I'm secure. After that I'll have to start picking up again. Have my binoculars all polished up and am all set for what ever it giffs. Should be mighty rugged but we have no qualms — merely routine business with us "seasoned warriors".

That's all for this morning — am going topside to keep cool and dry so this stuff won't drive me nuts — have taken a bath and doped my lesions and feel pretty good right now but am starting to perspire again so I'm going out in the breeze.

Love you sweetheart
Paul

15 Oct. 1944

Hello Honey —

Eleven months ago today I joined up with CA 28 and we're still going strong. Yesterday and today it's been storming — I am getting a big kick out of it — a high wind, driving rain and COOL for a change — gee, it's great.

I never tire of watching ships come along side so today I put on my rain-coat, went out side and "hung on" while they transferred official mail. It's a beautiful sight on a calm day but when there is a heavy storm — huge white caps — both ships heaving and tossing — it's a sight that makes your blood tingle. When the destroyer pulls away the spray really flies —

the entire deck is awash — Zinke took some pictures of them today — sure hope they turn out for I'd sure like some copies of them.

My room was flooded again today — didn't dog down my port tight enough so the waves crashed thru. Ships sure are built. How they withstand the tons of water that are slammed against her sides — makes a "distinctive noise" and sure makes her heel over. Have heard stories of raging seas — the old Pacific has a mad on now but it's marvelous — I was afraid my cruise would go by without a real storm — we have had a few ninnyhammers by comparison — it's the real McCoy now.

There isn't a speck of news — missed church this a.m. because I was getting the newcomers mess accounts squared away. Really wanted to go — don't know what the week will bring forth — we all have our fingers crossed — it's the biggest deal yet, they have already bared their teeth and have broken skin. Our gang will soon be right square dab in the middle of them ere long.

Am tired of skidding so will retire for the nite.

All my love
Paul

16 Oct. 1944

Darling —

It's still storming beautifully and is nice and cool — wish you could see us bobbing around, just like a bobber on a fishin' line. No mal de mer as yet and don't think I'll be affected.

Had g.q. tonight — the old routine is in again, so once more the uniform of the day is identification tags, sheath knives and life belts. Everyone is looking forward to the big shin-dig — hope our orchestra wins first prize.

Must have been a million tons of water hit us then — maybe you heard the dull crash — it was a dandy. Hope there are no mines on the loose. We're finding more and more of them as we go along. We have been lucky so far — perhaps there is something in a name.

I'm kind of pooped — everyone has the "dropsy" — it's hard walking these days, we should all go in for ballet dancing after this — you know, one step forward, a couple of skips to the side, hesitate, backtrack, run, bang against a bulkhead, slither, etc — honestly every one looks as tho they've had several too many. It's fun especially when you cross the open deck — dat's really something.

Honey girl — remember, I love you and am thinking of you — keep the home fires burning for it "ain't a fitten nite for man or beast" tonight.

Love you so much
Paul

17 Oct. 1944

Hello Honey —

Oh what a beautiful day! Whoops — what's that old saying — "God help the sailor on a night like this." Darling we really are in one and the worst is yet to come according to the "barometer".

It's just daylight so I took a peek to see what it looks like out side — Yi-e-e, there's a flood someplace. The waves are rolling over the foc'sle, well deck and fan tail — all hands ordered to stay off. We seem to be in a valley — mountains of water on either side — can't see a damned thing but water — all other ships are absolutely invisible. Hate to think what the smaller ships are going through out there — must be terrific, judging what it's doing to us. The crash of water against the sides — tonight I'm putting cotton in my ears so I can sleep — my inboard bulkhead keeps snapping like one of those mechanical crickets we used to play with — makes an awful noise. Then the sliding of chairs — boxes, etc — all in all it isn't conducive to sound and "restful" sleep. Now when I'm asked "were you ever in a storm at sea" I can answer — yea, verily with gusto.

It's time for breakfast so will go wrestle my victuals — case of hand is quicker than the eye and a big mouth helps — am sure I'll hit my oral cavity. Will talk to you later.

Good afternoon little sweetheart — goody — it's an official typhoon and are we having fun! Extra life lines have been strung — "this and that" is being done and away we go. The weather is to increase for 24 hours — hold for 72 and then clear up — after that I can claim being a real salt. Just before taking a nap this p.m. I was out watching the waves — remember our silos, the catapults sit on top, believe it or not the waves were that high — the sea is really boiling.

The "peculiar set-up" makes it doubly thrilling and I think it's the most exciting so far — hope I can remember what it was all about when I get home.

Had fun filling a tooth this a.m. — was an emergency so I went ahead.

Before I started this letter for the second time I shaved — showered and shampooed — feel like a million dollars and all clean for what ever giffs it. Big business in the a.m. at sunup — will drop a few tons of calling cards getting ready for the big day. It's a dime novel thriller — typhoon with all its fury — mines — subs and planes.

All my love
Paul (Typhoon Lad)

SUDDENLY, THE WEATHER cleared and on the morning of October 18, *Lady Lou* boldly led the way into Leyte Gulf, first sweeping for mines, then bombarding beach landing areas.

18 Oct. 1944

Hello Darling —

Turned out to be quite a day after all and thank the Lord we ran out of the storm. It has been a beautiful day as far as elements are concerned — no rain, very little wind and a bright sun. Was actually glad to see old Sol after the past three days — even tho my rash broke out again.

The morning was slow, had to proceed with caution due to mines but after we got them swept up we started in with our bombardment. We came thru swell but others didn't — have been in sick bay all evening with casualties that were brought in — have one more to do and we are thru for the night. Am waiting for them to clean up the mess so thought I'd check in with you. This kid has a hole in his belly and the lead is lodged in his pelvis next to his spine — have to cut down on it and remove it — he's kind of in bad shape.

Lot of plane contacts tonight but so far none have come within reach of our guns. Expect they'll wait until early morning or at least until we are supposed to be asleep and then try to slip in on us. A "beautiful" dark night — maybe they can't spot us.

We were the first ship in and fired the first salvo. Rugged terrain and our work is cut out for us — quiet today but doesn't mean a thing. They are out here in great quantities and are just biding their time — no doubt will have a different story to tell if I get a chance to write tomorrow.

Time to go below and help out so will say good night for now. Love you honey and don't worry about me — I'm okay.

All my love
Paul

THE MORNING OF October 20, a huge amphibious force put the U.S. 6th Army ashore on Leyte. Compared to many other landings, opposition was light, although much ground fighting lay ahead and the great sea battle would not begin for four days.

20 Oct. 1944

Good Morning Honey —

A little early for my girl but this is war so I'll just go ahead and babble on. Was too tired last night to write, we had had somewhat of a rugged day, nothing serious or spectacular, just routine but it seemed to wear on us more than usual.

Everyone is pooped, altho this morning every one reports feeling rested — they all had from 6-8 hours sleep for a change. It's so infernally hot here, no breeze or a damn thing to help cool it off — just close and sticky. A couple of weeks in a liberty port would do wonders for all hands — after all, we have been living in a huddle for a right smart spell.

Had a full day and part of the night yesterday — bombardment, air raids, P-T boats, bombardments again — mines, etc. — a noisy and stinky day. The air is so close the powder smoke hangs over you so you can actually taste it — my room is a shambles again. "I was so discouraged" with my house work — I had everything fixed up so nice, and I thought securely — everything is on the deck again now. Fiber glass a foot deep — all my doors and drawers popped open — magazines, books, letters etc., scattered all over the place — "I could just cry."

We are at it again now so I don't know how I'll come out with this letter.

Think I'll just hit the high spots — had a burial last night — just finished in time for an air raid and P-T boat assault — no runs, no hits, no errors. Our lunch was interrupted — couple dozen came over — no damage, but fun. Lou's luck was again demonstrated in the afternoon — a lone Jap plane came in — made a run on us but as he pulled out of his dive, his wings came off — bombs went one way — wings — engine, etc., in various other directions — had possibilities — he fell fifty yards from us — whew!

Sweet girl — we're pouring it on thick & heavy so will have to close — will write later — should be a bang up day — hope it's "Lucky Lou" again — wish you could be aboard right now — pretty stylish but hard to write decently.

All my love to you honey — al long as I'm here — Jeepers! Good bye — Just came back from topside — the air has black measles — we're in for it — two bombs with our name on it missed us by feet — remember honey — I love you.

Paul

20 Oct. 1944

Hello My Darling —

A memorable day has passed and with its attendant thrills — quite a day and I'm a firm believer in names — "Lucky Lou" — I'll always swear by her.

Had to cut my note short this a.m. due to intense firing — both bombardment and being under attack — when the big guns go off we really squat in the water — throw in the others, we squat, twist and squirm. I missed seeing the plane come in but got topside in time to see her disappear over the mountain and could see where bombs hit the water. It jarred hell out of us but no damage — not allowed to give you the complete picture but he was so low that after we missed him we couldn't afford to shoot him down or he'd have crashed square dab on the quarter deck and we'd have suffered severe damage if not entirely wiped out. Guess it must really have been a show and to think I missed it — here I've been observing, but good, for nine months and then get duty struck all of a sudden — if I'd have followed my usual procedure, I'd have been there with bells on. I thought it was a good time to get off a note to you for fear I might not have time later on — result, one poor letter and no show.

The morning dragged — it was ages long — our guns were busy all the time but was so different than other times. The Marines & Army work differently — Army has to have breakfast and the 3 "S"s before they get in gear — the Marines say what the hell, Nell, let's go. Harry's boys did a good job though, "considering" everything — an ideal spot for them.

We had another air attack about 1600. During or rather just before the torpedo plane attack, a rain squall came up — sky overcast and a regular downpour — visibility zero — made for tense minutes. The weather cleared, had a good dinner and went to the foc'sle for a breath of fresh air. A beautiful night; gorgeous sunset behind the mountains and the water calm. As the evening progressed, clouds came up and a terrific display of real lightning took place — have never seen anything like it — thought we had nice lightning at home but this put it to shame. It was right scary — what with a steel ship under you and all the guns and superstructure to attract it. Decided there wasn't a damn thing I could do about it and no place to go so decided to stay "aboard" and watch the performance that was taking place. We were getting ready for whatever the Japs had up their sleeve — had seen this preparation a few times before but not on the scale or as clearly as tonight — was fantastic and really pretty. We were on the outside and one of the sailors wanted to know what we were trying to do, off like that "playing hard to get"? Sure enough, here they came, a whole flock of them hell bent for election — and we were at the polls! In short order the sky was filled with lead the most I have seen thrown at planes to date — your really can't describe it — the tracers are red and appear as dotted lines when a stream of them go out — can you imagine thousands of dotted lines at all angles in the sky? The sky was literally aglow with them — you couldn't see the origin of them due to the smoke screen but as they'd emerge from it they shoot thru a clear patch of sky, then be hidden in the clouds, then in the clear again — "in and out again Finnegan". They'd end with a burst — vivid flashes of lightning, clouds, shell bursts, gun flashes and smoke screen — a colorful and noisy evening, I'd say.

Foster and I watched it all from the foc'sle and agreed it was quite a show — neither one of us, or anyone else can figure out where all the shell fragments go — they must come down — it's a wonder a lot of damage isn't done by it.

We stayed out about a half hour after the firing ceased and watched the lightning. We finally got into the screen and how the hell they keep from running into another ship is beyond me — it's the damndest feeling you ever had — worse than an air raid when it's so dark you can't see the plane until it's right on you — luck of Lou, says I.

Love you
Paul

21 Oct. 1944

My Darling —

What a pleasant surprise and a fitting climax to a more or less interesting day — had a marvelous letter from my one and only — gee honey — it's a great war.

I'm bad again — unclean — have fiber glass rubbed in along with the others and I'm really having a miserable time of it — hope I get squared away before I hit the states — I sure hain't purty right now.

What would you "love to put" in the local paper? I write you things that actually happen or as I see them — have guarded against saying anything I couldn't back up so I won't have to retract anything or be made a liar of. If it's something that doesn't mention the ship, operation, locality or time — I don't see any harm in it, if it's of any interest to the folks.

Sorry to learn Kingfisher has had so many casualties — don't know the conditions in Europe but do know what the boys are up against out "here" — it isn't spectacular and we're not fighting human beings — it's merely cruel, heartless extermination — "quarter is neither asked nor given". If the dads & mothers could only see their boys in action, they couldn't help but be rightfully proud — they are absolutely the best in the world and it's a shame they all can't come back. Think I have told you how I have watched them by the hours — as they steam by on their way in — as they land — their tactics in the field — actual contact with the enemy — wounded being brought board — some dying as you hold them — honey, even as they go out they never whimper — the Padre is with them and it's all over.

Seem to be wound up tonight and it's way past my bed time but I wanted to talk to you on account I love you. The Nip planes are more bothersome out here — nearer their goalline. Several gold stars today but mostly Australian — am not counting Nipponese, can't be bothered. Am still fascinated by the sight of planes exploding — as long as they are not ours — mighty pretty. With all these mountains they can slip in undetected until they are right amongst us — then wham! You never know when or from what direction — they seem to have had us singled out on several occasions but our Luck held and waiting for the next run. Can't get over the one whose wings came off as he pulled out of his dive — we'd have been goners sure.

Heard MacArthur broadcast today "I have returned" etc., etc.

Look out — the address system is squawking — here we go sure enough —

Bye
Paul

MACARTHUR'S SPEECH was actually made October 20, shortly after he arrived on Leyte. His emotional words to the Filipinos — "I have returned . . . Rally to me!" — were not particularly well received by his audience in the 7th Fleet because MacArthur failed to mention the Navy's considerable effort that made it possible for him to wade ashore into the face of friendly cameras.

22 October 1944

Honey Girl —

Another day is about over and a new week starting — wonder what it will bring forth. The past week has been a honey, what with typhoons, "history making" and dodging bombs and torpedoes — a few mines thrown in for good measure. The little yellow bellies are a nuscience (? — that stops me — you know what I mean — pests). They come over at all hours and drop a few bombs or torpedoes — we just got out of g.q. a few minutes ago, probably will be back in before I finish this letter. There are three less Jap planes as a result of their sortie tonight — have forgotten what the score was during the day — the days are all alike and the activities too, so they just don't register any more. Have been trying to figure out a way to describe what antiaircraft fire looks like when they all let go, maybe if you recall the chimneys (or ies) we have seen shoot out a shower of sparks — literally boil out and in all directions — that will give you an idea what it looks like when "several" are in the air and coming in all directions.

Remember that railroad alarm at the crossings in Kingfisher? That is the way our g.q. sounds "ding-ding-ding-ding" — next time you cross the tracks pay special attention and sing the bugle call and you have a general alarm as it sounds in the best of circles. Not especially loud but the steadiness of its ringing brings you out of a sound sleep in a hurry.

The plane we got tonight was a fancy one — apparently he tried to drop a flare in the "center of activities" but it fouled up on his plane and remained there so here he came, dragging a bright light through as concentrated barrage of a.a. fire as I've ever seen — believe it or not, he went thru miles and miles of fire unscathed — finally came in range of certain of our guns and "Lou" let him have it, brought him down just as he was about to disappear in the safety of the mountains — it was fascinating to watch his progress thru that hail of lead — reminded me of a broken field runner, nothing between him and the goalline but the safety man and he brought him down — a direct hit, terrific explosion and then a mass of flames on the beach. Usually all you can see is a shadow off and on, but this one carried a beacon and you could follow him all the way. Fun, but if he'd have been a white man, I'd like to have seen him get away — he earned it. Must go to bed and get ready for "ding-ding".

All my love
Paul

24 Oct. 1944

Good "Mid-Morning" Honey —

Missing writing yesterday because it was just a routine day, not much excitement although we had our usual air raids and a few planes shot down.

The water was beautiful — scarcely a ripple in it. We had a short trip to make and once more it was like a pleasure cruise — the water is simply gorgeous as we plow thru the swells and the wake we leave looks like so much jello.

Thought I'd better get in my two bits worth while I had time — we have had two g.q.s already this morning and looks like a busy day. So far has been a gala day — the busiest yet and most promising. "Company" is coming in — they're on their way and maybe at last I'll be in a surface engagement. Dozens & dozens of planes have been over — a lot of them have been shot down — the air is clear right now so we are having a breather. It's really a thrill to see a swarm of them — the red circle isn't near as pretty as the Star & Bars but they burn better. You watch them with mixed feelings & when you actually see the bombs released & follow their path downward — after they miss you, you find you have held your breath — some fun.

Love you
Paul

PAUL DID INDEED have "company" coming, because the Japanese had decided on a major effort to destroy the Americans' Leyte invasion force.

Japanese Vice Admiral Nishimura planned to enter Leyte Gulf from the south through Surigao Strait. Waiting for him in the predawn hours of Wednesday, October 25, would be Lieutenant Commander Paul C. Bonnette, an Oklahoma City dentist, with a vastly superior force of eight cruisers, six battleships, 28 destroyers, and 39 PT boats.

Admiral Nishimura's ships steamed through the 15-mile-wide strait in single file, while aboard his flagship, the USS *Louisville,* Admiral Oldendorf prepared a battle line of cruisers and battleships to cross the Japanese "T."

Oldendorf's big guns did not get first crack at Nishimura. PT boats and destroyers, darting and slashing in the darkness, used torpedoes and shells to extract a terrible toll on the enemy's single column. They also advised Oldendorf of Nishimura's location, course, and speed.

Despite his losses, Nishimura drove ahead, while Oldendorf's classic battle line waited.

At approximately 24,000 yards, the enemy came within range of the *Louisville's* main battery, but Oldendorf waited for his ships to become perfectly positioned. The range closed to 20,000 yards, then 18,000 and, as tensions mounted, to a scant 16,000 yards.

At 3:51 a.m., the Japanese came within 15,600 yards of the *Louisville,* and Oldendorf gave the order to open fire. All nine of the *Louisville's* 8-inch guns belched flame into the darkness. Again and again, 37 times in all, *Lady Lou* lifted in the water and shuddered back to her port side as the main batteries launched tons of steel at the hapless Japanese.

It was all over in 19 minutes. At 4:10 a.m., firing ceased with the remnants of Nishimura's force staggering in retreat.

Accounts differ, but the ship's history states: "In this spectacular night engagement the Louisville fired the first shot from a heavy ship and more main battery rounds than the total of all the six battleships added together."

"What a ship!" Paul writes.

26 Oct. 1944

Darling,

Think I last wrote you the morning of the 24th and had just come from g.q. The way it turned out I just barely finished your letter when we went back in. All in all we were in seven times that day — fun each time, but the payoff was 0300 yesterday morning. Expect you know all about it and I can't say anything more.

Feel like a real veteran now — had a marvelous experience and feel like "mission completed" and am ready for home. It's so quiet now — guess it's the let down after all these months of anticipation — everyone is completely pooped and I mean pooped. The past nine days have been mighty rugged — we knew it would be and were all set — then the climax — anything from now can't be anything but "anti"-climax. It's been marvelous — the war isn't over by any means and the hardest part is yet to come but we are now in position.

Can't believe we actually have gone through all this — Lou is our honey and the bars she has won for us are proud ones — she's a "fighter gal" and I'm proud to be one of her "hands". Her luck has been phenomenal — hope it continues — what a ship!

Saw a dandy water spout yesterday during all the turmoil — peculiar outfits.

Can't seem to think of a thing to say — am still going around in circles — kind of slap happy or punch drunk.

Love you
Paul (veteran)

28 Oct. 1944

Darling —

Have you heard any newscasts or read an account of the action wherever MacArthur is? Night before last and last night I listened to them for several hours as they were being released — we were all so damn mad, disgusted and burned up we are still seething. Had the same trouble trying to write the first night of the broadcast — honey it was so maddening — the mis-representation of facts of the action — hell, guess I'll skip it before I get mad again. Tried so hard not to believe the stories on Dougout, but you can put me down definitely as an anti-MacArthur — the lousy S. of a B. — "I have returned," poop, you know what I mean — damned publicity hound.

Had to call time out for a while, had our burial this a.m. instead of the usual time, which is sunset — too hot to keep the body and also "too hot" in other ways. It's the real McCoy out there these days and I can no longer say I haven't been scared — my knees played Home Sweet Home last night — that's for sure! As Charley, my colored boy in his inimitable way said, "Doctaw. Ah was so-o-o-o scared I couldn't move." I think he spoke for all of us. We stood there fascinated and got off with only one killed and eleven wounded. Lady Lou is still riding her luck and is one obedient girl — if she hadn't answered her rudder on those two occasions when a flip of her hips and a twist of her shoulders meant the difference between success or failure of these suicide crash dives — honey, they are terrible. Can't give you the dope — we are in for a lot more of them thanks to the "Wizard" — "I have returned."

I'm getting mad again — the people at home believe all the crap he releases — the Army! S - - - -! I'm burned up with the war correspondents. Why in hell don't they go along with the action instead of sitting on their fat - - - - s and getting their dope from the big shots that weren't anywhere near the scene and claiming all the credit. They had guts enough to ask where in hell were the cruisers during that epic battle of "- - - -"? Honey I'm sorry — I'm going to have to get on another subject and calm down a bit. "The General" stepped from his launch, a sniper only fifteen hundred yards away shot at him! Gee, that's awful! Poop.

Yesterday between air raids Johnson decided to fish out my port — rigged his line very carefully and turned to for a little serious fishing. He was called away after a while so I drew a can of salmon from Grubb, the supply officer, and tied it on his line. You should have seen his face when later he started pulling in his line. He though sure he had a whopper — then when the can of "prepared fish" hove into sight, he was fit to be tied. Much fun — not very exciting but after all, it's the best we could do.

Wonder what tonight holds in store for us — bright moon light — intermittent rain — squalls and lots of beautiful clouds — an ideal set up for enemy planes. There's a large squadron of suicide pilots out here and the nights are just made for them. We thinned their ranks last night but there are many hundreds more so we can expect a busy time for some time. Apparently they are mad at the Navy and are making an all out effort to get us — we have a lot to be thankful for but we won't go into that. Our fingers are crossed — we'll make it — we really are veterans now in every sense of the [*word*] — I'll wear my bars and whatever stars we get with pride now — we have an "impressive record" and don't have to back down from anything or anyone — have lost track of our business deals but we have had a bumper crop.

All my love
Paul

30 Oct. 1944

Hello Honey —

Am in much better physical condition tonight — damn near became sea sick last night — it was after nine o'clock and no reason not to turn in so I hit my sack and was okay. We had a terrific storm but ran out of it in a few hours — the ship did the "cork-screw" and it's really wicked — wow! Even the old salts became ill so I don't feel too badly over it — I broke out in a profuse sweat and when I saw my green face in the mirror — I jumped into bed and turned out the lights. Almost fell out of my sack several times but managed to dig in and stay put — it's typhoon season here and I'm glad we are leaving it. It's really funny the gyrations you go thru — one minute you weigh a ton, next you are light as a feather and float — then you stand on your head — roll over and up straight again — it's worse than being on a binge. The storm completely wrecked one of our planes so you know it wasn't just an ordinary squall. We're still rolling quite a bit but it's more like riding in a cradle and very comfortable.

Very, very quiet today — a little breather but we're still vulnerable — seems funny, no. g.q. or air raids for almost 24 hours!

Have you run across our Admiral's name in the news? Understand he finally has been recognized — sure hope he gets credit for all he has done — he is too damned modest usually but think he finally stirred himself after those news releases that had everything screwed up.

Counted my wardroom cash last night and believe it or not — it came out to the cent! Maybe I should do my bookkeeping during a "tropical disturbance" each time. Everything was juggled so perhaps that is what happened to the books.

It's a beautiful night out — marvelous moon — Zinke and I took a "long walk" and chewed the fat ninety-to-nothing. Walking was a little difficult due to the rock & roll of the ship but it felt good, think I'll get in the habit of doing it each night. I'm feeling [*splendid*] — you should see my hips — I ain't got any. The Padre says I have a very "trim figger" now. Still have my little pod from my appendectomy and am going to start working on it in an endeavor to reduce it. If I have to swim in a couple or so weeks from now I don't want any excess baggage to hinder me for it will be a long ways home.

All my love
Paul

31 Oct. 1944

Hello Darling —

Two whole days and nights without an air raid — can't get used to the silence — the only sound you hear is the swish of the water and the blowers aboard ship. The blowers sound like someone's deep and powerful breathing — the only sound and it seems miraculous to me how they can quiet down the thousands of horsepower we have.

Had an awful time getting to sleep last night. Took a nap in the afternoon and then all that fresh air at night — was too much for me. Finally got up again at 2330, swiped a sandwich, smoked a ciggie, read a story and then went off to sleep. Tough life for sure.

We are getting a new skipper and ours doesn't like it one bit — he is mad as hell. Understand he may get the Navy Cross for the really marvelous way he handled the ship during the suicide attacks — he was the difference between near misses and direct hits — "goodness" it really was close.

Honey girl — I have to finish my books yet tonight so I can collect mess bills tomorrow.

Love you sweet girl
Paul

THE *LOUISVILLE* spent November 1-2 taking on provisions and ammunition at the Ulithi Atoll fleet base, some 900 miles east of Leyte. She then joined Task Group 38.3 to take part in November 5-6 air strikes against Manila and other points on the island of Luzon.

3 November 1944

Hello Honey —

First I want to tell you how sorry I am for the anxiety I caused over my hands. Thought I had made it clear it was purely impetigo. Am pretty well cleared up now — don't look bad and am comfortable — have my fingers crossed however. Will clear up the very elegant expression "Pissed-Out".

You read it wrong — it's "Pissed-Off" my dear, meaning irked, burned up or what have you — it was nothing serious, we're all squared away now and are happy again.

Every once in a while things get fouled up by someone's meddling around in some other department where they have no business — no body got hurt. In the Padre's case someone made all arrangements for Mass & Divine Services and didn't tell the Padre a thing about it — he had made his own arrangements and of course "he was out of line" — he being only the Padre, and may add, was interested to a certain extent. My pouting was along similar lines — had my appointments all filled and "some one" made a flock of appointments for fellows off another ship without my knowledge — no, they didn't keep the appointments.

Out here, we have decided suicide dive bombers are more dangerous than flying bombs, on account they are steered and know where they are going. They really are hell bent for election. The only way you can stop them is blow them up before they get to you but even at that their momentum is so great they keep right on coming and takes some tall, split second maneuvering to keep them from hitting you. The last ones that came for us were completely riddled with bullets but they didn't blow up — one of them "bounced his wheels" on the turret over my quarters but slithered over the side of the ship & then blew up — jarred hell out of things and it rained bomb fragments and bits of plane for a long time. The skipper turned just at that second when it meant either the plane crashed the deck or fell over the side — whew! Over the side won — goody!

Our encounter with the Jap fleet was fun and had its "apprehensive" moments — especially when the word was passed "Enemy ships closing in on the starboard — stand by for rapid fire of "- - - -"-inch guns!" At that particular moment I was laying out battle dressing, etc., but couldn't help but think — my station is on the water line level and only the skin of the ship between Mr. torpedo and me — I was on the starboard side too! Nothing happened, so when I had my station all set up — went topside to watch the battle. It was beautiful — pitch dark except for gun flashes and flames from exploding ships. Wouldn't have missed it for the world — may get to see some more but the first is always the most thrilling.

Our guns knocked me on my fanny three times but was too busy watching thru my glasses to get hurt — it's a funny feeling when you miss the words "Stand By — Fire!" & then pick yourself up off the deck, blinded from the flash and shook up by the concussion. Glad I'm a religious plugger-up-of-ears-with-cotton-sailor or I'd have troubs. Am going to try and get a picture of the night firing — it's really something.

Sure am wound up tonight — haven't told any military secrets & we had permission to mention the suicide bombers — the big sea battle is common knowledge too so as long as I don't say "which one" — can't see any harm in comment on it — jeebers, it was swell!

All my love
Oodles of it
Paul

4 November

Dear Honey —

Not much to allow today — very quiet day, about the only thing of interest was seeing a Jap mine explode — we skirted it and a destroyer blew it up. There are subs out here but we still are riding high.

Asked the chief engineer (Westcott) yesterday if he had any idea how far we had traveled since leaving the states. He said he had roughly figured it last month and a very conservative estimate was better than three times around the world — nearer 100,000 miles! Boy! Did I ever get sea duty — wow! A hundred thousand miles and nary a port — it's all been enemy waters — constant threat of planes & submarines — think we have earned a visit to a liberty port and some relaxation — don't you? I had no idea we had been that "busy". Wonder what the official [*mileage*] will be when I get off — hope I don't forget to look it up. No wonder Lady Lou has varicose veins and arteriosclerosis — she isn't a spring chicken any more but golly she's a honey. I have an affection for her I can't explain — something like the way a person loves dogs or other dumb animals — gee, I'm proud to be one of her boys.

Had g.q. tonight — head lines tomorrow! Not as a result of "as of now" but come sunup, my goodness. The way the kids are singing you'd think we were headed for the states instead of "lights out for some —" — can't get over what a gang of real folks they are — I'm speaking of the enlisted men, from the lowest one up thru the officers. If all ships have the morale we have — no one can whip us that's for sure.

All my love
Paul

SUDDENLY, the censors clamped down on references to Japanese suicide planes. Not only does Paul back off the subject, he instructs Dorothy in his November 6 letter, "don't mention it to anyone."

6 November 1944

Little Sweet-heart —

Yesterday had three g.q.s but very boring — all the planes were taken care of before they got to us — watched the a.a. fire on the horizon and that's all there "are" to it. The job we are on is very monotonous — it's important but we don't have any excitement, will be glad when we get back on our job again.

Have had rough seas ever since we've been out this time — have our extra life lines rigged and my room boy is getting housemaids knee from swabbing up my room. In one or two of my letters I talked about the "new method" Jap pilots are using — I was told it was all right to mention it. Since then it is taboo so don't mention it to anyone — I don't know which letters it was in.

All my love
Paul

7 Nov. 1944

Hello Darling —

It's still storming to beat hell out here — my poor little legs are so weary from bracing against the ship's movement. It's kind of rugged trying to do dentistry in these rough seas but put in fifteen fillings & three emergency extractions this morning.

Jeebers — you ought to hear the crash of the water against & over the ship — expect it to come on in any minute. Expect a 75 knot wind tonight so I think I'll put my sideboards up before I go to bed — may have to give up writing — old Lou is kicking up her heels. Was afraid I'd finish my sea duty without experiencing a real storm — my worries are over — wow!

My damn bulkhead is starting to bang so I'm afraid I'm in for a hard night — should take a sleeping tablet — but afraid I might sleep thru g.q. — that would be bad!

Wonder how the election will go — Dewey sure has made some asinine statements — all politicians are alike — they're a mess.

Radio Tokyo & Tokyo Rose sure are slinging a lot of bull — their newscasts are fantastic and get a bang out of listening to them. Wonder who they are trying to spoof. They sure sound good over the air — the U.S. sure is taking a beating.

It's just too rough to try & write — will play a few hands of gin rummy & call it quits. Have you learned to play the game? It's fun so better get in gear. Hope I have some letters waiting for me — can't wait on it so it better be there.

Should get submariners pay these days — we're submerged most of the time — one of the Captains just stuck his nose in — said it was a real typhoon — I didn't argue — I know it isn't just a whirl wind!

All my love
Paul

LADY LOU RETURNED to Ulithi on Thursday, November 9. She took on ammunition and 165,000 gallons of fuel oil and spent the rest of the week resting her crew and patching her typhoon damage.

10 November 1944

Hello Darling —

Don't feel pretty good today, was a bad boy last night — this torpedo juice ain't good for one the next day. Had fun tho — had dinner with Tom aboard his ship and spent the night — got home at 0600. A thirty minute ride in a bobbing whale boat and a hangover — bad combination.

Really had a swell time — Tom, his skipper and I, up in the skipper's quarters — 0200 we were scrambling eggs.

We had a god awful storm for two days — can't tell you much about it — wow! I don't like storms like that and racing against time right into it — no sleep for two days and nights — I'm not kidding when I say it was terrible — lot of sickness but my record is still intact — guess my early training on chili and cokes gave me a cast iron gut. Lou never will be the same again but she made it — poor girl, this last time out aged her.

Paul

15 Nov. 1944

Little Darling —

It's so ungodly hot here — worst we have been in and my poor rash is giving me double hell. Was all cleared for a few days and then bang! Unclean again. I'm so tired of itching, and being raw — it's hard to sleep — hard to stay awake — all in all I'm not very happy.

Have the duty today so will go tomorrow and wind things up. They call the club Crawley's Tavern — I think Crawley of Notre Dame fame manages it. It's quite picturesque — native, etc., but not as fancy as some of the others. Lot of native huts around and are different from those I have seen before. They are more substantially built. I guess to stand up under the terrific storms they have [*to be*]. They evacuated all the natives to another island and haven't seen any as of now. Was supposed to fly this afternoon but found I had the duty so naturally couldn't go. We'd planned on setting down by the native village and getting a first class tour. Trink met the Princess the other day and said she really was attractive — even more so than Lola.

The return trip on our two nights was a lot of fun — was just at sunset — water calm & a beautiful sky. We poked along in the skimmer, everybody singing and happy. We have Sleep Hall aboard ship — he conducted a big time band for seventeen years before being called into the service. His theme song is Sleepytime Gal — I know I've heard him on the air. Anyhow, he was in the boat both times & led the singing — was fun.

Promise to get on the beam with my letters stat — the storms thru em off — itch, etc. But internally I'm hale and hearty — just ugly as sin & "itchy-bitchy".

All my love
Paul (The "Unclean" One)

THE *LOUISVILLE* left Ulithi on November 17 bound for a high-level conference at Hollandia.

17 Nov. 1944

Hello Honey —

Esch has had his orders changed. He was promoted to Lt. Comdr & named gun boss of the Louisville — Comdr. Bowers, former gun boss, was ordered to Washington & has already gone. The Padre received orders and is awaiting his relief. He goes back to the states for a little state-side duty. He has been at sea over two and a half years so I don't blame him for being happy altho I hate to see him leave. The saddest blow of all — poor old Long Tom Murphy also has orders for Dec. 1st. He is about my favorite — plain nuts and a pest but fun — really hate to see him leave.

Before long no one of the old gang will be left — myself included. Everyone is pooped out and burned up with heat — no rest in sight so we all hope we'll get a premature yard period — could be. We need so many things done — maybe the powers that be will shoot us along. It's a damned cinch something ought to be done about getting some liberty & recreation for the crew. The officers are having a bad time getting a little relaxation but the poor crew they really have the slippery end of the stick. They're such a swell lot and have never let us down — it's a shame to wear them out completely.

The captain just stuck his nose in and inquired about my heat — the fellows are beginning to prowl so I'd better look to finishing this letter. It won't get off for a few days so I'll have a chance to write several & try to get caught up.

All my love
Paul

18 Nov. 1944

Hello My Sweet —

Another day and another dollar — so goes it out here somewhere. An uneventful day other than working on one of the "hi-powered" captains. Had fun and he was pleased with my work and said, "You have a very gentle touch, if I may say so" — tee, hee — I said sure, go ahead. I'm big-hearted that way.

We didn't have an initiation this time but never the less I sleep with my shell-back card handy — just in case.

In one of your letters you asked if it wouldn't be all right to mention the places we had been after it was all over with — the answer is NO because it would indicate in a small way part of the strength etc. You'll just have to hold your curiosity until I get home and maybe then I can tell you if I haven't forgotten. It's sure awful to try and remember dates and actions — time or distance doesn't mean a thing and I find I'm mixed up already. During the actual happenings I'd bet any amount I'd never forget each little detail — I'd have lost.

You mean to say you don't know "Dougout Doug"? General Douglas MacArthur — "I have returned" MacArthur — shame on you honey. He and his 7th Fleet are the only ones fighting this war! His fleet did a good job on Surigao Straits — will have to hand him that much.

Don't know much about carriers — you were on a CV [*fleet carrier*] in San Diego — they are huge, a CVE [*fleet carrier, escort*] is an escort carrier and are used mostly for escort duty and ferrying planes. They furnish plane protection for amphibious fleets etc. A CVL [*fleet carrier, light*] is a light carrier & is used for various duties such as carrier task forces, escort duty etc. The CVE's are the smallest and slowest of the group but very essential. Don't see any military secrets in that information so will pass it on to you.

Have a beautiful morning of extractions for tomorrow so I think I'll turn in so I can do a good job — Zinke wants to watch and learn how to inject so must be on my toes.

Paul

THE *LOUISVILLE* ARRIVED in Humboldt Bay (Hollandia) the morning of November 19. Admiral Oldendorf disembarked for several days of meetings with General MacArthur. The *Louisville* left Hollandia on the

Dotty B and her new niece, Sandra Sue Stetler, in Oklahoma City, November 1944.

21st for a week at nearby Manus before returning for Oldendorf and his staff.

20 Nov. 1944

Little Darling —

What fun I had yesterday — was as nice a day as I've had in a long time. Remember when I talked to you Saturday, I said I was going to get a good night's sleep because Zinke was going to watch me extract — everything went off slick, had ten patients and popped them bang, bang, bang. Zinke was quite impressed with the system I have set up and the ease with which I took care of them. The patients put on a good act and bragged for me so all in all I had fun. Was thru at 0930 so I strolled out on the well deck to cool off — my clothes were sopping wet. We were just steaming into the Bay, the exec was standing there watching the scenery and wanted to know where in hell I'd been to get so wet. Told him I'd been having fun with my Sunday morning extraction clinic. He pointed out a bush on the beach and said he thought there was some beer stashed away behind it and if all went well, we'd investigate in the afternoon.

Got cooled off, drank a cup of coffee, then Church Call was sounded — hadn't planned on going but a simple, and I believe sincere, remark one of the fellows made kind of put me in the mood so I went. Glad I did, for it was the Padre's last service for Protestants — he's due to leave any time and when we are in port we exchange chaplains. He gave a nice talk — reviewed his year aboard the Louisville — he felt kind of bad about leaving but 2 1/2 years is quite a spell to be afloat. Oh yes! The remark Waite made that caused me to go to the services — "Well, Doc, I've prayed so much the past few months since I've been aboard the Lou and everything turned out all right — just kind of hate to let him down now." Honey — we have been so awfully, awfully lucky I do believe he is looking out for us.

After services we had a good lunch of assorted cold cuts, baked beans, potato salad etc — hit the spot. Then at 1400 we boarded a launch and set out for the beach. It was awfully hot but we hiked a couple of miles, up and down mountains over a new road — you could hear the monkeys and birds chattering away in the jungle. Really got a kick out of it — when we were here before we were only in a few hours and it was raining so we didn't get a chance to go ashore.

The Club opened at 1600 — we were there with bells on and a good thirst from hiking. The Club is nice — a bar for Comdrs & above, one for Lt. Comdrs. & ladies with escorts and one for junior officers. A whole flock of Red Cross workers were there — they sure look tuff and from all reports, they are that. The beer was nice & cold & had glasses to drink out of which was a treat. Ran out of beer so they served brandy & gin. Met some nice fellows from other ships. We missed the 1730 boat so decided to stay and close the club up — we got back to the ship about 1930 after a big day — I topped it off by falling in, but had fun.

It's pretty here — like the bay, it's very picturesque. The dutch are very "co-operative" — they will not accept American money — the medium of exchange is their own — the B - - - - - - s!

Had the medical watch today so I stayed aboard and knocked out a lot of work so tonight I'm tuckered out. Saw a lousy show this evening — "Here Comes Elmer" starring Al Pearce — wish I'd skipped it and started talking to you sooner.

Nothing scheduled for tomorrow other than work as we'll be underway — like the hustle & bustle of getting underway — fun.

All my love
Paul

21 Nov. 1944

Hello Honey —

We just came from a practice g.q. so I took a swell shower and shampooed my hair — now I feel like a million dollars. Johnson and I were just talking about how different the guns sound in practice and the real McCoy. Seems ages since we were last "bombed at" but I guess just a little over a week — just can't keep track of time or events — they just happen and we're here, so what?

Saw an unusual sight this afternoon — Zinke and I were on the foc'sle watching them get ready to get underway. We had been watching a huge school of barracudas or gars playing around — all of a sudden a huge splash and a fish about four feet long leaped out of the water — you know how high we stand out of the water at the bow — this fish was about fifteen yards out and leaped straight up to the level of the bow, then jack knifed & dived straight down. It was beautiful. It seemed suspended in the air at the top of his leap, then gracefully turned and down he went. If we'd have had a "still" picture of him you'd have sworn it was a fish suspended by a wire and super-imposed on another picture of back ground. Something sure must have scared hell out of him to cause him to go that high.

Hate to leave this place — it's so pretty, green mountains and lowhanging clouds — about as pretty a place as I've seen — that is from the bay. Not too healthy on the beach, every one is yellow from [*atabrine*].

Must not have gotten all the soap off for I sure am itchy-bitchy right now — have felt good lately so it's about time I break out again.

Must be getting near chow time — they have come in and closed my port so it must be "rig for darken ship". Sure lead a tough life — "colored valet" and everything.

Must get on some clothes. Have my foundation garment on but must add to it before I'll be presentable to the wardroom.

Honey girl — I love you more all the time — keep the home fires burning for the time is slipping by.

All my love, sweet
Paul (Clean-kid)

PAUL ARRIVED in Seeadler Harbor, Manus, on November 22. We know he visited several neighboring islands, because on the 23rd he talks about walking up hill, on the 24th he visits "Lonesome Isle" which is "perfectly flat" and on the 28th "visited a new island."

23 Nov. 1944

Hello Darling —

We're all standing around with our tongues out — there is a chance we may get a crack at a few beers yet this afternoon. This shortage of boats is serious for thirsty souls — it's too late now but it would have been nice if I'd have ordered one for Xmas.

The boat has gone after mail and should be back any minute. Sure hope it brings many letters from my honey.

The Padre's relief came aboard just a while ago — he was so excited he couldn't remember names when he tried to introduce us. The new one speaks with an accent — don't know whether his name is Strauss or Stradberg. He doesn't wear a rabbi's insignia so I guess he is German. Seems like a nice fellow — first sea duty but he'll have about a month to get used to the ship before boom-boom.

Looks kind of interesting out — we are shifting berths so must go "supervise it" and see that we drop anchor near the beach.

For now, bye-bye — will drink a cold beer to you if I get near one.

All my love
Paul (Thirsty keed)

P.S. — Just returned from the beach — lousy, no beer — a few bourbons and back home. Have written you about this island before — to me it's "Lonesome Isle" — the sunsets, the water at dusk are beautiful, but honey no fun — you and I could have fun here — could easily change the name to Paradise Isle. Honey — if you only knew how I miss you in a spot like this — but no — miles and miles between — more love.

Paul (lonesome wan)

24 Nov. 1944

Darling —

Had quite a day yesterday — spent the entire day on the beach and wore myself down to a nubbin. Left the ship at 0800 on the utility boat and putputted an hour and twenty minutes until we finally docked. Had to arrange for six sets of dentures so I contacted the Fleet Dental Clinic first and made all arrangements for the work. Zinke was with me and we had signed out for the day so we went out to the Base Hosp. Walked all the way, it was several miles and all up hill — hot! Wow, but a heavy down pour came along and cooled things off a good deal. Had Thanksgiving chow with some of the hosp. and then made some ward rounds — some pitiful cases and everything looks a lot worse due to everyone being so yellow from atabrine. Left the Hosp. about 1400 for the Fleet Club and a quantity of beer — did it ever taste good! Met a group of men I knew — they were heading for the states so had to join in the party. Had a lot of fun — everybody was telling wild tales to the men that were taking over — all in all, a good time was had by all. The boat was supposed to pick us up at 1730 but didn't show up until 1915 — missed our Thanksgiving feed on the ship but made out all right.

Broke my glasses a month or so ago and have been wearing my old ones which drive me nuts. Took them in yesterday to be fixed so they suggested they make me a new pair. Will get them tomorrow — good old g.i. glasses, round lenses but I hope plastic frames — this hot weather and salt spray won't effect them like the metal frames. Have to keep wiping the lenses and as a result the metal breaks, partly due to corrosion and partly to the bend.

All my love
Paul

26 Nov. 1944

My Darling —

Went to the beach Saturday on business and then a little beer, had fun but had a hell of a time getting back to the ship. Seems every time I plan a nice "party" for Cutts, the boat schedule gets screwed up and everything gets messed up. Had planned on the 1730 boat but it never did show up — finally got back to the ship at 2200. No dinner, movies or a damn thing — got over that all right but last night the exec jumped me about calling for a boat and a lot of blah about they couldn't be sending boats out at all hours for officers that missed the regular run. He said he had received a copy of the message and "left word" for me to see him whenever I got in — no one gave me the word so the first I had heard of it was when he just mentioned it. Told him I was ready to see him then and get squared away — the result was — the message was all garbled, worded wrong etc., and I got credit for it. There were nine of us stranded, both enlisted men and officers. The enlisted men had been waiting since 1600 on the dock — at 2030 still no boat and none available in the boat pool so I got busy — we got home. To top it off, Zinke got stranded last night under the same circumstances and went to the exec and raised hell so I think everything is squared away now. He didn't even know the boat mixup until I explained what happened to us and then when Zinke came in mad as hell — they're having a conference now to straighten it out — great life and one of the reasons I'd rather be at sea than in one of these places.

Got my glasses — they're beauties, perfectly rounded lenses — gold frames, the temple attaches just below the center of the lenses. Will save them for the museum — they are funny looking but excellent lenses and an ideal working sea-going pair of glasses.

Went over to Lonesome Isle yesterday afternoon, had an awfully nice time — drank nothing but beer and it was nice and cold. The whole gang of us sat on the beach and watched the rollers come in and the sun set — it was perfectly gorgeous — one of the prettiest I've seen. It is consistently beautiful — that's why I call it Lonesome Isle. It's so pretty makes me long for you so much.

The island itself isn't much — perfectly flat but has a coconut tree grove on it — lots of green bushes and looks almost landscaped. There is a wide channel between it and the next island — that is where the breakers come in — I know you'd enjoy it here — sure would like to buy it for our own.

The censors have allowed we could tell you about the action at Leyte Bay and the Battle of Surigao Strait — from that you know we were in the Philippines — the Lou fired the first salvo when we reoccupied the Philippines & also fired & sunk the first ship in the surface action in the Straits. Oldendorf was the tactical commander of the fleet and deserves all credit for the success of the action. The "other" big shot was miles away but sticks his nose in as the boss — poop!

Love you little girl
Paul

28 Nov. 1944

Hello Honey —

I'm so busy of a kid these days — the nights just aren't long enough. Yesterday afternoon the wardroom had a picnic on Lonesome Isle — the other half goes this p.m. I'm going for a few minutes this afternoon.

Murph shoves [*out*] in the morning and he wants to "buy a going away" drink. Sure will miss the monkey — he said when he reaches the states he would send you a wire — when the Western Union boy shows up, don't get alarmed — it won't be an "I regret to inform you."

Visited a new island this morning and met some good eggs — have been invited back to go into the bush with them to see the natives. Hope to go Thursday all day — should be fun.

Saw a cute show this evening — Eddie Cantor in "Show Business" — I thought he was good and particularly enjoyed Joan Davis.

My poor legs are tired and stiff — sure have walked a lot this past week — may not get splints after all. Have a pretty good crop of heat bumps — nasty things, but am fairly comfortable. It's just hotter than the hubs of hell here — no breeze, just good old hot sun, must be some "water" around for it seems to be a bit humid.

Love you little lady and miss you so damn much — if our luck holds out will be seeing you one of these days.

All my love
Paul

ALMOST ALL OF PAUL'S letters were written in ink, front and back, on either "U.S. Navy" or *"Louisville"* letterhead paper. The past few letters have been on flimsy paper that won't accept ink on both sides.

29 Nov. 1944

Hello My Darling —

This sure is terrible writing paper but we ran out on the ship so I have to use it. We'll have some in any day, so maybe you can put up with it for a while.

Saw a cute show this evening — "Music in Manhattan". We are getting some swell pictures lately and everyone enjoys them a lot. We're all getting restless again but will have to restrain ourselves a couple of weeks yet but you never know.

Must get my books in shape on account of Friday I have to collect mess bills again. They turned out swell last month — think after the first of the year I'll resign and break someone else in because my "theoritical" time is getting short and I don't want to be all fouled up at the last. I've enjoyed it in spite of the headaches and learned something about keeping accounts.

I'm itchy-bitchy again — am going nuts, have a day or two of comparative freedom from the lesions and then they let go again — the nasty stuff.

All my love sweet girl
Paul

1 Dec. 1944

Dear Honey

Had an awfully nice time yesterday evening. A small party of us went over to the club — it's a good thing we did for it's the last beer for an indefinite period. It rained like hell so the club wasn't crowded. Esch, Fisher and I had a table all to ourselves and had fun slinging bull and drinking beer. It's about the first time we have had a chance to drink like gentlemen. Usually you have to stand in line and then when you get to the bar — no beer.

Three of the fellows had dates — Army nurses & were good scouts even if they looked like hell. They lead a rugged life and it shows on them — couldn't see a thing about them to get excited over. I like my little girl and am marking time till I see her again.

All my love sweet girl
Paul

THE *LOUISVILLE* LEFT Manus on December 1 for the 24-hour trip back to Humboldt Bay, Hollandia, New Guinea, where she stayed until late evening, December 7.

2 Dec. 1944

Darling

There isn't much to write about these days but thought I'd better make hay while the sun shines. Speaking of sun-shine, we're still getting plenty of it but it seems fairly cool — there's a nice breeze blowing so when you go topside you do have a chance to cool off. It's still my favorite spot for some reason or other. There isn't a thing to do but it's sort of cozy and the scenery is pretty.

We're anchored less than a hundred yards from a huge hill — lot of big rocks, lots of trees and under-brush — tonight the moon is out in all its glory, peeking from around the mountain & casting its beam on the water — mighty pretty honey girl, and sure wish you were here.

Mail hasn't caught up with us yet and to top it off a cargo of air mail had to be tossed overboard due to foul weather — sure hope none of your letters were on it. It beats hell how we get fouled up — the mail is sent to us "here" and before we get to "here" it is sent back "there" — from "there" it is sent "elsewhere" etc. — that is about the only bad thing about cruiser duty, especially Lou — she never sets still very long in a place. I still like her though.

I love you
Paul

6 Dec. 1944

Darling

So "hep" me — I'm going to get a letter written today if I have to call in my congressman. Have started a letter a day the past four days but something always came up and had to stop. Think my last letter was on Saturday — what did I do the past few days — had the duty Sunday, Monday afternoon went to the beach to drink beer but had to settle for bourbon, yesterday I left the ship at 1300, went to the beach in quest of shirts and trousers — turned out to be one of the nicest afternoons I've had for ages. There were three of us and started out with a bang — there was a heavy sea, we went along side a destroyer to deliver a passenger — the swells were huge and as we came alongside the ladder was dropped to the bottom of the trough and as we came up, the side of the whale boat caught underneath the ladder and tipped us up so that we were thrown flat against the side of the ship. We shipped a lot of water and to top it off we were carried under the water scupper or spout and gallons of water poured in on us. The boat didn't capsize but we were wet as drowned rats — we continued to the beach however & went on about our business.

The town itself was interesting, reminded me of a boom town — huts thrown together — mud up to your knees — natives standing around & sea bees & soldiers selling souvenirs. The kids had monkeys & parrots but I didn't get you one each of either. The souvenirs weren't anything — obscene pictures, Jap condoms, shells etc., so I didn't buy anything. We browsed there a while & then started looking for the Army quarter-masters Hdqs. — found they were located away back in the mountains — ten or twenty miles away. We hitchhiked out there and the trip was beautiful but I was scared stiff. Out there they drive on the left hand side of the highway and you know how they herd these jeeps — well, they haven't improved their driving technique — it's worse if anything and on these hairpin turns, dust so you couldn't see your hand in front of your face and then dodging in and out of traffic. Traffic was awfully heavy — jeeps, trucks, gun carriages etc. — sheer drops of hundreds of feet — soft shoulders and left side driving. I longed for the safety of the ocean with all its typhoons and what have you.

The rain doesn't make sense out here — rained like hell in one spot so there is mud up to your knees and a little ways farther, dust up to your knees. The country was awfully pretty — lush green — thick jungles etc and a U.S. highway cut thru it. We reached the top of one peak and could look down on the Bay — a marvelous view of all the shipping. The native men have the right idea — they make the gals do all the work — saw dozens of them coming down the trails in the bush, loaded down with huge bunches of some kind of green leaves & herbs. The kids had malaria control tanks strapped to their back and were spraying the pools of water with oil. Quite a native village set back in the bush but looked deserted so we didn't go back in there.

We got our two shirts & pants and then started the long way back — as usual got lost a couple of times but it was fun and I'd never been before so I didn't mind. Decided to go to the club for a beer to cut the dust but all they had was bourbon. I looked like hell — when I started out I was wet from the dunking and then thru miles & miles of dust — you can imagine what I looked like — wasn't pretty.

Honey — I cheated a little bit today — your xmas boxes arrived — no letters but one box with perfectly chosen pecans — it came thru swell, just one side popped open. The other box, poor thing — I had to go to the post office & identify the remains. The only way they knew I was involved was when they ran across a card with your name on it. There was a big pile of broken & messed up goods — they had two similar boxes, one had your name in it so I took both of them — one had "Rally's" chain in it; the other a pair of mustache scissors. There were six pairs of socks, three hankies and two books — and a pair of rope slip-in shoes. I knew I had socks & a chain coming — there were no claimants for the other things so I took them for good measure. Thanks so much honey for the gifties — it's stuff I needed and you are the thoughtful one — I'm having a fine xmas. I'm glad they made it this far — there wasn't any box or wrapping left for identification purposes so I'm just lucky. Now if I only would get some letters from you I'd be very, very happy.

I have the medical watch today & must go to sick bay in a minute — will talk to you later — until then, love you good and much.

All my love
Paul

LATE DECEMBER 7, the *Louisville* sailed back toward Manus. Shortly after 9 p.m., the #1 stack's canvas cover caught fire. It was a minor event, and the flames were extinguished in less than ten minutes, but the damage control party gained experience which would soon prove invaluable.

Arriving at Manus shortly before noon on December 8, the *Louisville* was moored next to the battleship USS *California* for a scant six hours, just long enough for Admiral Oldendorf to move to the *California* as Commander Battleship Division Two. He was replaced on the *Lady Lou* as Commander Cruiser Division Four by Rear Admiral Theodore E. Chandler.

After the ceremony the *Louisville* was underway, passing through Seeadler Harbor's anti-submarine net at 5:04 p.m. on her way to Leyte Gulf.

8 Dec. 1944

Hello Darling —

Lou is living up to her "cognomen" in a great big way — sure hope she doesn't let us down this time — think I'll finally break out my life belt and see if it fits — haven't tried it on yet — one never knows these days — getting pretty rugged.

There is so much commotion aboard ship — we changed admirals and housing & eating problems confront us now. I'll get into that later. Will tend to "our" business first so if don't get a decent letter off, you will have the info you need.

Am having a hell of a time with the sea — it keeps coming in my port but it's too hot to close it so I'll keep on taking my salt water baths. Quite a storm going on, hasn't reached typhoon proportions yet but it's plenty rough and we are getting closer all the time.

As stated earlier in my letter — we changed admirals.

In spite of what the various skippers gave out as to who won the Battle of Surigao Strait you can draw your own conclusions when you hear that Rear Admiral Oldendorf is now Vice Admiral and placed in command of "- - - -" but not better than "- - - -". The clipping you sent caused quite a furor — the one about how the battleships won the fight — casually mentioned "with the aid of smaller vessels" — poop! Again I say — who got the promotion? The funny part is Oldendorf will be with & superior to the officer that released it! Fun — I betcha. When he left the ship we had the usual "change of command" ceremony — just before he had his flag pulled down he said quote — "I hate to leave the U.S.S. Louisville — I wish to thank all the officers and the crew for the marvelous support they gave me during these past hard and dangerous months. The Louisville is a lucky ship — a good ship and a shooting ship — always remember, a hit by an "- - - -" shell is far better than a miss by "- - - -" shells." It was a nice little speech and everyone felt good over it — he goes from a "- - - -" shell to the "- - - -" shell ship — tee hee.

All my love
Paul (plain)

OLDENDORF'S QUOTE was: "A hit by an 8-inch shell [*those which are fired by heavy cruisers*] is far better than a miss by 16-inch shells [*those fired by battleships*]."

Chapter 5

It Was Awful

AFTER LEAVING the relative security of the Admiralty Islands, the *Louisville* spent most of December in the Philippines at a sweltering anchorage in San Pedro Bay, Leyte Gulf. She received a new captain, Captain R. L. Hicks; the calls to General Quarters seemed to be endless as Japanese planes droned overhead and lurked in the late afternoon clouds. There was an exciting, but fruitless, dash to Mindoro in search of a reported enemy surface force.

The New Year, 1945, found *Lady Lou* bustling in preparation for another major campaign, the invasion of Luzon. On January 2 she steamed out of Leyte Gulf to lead the massive invasion force northward, and on January 5, with flags snapping and guns blazing, the USS *Louisville* sailed into hell. No, not hell, wrote a war correspondent — "It is worse than hell."

10 Dec. 1944

Honey Girl —

G.Q. days are upon us again and looks like we are in for a siege of them — anything can happen any time. Finally have the damage control parties interested in rendering first aid and had to give a lecture & demonstration tonight. We're winning the war that's for sure, but if the smugs at home think it's a walkaway, all I can say is they better keep up production and shipyard workers & other war industries better stay on the job. It's an entirely different war than the European Theatre — we're not fighting human beings out here and they don't give up — they're out to take somebody with them when they go out — they don't give a damn for their lives, no sacrifice is too great for them.

We eat early chow these days — lunch at 1130 and dinner at 1630 — I like it because we can have our ports open so it's a lot cooler and we're all thru eating before the Japs are due to come over. We've missed so many meals and they finally got wise and moved the time up. I can observe a lot better on a full stomach.

The water was beautiful today and had a gorgeous sunset. The flying fish were out in force and they too seemed to be enjoying the nice weather. They are most interesting — wish we could watch them together.

Had planned on going to church this a.m. but it was one of those days nothing went off right. It was extraction day and I broke every tooth I took hold of — had one horizontal impaction and it's the only one I did a slick job on — seven minutes from the time of incision to finishing suturing.

I have a fellow sharing my room to the extent of storing his luggage & clothes and he and I sling a lot of bull which is hard on letter writing — he just came in so I'm saying good night honey.

All my love
Paul

12 Dec. 1944

Little Darling —

The fellow staying with me is quite a nice chap — is district attorney from someplace in Louisiana. They got to talking about fishing last night and we are invited to try our luck some time. They guarantee all the bass we can handle. Ain't never been to Louisiana so guess we can at least look at the scenery.

Real heavy sea today with intermittent rain squalls — we're in the area where typhoons hold forth — fell out of my office several times but managed to complete my schedule without any casualties.

Soon will be on my 14th month — can expect word from my relief any time now but probably will be a couple of months yet — when I start a new month I feel it's already over with because it does fly — we'll have enough on our minds to keep us from getting too bored the next couple of months. Lot of subs out here to add to our entertainment but nothing has happened as yet. About all it has amounted to is a lot of zig-zagging and changes of course. Breaks the monotony and keeps us on our toes — good, clean fun.

Until tonight — all my love
Paul

ON WEDNESDAY MORNING, December 13, the *Louisville* dropped anchor in San Pedro Bay, Leyte Gulf.

14 Dec. 1944

Dear Honey

If a sound recording could be made at the present moment, you'd hear the ding ding of the general alarm and the various and sundry noises associated when men hurry to their battle stations. Didn't start out so good so I guess the brig will do business today — can't seems to get it thru the mess attendant's head that coffee is very vital to the success of the war — the past few mornings we have gotten up with the idea of having a couple cups of good coffee to wake us up and start the day off. But no — they sit on their fat, black do-dads and say Yaz Suh and the next morning it's the same thing over again — bet there will be fresh coffee in the morning.

Tomorrow we have another change of command ceremony — Capt. Hurt leaves and I'm sorry. He needs a rest — looks twenty years older since the 1st of the year. Before long none of the old gang will be left. I'm beginning to feel like an old timer myself. It was eleven months yesterday we steamed out of San Francisco Bay, as the old saying goes "a lot of water has flown under the bridge" — should say has flown by the bridge of old CA 28 — and what water! Soon be a year since I kissed my darling good bye — as I have often said, it doesn't seem possible until one gets to thinking about it and then it really is so. We have been trying to figure out how many stars we have earned. The scoring has been changed so I guess we are entitled to six — used to be one for every action but now it's for groups of islands. Six is damn good and they are stylish ones so if asked if I saw any action I can truthfully say "but good" [*during Paul's tour of duty, the* ***Louisville*** *earned seven battle stars*].

Yesterday was quite a day — an air of expectancy hangs over the gulf — you know, something in the air — you can feel it and things can let go any minute. It was a long day, nothing particularly exciting — a few bombs but mainly the tenseness of the situation. In spite of the threat of attack, dozens of native canoes came out to sell us trinkets, coins etc. They had some rather nice hats — huge cone shaped affairs but couldn't think of any dress it would go with and besides I was afraid they are full of bugs & too, they were too large to send home — therefore, no hat.

We owned a monkey and a parrot for a "few minutes" but the exec wouldn't let us keep him, which is just as well — he was cute tho — I mean the monkey. Several quite attractive native gals were out — two looked like twins, both dressed in neat, white dresses and quite attractive. The kids really went nuts — it's the first time they have seen a decent looking gal — you know, well built, clean looking and beautiful teeth with this exception of a gold crown on their upper right lateral. Think they would have "fun" if they were turned loose together.

Am having an awful time with my paper — a fan keeps blowing it and it's driving me nuts so I think I'll delay writing until tonight.

All my love
Paul (g.q. kid)

THE JAPANESE "special corps" Paul writes about in the next letter refers to the kamikaze suicide attacks that have been taking a steady, nerve-wracking toll on Allied ships and lives for over a month.

14 Dec. 1944

Hello Honey —

So far so good — we're still hale and hearty after two days of "what have you". Had four g.q.s tonight — one caught me in the shower soaped up beautifully — the damn Japs have no consideration of one's toilet; grabbed my pants & shirt and scooted across the quarter deck with my shirt tail flying and shoes in hand — no runs, no hits, no errors.

Had the admiral & two captains down for lunch today — the admiral and new captain seem to be awfully nice, am particularly pleased with Admiral Chandler. Think we will continue to be a happy, lucky and shooting ship — sure hope our luck doesn't go with Captain Hurt. He leaves tomorrow, have the change of command ceremony at 0800 — he sure looks worn out & rightfully so for he is a hard worker.

The sunset was gorgeous again, it's really out of this world — the clouds are beautiful (if it wasn't for what lurks in them) and the way they catch the sun's reflection is really something. For a short time it was all gold & blue — light, blue sky, darker blue clouds & finally dark blue water. As the sun dropped behind the mountains the rays changed to a bright golden — brassy — orangish which lent a bronze cast to everything — water included. The beauty of the clouds is in our favor for they are fascinating to everyone so we keep a sharp lookout for enemy planes — the devils — honey they are that — wow! Their "special corps" has a distinctive uniform, yellow & green silk tight-fitting coveralls, guess it adds to their glory when "mission completed".

I see my page is running out — have to check my uniforms for missing buttons and do my stint of sewing ont and be ready for the ceremony in the a.m. We're early risers these days and on the go all day, so by this time of night we're ready to fold — never know when we have to hit the deck.

May get a thrill tomorrow — if things turn out right I'll get to go ashore

& spend the day. Sure would like just to say I set foot on "- - - -" and maybe pickup a trophy for my girl.

All my love
Paul

IN THE EARLY MORNING ceremony on Friday, December 15, Captain R. L. Hicks became the *Louisville's* 12th commander when he formally relieved Captain S. H. Hurt.

15 Dec. 1944

Dearest Honey —

The captain left just a while ago — kind of a sad occasion and a lot of near tears, myself included. He was a swell skipper and made a nice little speech and was quite choked up — he hated to leave, was a year ago today he took command. Said the people of the U.S. owed the Louisville & her crew a great debt for what she has done this past hard & dangerous year. He had waited thirty years for a chance to do what has transpired this past year & now it's over. Can't remember all he said but spoke of the remarkable record the Lou has compiled — a truly great ship.

It is now hours later — just finished taking a shower and feel like a white man again. Caught my boat this a.m. in "past due" time and had a thoroughly enjoyable time — had lunch aboard the LCI [*landing craft, Infantry*] that took us in which was an unexpected pleasure and a life saver. Arrived at the beach and had to tie up alongside a merchant marine and then climb over & thru her to get on the dock. Enjoyed that little experience, hadn't done it before — I'm glad I'm Navy.

I thought [*Tijuana*] & Nogales were a mess but you should see "- - - -"! Supposed to be a "city" of 30,000 — counting all the kids. I'll bet it's nearer 1,000,000. Zinke and I just wandered around, wading in mud over our ankles — we limited it to that height by dint of carefully picking our steps. Saw a jeep completely disappear a la slap-stick so we watched our step. Filthy! No sewage or waste disposal and they have had the heaviest rains in 24 years — stink!

The Army is billeted "downtown" and it's a mess — yea Navy — sure am glad I wasn't procured & assigned to the Army. Honey, you have no idea how terrible it is — God help the Wacs — Red Cross & nurses that are here. Tried to buy some trinkets — all they know is six dollars & that for a pair of wooden clogs or whatever you call them that sell for fifty cents in the states. They have the usual condoms and cigarettes but have no use for either so I made no purchases. Tried to find the Army hospital but no one knew where it was — not even the information center run by said Army — poop. In our wanderings we ran across a house with Medical Center on a sign out front — could see a dentist hard at it so I decided to call on him. He had a reception room full of patients but he was very cordial and as he was busy called his daughter who was the wife of the physician. She was very pleasant, very charming & well educated — her husband was out at the time but was expected back at 1600. We had to shove off so missed him. The dentist soon joined us for a brief visit, offered us coffee but had to decline due to having to catch our boat back home. He extended us an invitation to come back Sunday and have dinner with the family — if we are around, we may take him up — they were awfully nice and clean.

The homes are extremely bare of furniture, carpets etc., but clean. No window glass or doors in evidence so I guess there aren't many vermin or varmints around but how in hell there can help but be is beyond me unless they drown in the green, scummy, stinking pools of water in the gutters. No sight of pavement or sidewalks but plenty of creamy gray mud. The native children are really handsome & cute — look like miniatures and everyone is friendly. Everyone is small — saw a lot of the kids coming from school and some of the girls were really pretty — neatly dressed — well built and everybody goes barefooted. The morals are very high for the most part but of course the city has its "districts" — one of the store keepers very generously offered to direct us to a house where only officers were "entertained" & by the most beautiful and "talented" girls. We were not looking for "pom-pom" so we declined. If you molest the native women, especially the married ones — the men folks have a bad habit of chopping off the guilty one's head — several niggers have had theirs lopped off so I guess "crime doesn't pay"!

On our way back to the ship we came by a devious route — choosing residential and side streets we came across a beautiful villa — two stories, pale green & light brown, iron picket fence beautiful grass — trees, etc — really nicely landscaped & oh, yes — a garden on the roof. Armed guards were at damn near every door, window and gate — no it wasn't a prison and I can't imagine who was billeted there. If "I return" Sunday I'm going to try and pay him a visit just for the hell of it — you know, one military man to another — would also like to meet the president, just for the more hell of it.

That's about all I can say about my excursion. Maybe I neglected to mention the pigs, chickens & what have you that have full run of the houses — except of course the Medical Center. Really would like to go back & see them & learn some more about when the Japs took over — will take a couple cartons of candy bars for their hospitality.

Didn't sleep so good last night — my impetigo & rash raised hell & we were in & out of our sacks a good deal — we're still riding high — watched many score bodies being removed from a less fortunate ship yesterday — it's a great life honey and I'm so glad to be on "lucky Lou" — may her luck continue until she is pensioned — you have no idea of her miraculous (?) record.

Honey — don't worry about me — it's ticklish going but no more than I expected and I'm on the best damn ship in the fleet — we'll come thru.

All my love
Paul (mud dobber)

17 Dec. 1944

Hello Darling —

It's one of those dreary, rainy Sundays that normally one would turn over and go back to sleep. Did we? Hell no! The bugler, loud speaker and alarm did business as usual so we were up early. Did my extractions & cleaned Art's teeth, had planned on going to divine services but I was hot, sweaty & unshaven — services were being held in #1 mess hall where it's hot so I decided to talk to you instead.

It's very quiet out here as far as we are concerned — we're just setting here marking time — lots of planes being shot down but so far they have left us strictly alone — they must be aware of the reputation Lou has earned and steer clear of us. We are very much on the alert however — the sky is ideal for unannounced visitors so we're taking no chances. Wonder if I'll ever be able to look at the clouds, especially the low-hanging ones and feel secure — things happen so fast & sudden — just no warning at all — much like it must have been before radar.

The pecans you sent went over big — was sitting in my room one evening writing to you when the exec dropped in. He was looking for my neighbor (chief of staff) but he wasn't in so he came in and slung bull with me. He spotted my can of pecans and started drooling — offered to open them but he said not to because he was afraid he'd eat too many & the rest would spoil. We sat around and talked for some time and finally he burst out with "Ah hell, let's open them." None spoiled — there weren't any left, what few remained I gave to some of the fellows there were still around. The next night we had dessert consisting of vanilla ice cream & chocolate sauce — the exec bemoaned the fact he weakened the night before and ate all the pecans so I broke out another can & served them — the whole ward room got a sample so your giftie made everybody happy. Still have one can left and am saving it for our next beer session — should be a bit of all right.

Gee darling — you reckon maybe I'll see you in a few months — will you marry me? It's your "patriotic duty" to help the "morale" of the armed force. Please note singular & I'm it where you are concerned so you must say yes. Guess I'd better bring this letter to a close — too many interruptions, everyone is restless — it's raining still & we have no place to go so they're just milling around.

Sweet — should take a nap but am afraid I won't sleep tonight — went to bed early last night but had to get up in a couple hours due to ding-ding-ding! I was so sound asleep had an awful time getting into my clothes and finding my way to my battle station — no runs, no hits, no errors.

All my love
Paul (Lonesome)

18 Dec. 1944

Dear Honey —

They are really working my tail off, smaller ships without dental officers are flocking over. Was nice to a few of them and now they are sending their friends — perhaps they think they are doing me a favor — poop. I'm booked up until the first of the year, including xmas day, with my own personnel and when they run these ringers in everything is all messed up — poop again. If it wasn't for Lou being such a swell ship and held in such high esteem by all — I'd tell them to go to hell. Guess that is why she is the girl she is — everyone is zealous to maintain her good name so we all turn to and stand by her.

The mail situation is still acute — there's a bottleneck some place again and all the xmas mail is held up. The Army gets theirs by air, to hell with the Navy — would like to kick a few teeth.

It's chow time and my "practice" is due to arrive soon so better close for now. If I'm not all in by night I'll talk to you again later. These g.q.s plus tension, plus heat, plus no recreation is sure putting rings under the fellows eyes — it sure isn't from dissipation, that's for sure.

All My Love
Paul (dentist plus)

20 Dec. 1944

Hello Sweet Girl —

Haven't been to the village since my first trip. Looks like I'll have ample time to go back but doubt whether I will. Would give my eye tooth for a couple of cold beers, it's so hot here, absolutely no breeze and we have dropped anchor so we are dead in the water. Thank the Lord our anniversary will see us under way and we'll create a breeze with a change of scenery. May wish we were back here but doubt it — there'll be plenty of excitement and we'll only be too happy to be in g.q. Won't miss not having mail near as much either, too busy to worry about it.

Whoops! Hours later, my "moral" is high again — actually had a letter from you, mailed Dec. 2 so I guess they have located us again. It was read to the tune made by every gun on the ship except the main battery and "- - - -" planes are no more. We secured from that g.q. — I had just removed my clothes down to my [*skivvies*] in an effort to reread your letter in comfort & the peace & quiet of my compartment, when ding-ding-

ding and we were off to the races again. Looks like a busy night tonight but it's fun and exciting — breaks up the monotony & besides it's pretty fireworks at night.

'TWAS IN A RESTAURANT THEY MET —
ROMEO AND JULIET;
HE HAD NO CASH TO PAY THE DEBT,
SO ROMEO'D WHAT JULI-ET.

I'll be afraid to step out when I get home after living in the comparative safety of a ship — women drivers — streetcars — and what have you. Out here, the fellows that have dates have to wear a loaded pistol — get a kick out of it & always wonder if it is to be used on the girl "or else" or really for protection against the hazards offered by the sex starved men. Lot of wild tales are told and no reason to believe they aren't true — really rugged, it's dangerous for a girl to be out and after dark they have to have armed escorts.

All my love
Paul (G.Q. kid)

21 Dec. 1944

Hello Darling —

The power just went off — I'm writing this by the light of or from my port — jeebers it's hot!

The sky is ideal for air raids — completely filled with dark clouds so we no doubt will have business ere long. Wanna come home.

It's all I can do to keep from peeking into my letter box — it's too early for it to be sorted but guess I'm entitled to a peek. Waiting for mail from my honey is more thrilling than shooting down Jap planes.

Had a swell day in the office this morning — mail and the air raids started my red corpuscles going and I knocked out 21 fillings plus the various & sundry odd jobs associated with dentistry. Nothing like letters from your best girl and being under attack to boost one's morale.

All my love honey
Paul (anxious kid)

22 Dec. 1944

Little Honey —

The glare, heat and perspiration sure is hard on the eyes. I've used up gallons of boric acid on mine to wash the "goo" out of them. They're still blue, both of them — had "checked my bags" but have some small "over night bags" now. Rather a strenuous life — g.q.s in the mornings have me all crossed up. We have this set up — reveille sounds over the speaker each morning before sun up by a good margin so we are alerted — if the screen is clear we don't have to go to our stations — if a red flash, away we go. I tried being alerted and going back to sleep — sure there was business — the next time I got up, dressed and was all set — business? Why no!

Beings I have the welfare of the ship at heart, I get up at reveille each morning and stay up — sure enough it's two hours of sleep I lose but I enjoy slinging bull with the watch officers over a cup of coffee & watch the sun rise — if it will keep the Japs from coming over in the mornings I'll gladly sacrifice the sleep. Haven't found anything to keep them away at sun down or that period just after.

The water is filled with native dugouts [*canoes*] and they became such a nusience (?) we had to turn the fire hose on them to drive them away — they didn't have a thing to sell — just beggars. May go to the beach Sunday and wander around — it hasn't rained in several days so maybe it's dried out enough to get around a little more comfortably.

Tomorrow night at midnight I kissed you bye — a whole year without seeing you — golly that's a long time. Sure shouldn't be more than six months more before my relief shows up — then we'll have soft music and low turned lights.

Love you little sweetheart
Paul (guess just plain)

23 Dec. 1944

My Honey —

What great event took place one year ago tonight come midnight? We had a last cup of coffee together aboard the Lou, all men had to be aboard at 2400 — all leaves and liberties were over. Kissed you good bye and you became a temporary widow. It's been quite a year.

Almost got caught in the shower again just awhile ago — had just dried myself and got into my [*skivvies*] when Ding-Ding-Ding off to the races. Grabbed my pants & shirt, slipped into my shoes & was at my station before the last ding. Bet I have a hell of a time when I get home — at least for a while if I hear a bell — guess I'll stopper my ears so I won't make a fool of myself — these days when the alarm goes there is no dilly-dally or shilly-shalling — we get in gear.

Have had chow and watched the sunset — a beautiful sky — kind of makes you hurt to watch it — changes color continuously until the last ray dies out. The changing water adds to the beauty — all kinds of reflections to make a scene of breath-taking beauty. It's hard to believe the multi-colored clouds — pinks, blues, grays etc can be filled with "dynamite" — the Japs haven't bothered us since just before chow — they'll probably come in now that I'm comfortable. Had planned on going to church in the morning but just received a message requesting 6 dental apts in the a.m. I sent an affirmative — sure hope they aren't merchant marines. If they are I'm going to throw them out on their ears pronto — they stink.

It's still quiet — maybe they will leave us alone tonight but it sounds too good to be true. They probably are resting up for xmas day & [*will*] swoop on us thinking to catch us napping. About all the difference from any other day will be maybe a small party to the beach for a beer.

My heat rash and impetigo have almost cleared up — I'm knocking on wood — finally roasted it out of me. Had tried everything — mild sun doses — medicines — baths — no baths, etc., but to no avail. Finally decided to burn it out by exposing it to the sun until I blistered. Right now I have a beautiful tan and free from itch — the trouble is the tan sweats right off so I'll be itchy-bitchy & white when I get home. Am feeling too good these days — if I just had my girl and a few rounds of golf — would be happy.

All my love
Paul (with coat of tan)

24 Dec. 1944

Hello Dorothy Darling —

Twas the night before xmas — so what? G.Q. as usual & again just had come out of the shower when the pests came over — we're getting so we don't even ask where or how many — just let em come.

Last night had no more than crawled into my sack when Ding and away we went. Stayed in several hours and spoiled a good night's rest. Be glad when we move on to new hunting grounds — gets old when you stay in one place very long — kind of get onto the pattern and it's the same old thing over and over again.

Tonight after chow I'll have my little xmas. Am sorry yours [*gift box*] was entirely broken up — better tell me what you sent — I retrieved 6 prs sock — 3 beautiful hankies, mustache scissors, chain & laid claim to a pair of mighty comfortable cloth slip in shoes and a book "Hi Ya Katie, I'm In The Navy Now." The last two items I don't know whether or not were mine but the mail clerk said take them so I did. Thanks a lot sweet girl and I can use each and every article.

We're sitting in the middle of the "- - - -" and will be blacked out soon — as yet, no snow and I've about given up — seems a little too warm any how, so it would melt right away.

Wish there was an officers club around — having a sneaking suspicion I'd throw a shoe — feel kind a low for no good reason — must be the "season" and I miss you so.

Had a busy day today — missed church again due to patients from other ships — I'm half way p - - - - off about it. Had to hold two services due to the huge crowds — had several dozen boats from other ships to attend. Our new chaplain is quite a live wire — protestant — & we're really having turnouts. He has organized a ship's chorus and is quite good — he's a good hand shaker and mixer.

We are having quite a number of the smaller ships over for xmas dinner tomorrow — officer and crew so it should be a gala occasion. I know they will enjoy it and I'm glad the exec asked them over. Maybe there will be some one from near home.

All my love
Paul

PAUL'S ACCOUNT of his Christmas Day — rum punch on the beach — doesn't match the ship's history which says: "Christmas Day found the ship and three other cruisers making a high speed run from Leyte Gulf to the area off Mindoro Island in a vain effort to contact enemy surface units which had bombarded our position on Mindoro the previous night." According to the end of Paul's letter, the *Louisville* got underway on the 26th. The ship's log agrees with Paul, noting that the *Louisville* got underway at 6:25 p.m., December 26.

25 Dec. 1944

Merry Xmas Darling —

How are you this bright & sunny day — hope Santa Claus was good to you. All is quiet on the Western or I guess it's Eastern Front so far. Had quite a xmas eve — went to g.q. five times during the evening and several more Japs joined their ancestors. We did have a white Christmas but it wasn't snow — a dandy smoke screen and very effective.

I'm now well supplied with tooth brush, dental cream, talcum, soap, cigarettes, hand lotion, hankies, white sox etc — a very nice xmas. Didn't get to open them until this a.m. due to g.q.s and air raids. The admiral has a birthday tomorrow but we are having him in today — a joint affair.

Am catching the 1300 boat for a little xmas cheer on one of the islands.

Tonight has come and went — this is the next day and everything is under control again. Caught the 1300 ship as planned but it was 1400 when we finally shoved — arrived at the beach at 1500 which left an hour and a half to quench one's thirst. Had a thoroughly enjoyable time — the beer was nice and cold, plentiful too — also had really good rum punch. For a thin dime you could get a bottle of Schlitz beer or a water glass full of punch. They served the punch in beer tins but we came prepared & brought our own glasses & p-nuts. The club was nothing but an over-head and a bar — the deck was sand but the background was pretty — set right on the beach with a native village just arrears. A nice rain squall came up and cooled things off and was fun drinking beer with a solid sheet of rain less than a foot from your face — there were no bulkheads so it was like being under a large umbrella. Met Bill Dunn of NBC and [*name unreadable*] of CBS and had quite a bull session. They're touchy on the D.O.D. subject and are on the defensive whenever brought up.

The trip to and from the beach was fun. Took another LCI back — a later one and what a trip & wow! What a climax! Went thru an air raid, got lost in the smoke screen and when we finally got home the word was passed — Dr. Zinke, Dr. Bonnette, Lt. Trinkle etc report to the exec's office immediately — started to report but another air raid took place — after we secured we reported to the exec and be damned if he wasn't madder than hell and marched us into the captain's cabin. Twas my first "Captain's Mast" and was my face red! Sure was a surprised little sailor but now I am a bonafide "salt". Seems we were A.O.L. (absent over leave or liberty) and supposed to be serious because we were in critical battle area etc., etc., subject to shove on "- - - -" notice. He lined us all up — Archer was first and was asked for his story — on down the line, me included. After he heard us all he gave us a song and dance, then dismissed us. This morning while having a coffee — the exec came in still looking sour and busted right by me without his customary "Good Morning, Pablo" — he had been awfully nice and friendly to me. I grinned & said "Good morning, Commander" as he went by & he did give me a gruff "morning". Drank my coffee when he came back through — this time he slugged me across the shoulders with his cap and sat down to a cup of coffee. I told him I was sorry about last night and he said it happened to every officer some time or other but what made him mad was everyone but "me" told a barefaced lie — I merely said I met friends — the beer was cold — got in a bull session — had transportation back to the ship and had no excuse to offer — so I guess what Comdr. George told us back in San Diego still holds — when you get caught it's merely "No excuse, Sir" and let it ride.

This letter was interrupted a ways back by a "flash red" and had g.q. Since then I have eaten, we are underway, watched the air strip get bombed, watched a.a. fire and we all have our fingers crossed. We stand a good chance of really winding up the old year in a big way in an extra curricular way. Can't tell you what it's all about but "Lou rides again" and it's a tough and ticklish mission. Sure glad I was A.O.L. last night instead of tonight — wow! We never know when things let go and I always get a thrill out of getting under way — no fuss nor muss — no packing, just get going.

Am glad we are steaming — I ain't never been "there" and it's a plenty hot spot — a fitting climax to a marvelous year. Just hope our luck holds

& I'm sure it will — the old gal knows something is in the air for she sure is on her toes and looking mighty trim.

All my love to you little girl
Paul

27 Dec. 1944

My Darling —

Thought I'd better get my communique off to you while the fuse is still spluttering and things are quiet — too quiet and that's what is bad.

Am seeing some beautiful scenery and the sky & water are gorgeous — it's mighty tricky business but it's fun — don't expect to sleep the night thru but everyone is looking forward to whatever they throw at us. Picked up some Jap prisoners this evening — they sure are mean looking and not very bright. It's the first live ones I've seen close up — they aren't pretty but seem well nourished and in good condition — they were all Navy personnel. They certainly are stoical — not a change of expression or glimmer — just blank and sullen.

Winding up our fifteenth day of the battle of nerves — think tomorrow we may have a showdown if not tonight — it can't be far off.

There isn't any news — I'm hale and hearty — rarin to go — am seeing all new country — should say water — was in hopes I'd get in these waters even if not far but I can add it to my sea stories — and the dawn comes up like thunder tra la [*this line from the song "On the Road to Mandalay" Paul decorated with musical notes*].

It's past bed time and as usual one never knows so I'm going to say good night for now.

All my love to you honey
Paul (Sea going kid)

28 Dec. 1944

Dear Honey —

Just woke up from an hour's nap — I'm still groggy and wet as tho I'd taken a dip but thought I'd check in with you and let you know we are still afloat. No runs, no hits, no errors last night altho they roused us out about 0200 and ruined our rest.

We disposed of our Jap prisoners this noon after thorough interrogation by an intelligence officer — sent them off on a P-T boat for further questioning by the Army.

According to radio news received here, [*Secretary of the Navy James Vincent*] Forrestal says the Jap fleet has been driven from Philippine waters — Oh Yeah?

Hours later — a rain squall came up and it really poured down for awhile — now it's clear but a strong wind and a heavy sea is running, am having an awful time trying to write but "correspondence must go on". Just came off the foc'sle — it was marvelous out there — almost cold, one had to hang on to keep from being blown off or washed overboard. It's a great life and I like seas like tonight — hated to come in but wanted to talk to you and then try to finish Green Light — I think it's a swell book.

Don't think I told you how we started the day off xmas — over the loud speaker, "Good ship, good crew — merry xmas — turn to" — kind of cute.

Mission completed up here so now we're heading back to act as bait again — perhaps mail day after tomorrow.

All my love & good night
Paul

30 Dec. 1944

Hello Honey Girl — Hello, Hello, Hello!

My goodness — had nine letters from you today! My moral is soaring by leaps and bounds — bring on your Japs — Whoopee!

All my love
Paul

31 Dec. 1944

Hello My Darling —

Had a nice day today — tough morning in the office and then went to the beach in the pm. Had four beers and took a stroll thru the native village — watched them pound rice the old fashioned way. The Japs had destroyed all their machinery so they have to resort to pounding it with clubs. It was a lot like they used to pound stakes when erecting a circus tent — several swinging in turn. They were very adept at it from the little kids on up. Cock fighting seems to be the big sport with much gambling. Watched them draw water from a crude well — everything very primitive — the kids carried huge containers of water fastened to a bamboo pole and carried on their shoulders. Tried to buy a "pretty" but there isn't a thing other than American cigarettes, candies, etc., the sailors had given to them. Saw a lot of water buffalo, native pigs, etc — kids predominated. All in all was very interesting — saw a beautifully crappy bar but did not partake and the line up for the sporting house was too long for me to wait so "I went on" — still pure.

They have a novel way of tethering their pigs — they "pierce the ears" and run a cord thru the ears and across the back of the head, each end of the cord has a button or knot in it so it won't pull thru — to this is attached a leash so they can lead or tie said piggie up.

Haven't had a g.q. so far today but the kids on the guns are restless and it being New Year's Eve we expect company any time.

Happy New Year sweet — am thinking of you.

All my love
Paul

1 Jan. 1945

Happy New Year, My Sweet —

Maybe good old Lou will get a little credit this time — a big shot from the New York Times, a friend of the Admirals, is riding with us on this next deal. Have forgotten his name and can't give you the Admiral's name, so guess you'll just have to read all the papers.

Sure enough, had company last night — just after I finished my letter to you — ding-ding-ding. Secured from that, turned in and was sleeping ninety to nothing but at 0200 — ding-ding-ding & away we went. Great life.

In case I don't write on our anniversary — I'm glad I'm married to you and have loved every minute of our life together, except maybe the time you fouled up my suits in Alpena — sent the wrong one to be cleaned — remember? No fooling, I'll be thinking of you — we're fifteen hours ahead of you out here but I'll make the correction. Hope my flowers didn't get fouled up. Am looking forward to the rest of the years together — bigger & better years.

All my love & thoughts
Paul

NEAR MIDNIGHT on January 2, the *Louisville* left Leyte Gulf's San Pedro Bay headed north to Luzon.

3 Jan. 1945

Hello Little Sweetheart —

It's a little early to get you up but "tis my wedding day" so I must be up & at them — you too. It's 0600 at home so you should be getting up so you won't be late for the ceremone-e-e-e.

Gee honey — twelve years ago — the big event — I'm still happy with you and love you more and more. Just hope I come thru the remaining big deals out here so I can hurry home to you.

It's a beautiful, powerful picture out here — makes the corpuscles run faster — wish you could see this phase of it — it's like a movie, how in hell they maneuver the way they do and not get lost is beyond me. This part of the operation is kind of slow altho we have some business every now and then. Did have a good night's sleep last night — heard them pull up the anchor and had a hunch we wouldn't be molested the rest of the night so I dismissed g.q. from my mind & didn't even hear reveille — the alarm clock got me up at 0700 so I bounced right out of my sack feeling like a ninnie. Think it was the last good night's sleep

I'll have for at least a couple of weeks — it's going to be rugged — the worst yet.

Had fun cleaning house last night — dumped out a lot of trash and secured everything else in readiness for the big boom-boom. My quarters really look nice now but come Saturday it will all be in shambles again. Such is life aboard a war ship — it's fun though.

All my love and happy anniversary my sweet
Paul (absentee)

THE *LOUISVILLE* WAS lead "big ship" of an 850-ship fleet carrying the U.S. Sixth Army, which would invade Luzon and drive the Japanese from the Philippines. Often in a zig-zag pattern and making from 12 to 15 knots, the fleet sailed from Leyte through Surigao Strait and turned to the northeast. Aboard *Lady Lou, New York Times* correspondent Frank L. Kluckhohn wrote: "There were fleecy clouds, blue skies and sea — beauty with just an undertone of danger."

By Wednesday night, January 3, that undertone was transformed into a terrifying gauntlet of frenzied swarms of kamikaze planes as the *Louisville* led battleships and carriers into the China Sea toward Luzon's Lingayen Gulf. The fleet sent up a curtain of anti-aircraft fire, but the suicide pilots bore in, strafing and aiming themselves. Most cartwheeled into the sea, but others got through and even with dead hands on the controls their momentum carried them into their targets, washing decks with flaming fuel and plunging bombs deep into American warships.

"We sailed boldly ahead," Kluckhohn wrote, "spearhead of the mighty drive capable of deciding the fate of the war with Japan."

On January 4, Paul wrote a chatty letter, fretting about Dotty B's cold. Only toward the end does he acknowledge that it is "mighty rugged" and "gray hairs are popping out." He would not write again for seven days.

The following six pictures were taken from a nearby ship, and show a kamikaze aircraft approaching and striking the *Louisville*. The National Archives lists the first picture as having been taken on January 5, 1945, and the rest of the series on January 6. However, the number, shape, and pattern of aerial shell bursts indicate all the photos are from the same sequence. Several sources, including a family album notation most likely supplied by Paul, say the pictures were all taken January 5.

National Archives Photos

4 Jan. 1945

Hello Darling —

Am so sorry you have had a cold and am glad you are almost recovered — evidently you haven't paid me any mind — I have told you repeatedly to take care of yourself — now get on the beam and take care of yourself — whatinhell do you think I'm fighting this war for?

No fooling honey — please be careful — I can't duck with gusto out here if I'm worried about you "to home". Woke this morning with a raw throat myself but is all right tonight — my port blower, pardon me, you of the laity — left nostril has been running right smart — guess the arid fumes of the smoke screen irritated it.

Am anxious to know how your New Year's party came out — have fun? Don't forget to stash away a bourbon & if possible a scotch for when I get home.

Golly Sakes — slippery end of the stick tonight — remember Eugene Stetler? One less of that clan — a real tragedy. [*"Eugene Stetler" is Paul's code for the fleet's aircraft carriers. One less of its "clan" could have been the escort carrier* ***Ommaney Bay,*** *which was hit by a kamikaze on January 4 and sank with the loss of 100 men.*]

Served warning on us and it isn't even near zero hour. Gray hairs are popping out — mighty rugged and only the beginning — must be on with my rummy game — might pick up a few quarters.

Take care little girl
All my love
Paul

THE *LOUISVILLE'S* LOG ENTRY for 1659 (4:59 p.m.) on Friday, January 5, 1945, reads: "Commenced maneuvering radically in formation for enemy plane attack." Seven minutes later a smoking, single-engine suicide craft broke through the withering fire. At the last instant, Captain Hicks swung his ship to take the impact head on. The plane smashed into No. 2 turret and skidded into the bridge area. Amazingly, only one man was killed. Captain Hicks was badly burned and 58 others were wounded. Commander W. P. McCarty, executive officer, assumed command. No. 2 turret's magazines were flooded to prevent flames from igniting the ammunition. By 5:44 p.m., all fires were out and the *Louisville* fought on, shooting down a number of planes and bombarding enemy shore positions.

Wrote Kluckhohn: "We sail majestically along in single file, fires and smoke ashore showing where our shells are landing."

On Saturday afternoon, January 6, the minesweepers had done their work and the *Louisville* steamed into Lingayen Gulf. Desperate Japanese suicide pilots began an assault that inflicted the worst pounding the U.S. Navy had suffered in nearly two years. Three battleships, a light cruiser, and five destroyers were hit.

Man of War, the book compiled by a number of the *Louisville's* officers and men, describes the sky that day as "a billowing cloud of smoke, flying steel and flaming planes."

The *Louisville* battled throughout Saturday afternoon until 5:30 p.m., when a kamikaze crashed high on her starboard side between the navigation bridge and signal bridge. Both its bombs exploded, killing 32 and wounding 56. Although horribly injured by burning gasoline, Admiral Chandler manned a fire hose until he was physically removed from the flag bridge to take his turn with the enlisted men awaiting medical attention. His lungs had been seared by the flames, and on Sunday he would die.

"It is not hell, it is worse than hell," Kluckhohn reported, "as we burn topside with this ammunition-jammed steel casing threatening to explode and many of our controls temporarily gone. Above me flames are burning high. Fragments are raining upon the thin metal covering overhead."

"On the bridge some men have been blown to pieces and others burned so badly they are unrecognizable but still living."

Writing in *Man of War,* an unidentified survivor recalled the scene:

> Lingayen Gulf became a holocaust. The forward portion of the ship was a tragedy of twisted plates, twisted bodies, and twisted minds.
>
> In the after half of the ship, men, choking and gasping for air as the thick smoke, stinking of burned flesh and paint, enveloped them, stood their ground feeding the anti-aircraft guns.
>
> Out of the flames, broken, burned bodies pulled themselves over blackened fire hose, through stinging salt water, along the buckled decks to the arms of those who mercifully injected

> morphine, applied rudimentary first aid, lifted them into the wire-meshed battle stretchers and lowered them to safer areas.

Kluckhohn wrote: "We lurch along, almost ramming other ships. But under the executive officer — Commander W. P. McCarty, the captain having been wounded yesterday — we don't even lose our place in formation."

Trained to a fine edge and tempered by a year of combat, the crew regroups. A 6:02 p.m. log entry reads: "all fires extinguished." *The New York Times* correspondent continued his report: "We are battered and scarred, mourning our dead and individually shaken . . . Men working with burned and bandaged hands will smile through faces covered with grease."

Kluckhohn then concluded his front-page story: "I am incapable of describing what war is like, but there is heroism aboard this ship and in this fighting force to which every American should pay tribute."

In a later dispatch headlined "Lead Ship at Luzon Saved By Heroism . . . Her Voyage of Deadly Danger Replete with Acts of Self-Sacrifice and Valor," Kluckhohn wrote about the officers and men of the *Louisville.* The story mentioned Paul, who was in charge of the midships battle dressing station, and such familiar names as Lieutenant Commander Arthur C. Esch, gunnery officers, and Lieutenant Commanders E. A. "Zimke" and William H. Johnson, the ship's doctors "who worked indifferent to anything but caring for the injured" (Paul and the ship's roster of officers spell the doctor's name "Zinke," with an "n" instead of Kluckhohn's "m").

An Oklahoma City newspaper carried the following story based on Kluckhohn's reporting:

> City Dentist War Hero Aboard Ship
> (Copyright 1945 by *The New York Times*)
>
> ABOARD A UNITED STATES WARSHIP OFF LINGAYEN, Jan. 10 — (Delayed) — A dentist is one of the most popular men aboard his ship. He is Lt. Comdr. Paul C. Bonnette of Oklahoma City. Both times his ship was hit he labored like a doctor of medicine, giving plasma to the wounded and burned while ignoring danger. He worked in the wardroom emergency hospital and the battle dressing stations.

> Generally speaking, dentists do that on these warships under such conditions. Although Bonnette's activities were outstanding, his courtesy and kindliness under the most difficult situations also were apparent.

On January 8, the *Louisville* committed her dead to the waters of the South China Sea and continued fighting, but her damage was extensive, and on January 10 she finally retired from the action to join a convoy of transports and damaged ships returning to Leyte Gulf. That same day the ship's log records more victims of the kamikaze attack as two sailors were "admitted to sick bay for treatment of nervous shock."

The New York Times reported the following "memorandum for all hands" issued by Captain Hicks and Executive Officer McCarty:

> Words cannot express the deep feeling of pride which we hold in our appreciation and admiration of the crew. Under the most adverse conditions of modern warfare and the fanatical acts of our enemy you stood up and fought it out.
>
> We will never forget our brave comrades who perished in their attempts to save the ship and the lives of the rest of us. Our heartfelt sympathies for their bereaved families and we will miss them in our daily lives.
>
> To all hands congratulations on the superb jobs of assisting in the speedy care of the wounded, in fighting fires at the risk of life and limb, in re-establishing and maintaining gun and ship control stations and communication.

From that day to the present, *Louisville* veterans are reluctant to discuss the events of January 5-6, 1945. A short letter to Dorothy dated January 31, 1945, from Lieutenant F. R. "Bob" Linthicom is typical. "Paul was splendid during our trouble," Linthicom wrote. "You can be proud of him. The less said about that period in our duty the better."

When Paul finally wrote again on January 11, he said he was dazed and exhausted. He summed up his endless hour with the *Louisville's* injured and dying as "awful." He acknowledges his sadness, then carries on his narrative as before.

However, at one point in later years Paul was moved to share at least one graphic incident with his family. After the second kamikaze strike, Paul ran to a screaming sailor whose flesh was cooked to the *Louisville's*

Lt. Comdr. P.C. Bonnette (DC) USNR
U.S.S. Louisville
% F.P.O.
San Francisco
U.S. POSTAGE
VIA AIR MAIL
JAN
12
P.M.
Mrs. Paul C. Bonnette
1700 NW 17
Oklahoma City (6)
Oklahoma
PASSED BY
NAVAL CENSOR

IN REPLY
REFER TO:

U. S. S. LOUISVILLE

11 Jan. 1945

My Darling—

In case any news has filtered thru to you and you are wondering—I'm absolutely all right, didn't receive a scratch—all the Medical Dept. escaped unscathed.

Please forgive me for neglecting you this past week—was mighty rugged & no time to eat or sleep for days—we're all dead tired and still somewhat dazed. Lord's luck held or we would have all been wiped out—was awful.

By the time this reaches you we'll be safe—after 31 days continuous exposure we're finally relieved. Will see Cutts in a few days—hope Clancy is still with him. May see Ade and a fifty-fifty chance of seeing "Sandy" Stetler. It's maybe a less than 50-50 chance but not at all impossible.

Golly Sakes—have quit gambling—lost thirty-eight to Bracken and around a hundred & sixteen to Pendleton—still have enough left for pretties if & when. Sorry for the short note but I love you just the same

All my love
Paul (Dad)

red hot deck. As he grabbed the sailor he heard the thunder of an approaching plane and the roar of its gunfire raking the ship. Paul ducked his head and felt the bullets pluck at his clothing. When he opened his eyes, he was holding only shreds of the sailor's body.

On June 10, 1945, Lieutenant Commander Paul Christian Bonnette was awarded the Bronze Star Medal. The citation read:

> For distinguishing himself by heroic and meritorious conduct as the Dental Officer on board . . . a cruiser during operations against the enemy in the Southwest Pacific area. . . . When his ship suffered severe personnel casualties, Lieutenant Commander Bonnette speedily and efficiently administered to the wounded and through his outstanding skill and knowledge, he was able to save the lives of many of the injured. . . ."

11 Jan. 1945

My Darling —

In case any news has filtered thru to you and you are wondering — I'm absolutely all right, didn't receive a scratch — all the Medical Dept. escaped unscathed.

Please forgive me for neglecting you this past week — was mighty rugged — no time to eat or sleep for days — we're all dead tired and still some what dazed. Lou's luck held or we would have all been wiped out — was awful.

By the time this reaches you we'll be safe — after 31 days continuous exposure we are finally relieved. . . .

Golly Sakes — have quit gambling — lost thirty-eight to Bracken and around a hundred & sixteen to Pendelton — still have enough left for pretties if & when.

Sorry for the short note but I love you just the same.

All my love
Paul (Sad)

THE *LOUISVILLE* DROPPED ANCHOR in San Pedro Bay on Friday, January 12. The next day, she transferred her most seriously wounded to the hospital ship USS *Mercy.*

13 Jan. 1945

Hello Darling —

Today has been a marvelous day — started off with a beautiful sunrise, gave way to a hot sultry cloudy day.

Am having an awful time writing this letter — had to take time out to win 25 cents from Comdr. [*name unreadable*] — then Zinke came in to have me listen to a recording of his wife & kids.

I claimed the right shower slip-ons & I'm sure using them — always strip down when I hit my compartment — hang my clothes a la fireman fashion so I can scat with the first ding.

A few more days and my "war days" will be over — in a couple of days my 15th month starts and by the time we're all set again it will be too late. Sure am going to miss all the excitement and tense moments — it's been a real experience — that's for sure.

A long, long time ago I ordered some sea boots & jacket — they showed up today and they're sure swell. Hope it's cold when I get home so I can wear them — otherwise will have to just pet them.

Had a marvelous speed boat ride this a.m. — water like glass — not a breath of air — smoke from the stacks went straight up — was real sport skimming over the surface. Not many more said rides left for me so I'm looking good but good and breathing in all the salt air I can.

All my love Sweet Girl
Paul (Hope I Hope)

ON JANUARY 14, the *Louisville* left Leyte Gulf to arrive in Manus on the 18th.

17 Jan. 1945

Hello Honey —

We're having pretty rough weather these days and lots of rain but it stays hot and sticky. My rash & impetigo is under control. Sure hope it stays that way. We're all on pins and needles these days — won't be long before we know the truth — hope I hope!

Did I ever tell you the New York Times correspondent's name? It's Frank Kluckhohn — thought maybe you'd run across some of his articles. Cute remark he made — "all I want is to walk knee deep in blondes and lay down." He had been thru all the African campaign etc etc etc., but his first time on a warship and he said it's his last — too tuff for him, he frankly admits he never was so damned scared and for so long in all his experiences — said he "just couldn't dig a foxhole in these steel decks."

For once we don't have to anxiously scan the clouds — all we have had the past few days are sub contacts. My birthday this year will be far less interesting and exciting than last year's — looks like nothing more than a quiet ocean voyage — destination unknown.

All my love
Paul (Happy)

19 Jan. 1945

My Little Darling —

What with butterflies, hang over and being in love — will not giff a good letter. Just hopes this gets off — time is short and everybody is so excited — will celebrate my birthday with Ade [*Paul's code for Hawaii*].

Had four grand letters from you yesterday. What a field day I had — gee, I'm happy inspite of my hangover. Am going to reception this afternoon in honor of his majesty's ships present. Maybe a little hair of the dog will do me good — wow! What if they only serve tea!

Had an awfully nice time at the club yesterday — all were "battle scarred veterans" and our first let down since the big deal — everyone seems a lot closer and there were a lot of hip-hip hoo rays!

Honey, I'm too excited to write so think I'll bathe, clean up and get ready for his Majesty — does one curtsy or give them the glad hand?

In the kitchen of the Lankard family “big house” in Kingfisher, Oklahoma, January 1945. From left: Fred Lankard, Dotty B, and Mary Sue Stetler.

Gee honey — do you reckon? Hope I hope — Feb. could be such a happy month.

All my love to you sweet girl
Paul (oo la!)

20 Jan. 1945

Hello Darling —

Am pleased to report my hangover is under control today — still a little washed out but am doing okay.

Had fun at the reception — the "guests" were pretty in their white shoes, socks, shorts, shirts, & caps — very cool & comfortable. Not a damned one of them had a coat of tan — all looked so well fed & pink cheeked — sure didn't look like a fighting group of sea going men — poop!

Sure wish we'd get our unfinished business done here so we could get going — am anxious to see Ade, perhaps he'll have some startling and pleasant news for me. Hope I hope!

I'm hungry & it's about that time so will drop this in the box & turn to — have hot dogs, trimmings & baked beans for lunch — goody.

All My Love
Paul

ON JANUARY 21, the *Louisville* set sail for Pearl Harbor.

Jan. 23. 1945

Honey —

We're really riding the roller coaster tonight — a strong wind is blowing which makes big waves and causes us to pitch and toss a lot — am glad I've had a year's training or it might go bad with me. The evenings have been beautiful, last night particularly. Sure am going to miss all this but I guess everything has to come to an end. Already miss g.q.s — air raids, etc., — life is awfully monotonous and I just hope we're not stuck out here somewhere for several months — wouldn't that be awful! So near and yet so far.

Have had a million interruptions since I started this letter — everyone is restless and milling around tweedling thumbs and "hoping" — one minute they're up and then down — it's a great life but sure is nerve-wracking. At least next week I'll have the novel experience of wearing a necktie — bet we choke the first hour or so.

Much singing and horse play going on — notice on the work sheet for tomorrow they have a series of "sex hygiene" lectures scheduled. Guess they are warning the boys against the "pit-falls" of civilization they'll be exposed to next week.

Speaking of sex — I don't recall a single instance since we have been out that our bull sessions turned to sex problems — not that the fellows would throw any "pom-pom" over their shoulders, but they just don't discuss it.

Have eaten — a swell meal of soup, tenderized ham, candied sweets, fresh peas, corn bread, iced tea, olives, ice cream with fresh strawberries. Sounds pretty good for sea-faring diet — nez pas? Did go to the foc'sle, damned near drowned myself & was almost blown off but it was wonderful. The sky was weird sinister — somewhere there was a sunset but all we got was a faint glow behind the clouds. Looked like the world was on fire & we were getting a faint glow. The sea is mighty rough — spray washes the decks and continues on up. Am doing some tall looking for I'm afraid this chapter in my life is coming to a close. It's been wonderful and I've enjoyed every minute of it — could have gotten along without the horror scenes very nicely but one has to expect that when you are on a major warship. Certainly have no qualms about going out again if time allows.

Am having two birthdays this year — we cross the date line on that day so we'll have two days of the same date. I'm not going to accept the added year tho — I want it with you and time flies so.

Looked at my blues awhile ago — they sure look like hell — mold spots, etc., have to hang them out in the sun after a thorough brushing. Where do you have your cleaning done? Warn them that if your boy friend comes home "unexpectedly" you'll expect one-day service on a top coat and uniform. Certainly am not going to wait around on the West Coast or

"East" Coast until I can get a uniform clean, I'se heading for my honey as fast as a plane will carry me — if and when. Jeebers honey — will know next week if I can be your valentine or there abouts! Talk about butterflies — even in the heat of battles I've never had them like this. This is the longest & slowest & most uninteresting trip I've ever been on — if we just knew what word awaits us and how long they'll delay us. When we're on a mission we don't think about home but on a deal like this — that's all we think of — golly darling, are you praying with me?

All my love
Paul (anxious)

25 Jan. 1945

Hello Darling —

How is my bestest and onliest girl this bright and sun shiney (?) and squally (?) day? We are still cutting capers and it sure is hard to write legibly — like being on a giant teeter totter with a few barrel rolls thrown in. Sure must be a terrific storm somewhere for we're tossing, rolling and pitching something scandalous. On my way from the shower, stopped in to see the chaplain — he sure is sick & has been most of the time aboard. Several more are real sick, yours truly is feeling fine but my poor legs are about worn out from bracing against the ship's movements — quite a trick to do dentistry but as long as I can't have any lady patients I don't have to worry about falling into their laps and convincing them it was an accident.

Better take my wind scoop in for the sea is coming in again & I'm about to drown. Sure silly weather in these parts — can't make up its mind.

Getting near chow time so I'd better dig out a clean uniform & be all set. I'm continually starved and my pod is showing again — when I get the word and it's "favorable" I'll do something about it again.

Must away honey girl — all my love & "best wishes" to you.

Paul (bouncing)

25 Jan. 1945

Hello Darling —

We are still having rugged weather — very little sleep last night; couldn't stay in my sack and the noises — crashes — bangs — splashes, etc were terrific. Just came in from my "nocturnal" salt bath on the foc'sle — sure swell out there, the bow went completely under and when it came up, tons of water poured over the deck. It's a magnificent sight — a full moon is out, when it comes out from behind the clouds it throws a light similar to a spot light and catches the ship ahead of us in its rays. Really an outstanding sight and have it indelibly inscribed in my memory.

Sure have been polishing a lot of teeth these days in preparation for liberty in a civilized port.

Almost fell out of my chair then — when we zig zag in this kind of weather, we really go to town, that's for sure! If I ever ride in a taxi I'll have to hire someone to rock it and sprinkle water on me so I'll feel at home — great life — think we're riding the dipper now — Wow! That wass a goot one.

Not much to allow tonight — no sleep last night & worked hard all morning so I'se tarred — think I'll try to read a while — catch my sack when it comes down and try and stay with it a few hours at least. Wish you could see us bounce around.

Am thinking of you — miss you much, wish there was something I could do about it — hope, I hope.

All my love, darling
Paul (optimo kid)

26 Jan. 1945

Hello Darling —

Just had a lot of fun — have been eating pop-corn and did it ever taste good! Someone sent Esch a big bag of it so we had the mess attendants turn to and pop huge quantities of it.

Nothing new to allow today — we're in our eighth day of heavy weather, three more days and we'll be in "- - - -" and calm weather. Finally get off the "cracked record" and the days won't repeat themselves — at this stage of the game it seems twice as long.

Everybody is antsy-pantsy — this suspense is terrible — it's catching us all short but no one is going to let that interfere. As the zero hour nears, my butterflies increase & I can hardly wait for the verdict.

All my love honey girl —
Paul (pop corn kid)

27 Jan. 1945

Hello Lamb —

Sure don't feel 42 — feel too good, something must be going to happen. It's actually cool out these evenings, damn near froze tonight out on the foc'sle.

It's still mighty rough out but I still like it — never seem to tire of it as I do of real calm weather & a mill pond to set on. At least we have the sensation of being underway when we're tossed around and right now that means something.

Sure looking forward to waking up Monday morning — should anchor about noon and then pins and needles for orders — hope, I hope. Looks pretty good at this writing but one never knows what the powers that be will do. We're all concentrating on but one thing — hope, I hope.

Still am g.q. conscious and the hurried patter of feet on the deck over my head still causes an "alert" in my mind — expect some day I'll get over it entirely. After all, a year of almost constant g.q.s — alerts, etc., causes one to listen for alarms and be all set to go. The door bell on Apt. 4 sounds like our Stand By! Fire! signal, so if I grab cotton & stand with my mouth open don't think I'm nuts when company comes.

My bed looks awful good — almost froze last night so guess I'll dig out some covers tonight. My blood must be salt water and sure doesn't have any antifreeze in it.

All my love sweet girl
Paul (birthday kid)

THE *LOUISVILLE* ARRIVED in Pearl Harbor on January 29, 1945. Two days later the long-awaited orders came down.

1 Feb. 1945

Hello My Darling —

Guess there is a Santa Claus after all — you no doubt have had a note from Bob Linthicom by now, telling you I was on my way HOME!!! Gee honey — it's too good to be true — even tho we are having a rugged trip — the rainbow is at the end and no one is complaining. The sea is awfully, rough, roll thru better than 20 degree from the vertical — that swings us thru an arc of 40 degrees — dishes (with soup int) etc., go scooting from the table — chairs & occupants slide across the room & then tip one each officer on his fanny. Lot of fun but sure hard sleeping — we'll all look like we have been on a real bender by the time we reach home.

Hope to catch a plane Wednesday (7 Feb.) & will be home that night or early a.m. Will wire you time of arrival — golly, hope I can get a reservation & then not get bumped. As of now we get 20 days including travel time. Will make arrangements for a hut before I leave here so we'll be all set when you and I return to the coast. Gee honey — back together again! May not be for long but at least we'll see each other for a while and I'm all in one piece.

Tried to do some shopping in Honolulu but it's terrible — tried to get some lizard skin shoes for you — they only wanted $48.66 for them and they didn't even look halfway decent. I was only there a very short time — everything was so high I just didn't buy a thing. Feel kind of bad about it, but Honolulu is lousy and everything is shipped in from the states anyway so phooey to them. Had a run of luck so won't have to cash a check — if I'm held up in getting a reservation I may get to pick up a trinket or two — it's a lead pipe cinch I'm not going to dilly-dally at this end of the line.

Can't seem to think clearly — coherently or I guess just plain think — heading for my girl — Whoopee! Do you think next week will ever roll around? The trip from Manus seemed months and this leg on it will be ages. If it ever calms down enough I have "oceans" of dental work to do — right now it's all one can do to stand up or keep off his fanny. Noticed when I was walking "downtown" sure was loppy and my coordination is terrible — will get me a white cane & a seeing-eye dog so people will look out for me.

We have a big inspection Saturday — dress blues and all the frills — back to civilization once more. Am damn near freezing now — wonder what I'll do in Oklahoma! Wow! I'll take a chance.

The USS *Louisville* (CA-28) arrives off Mare Island Navy Yard, California, on February 6, 1945, for repair of kamikaze damage received the previous month. The photo is annotated with crash details.

U.S. Naval Historical Center Photo

The USS *Louisville* off the Mare Island Navy Yard, April 7, 1945, following the repairs of battle damage.
Courtesy of A. D. Baker, III, 1983, U.S. Naval Histcrical Center Photo

Didn't know it was so late & then too we have to set our clocks up — the sea is rougher than a boot — the kids on watch over my head tap dance to keep warm — looks like a bad night so I'll close for now — probably won't write again — next communique will be a wire with vital information. We get in some time Tuesday so will try & get a wire off that day or as soon as get my reservation — Bird Balls! My bottle of ink just turned over — that does it — good night sweet heart — keep the home fires burning bright — all my love.

Paul (homing pigeon)

4 Feb. 1945

Hello My Sweet —

Can't stay in my sack so thought I'd talk to you a few minutes while we're still right side up. "God help the sailor on a night like this" — sure are doing our stuff tonight — we're hovering near the capsizing point — glad I don't know enough about this and that to worry about it — the captain is worried — that's good enough for me.

Leave starts 8 Feb. for twenty days — sure hope I can get a plane out early that day — won't fool with trying to get an Army or Navy plane — I want to get to 1700 stat. Am not going to try & call you — takes forever to get a call thru — will wire as soon as I get the dope on how & when I'll arrive. Keep your fingers crossed so I'll get an early plane and don't get bumped off — wouldn't that be awful.

Soon will land. Wow! Will go in with the first wave, that's for sure.

All my love
Paul

THE *LOUISVILLE* STEAMED under the Golden Gate Bridge and dropped anchor in San Francisco Bay on the morning of February 6.

The *Kingfisher* (Oklahoma) *Times and Free Press* reported on February 9 that Lieutenant Commander Paul C. Bonnette was "spending a short leave in Kingfisher" and that his wife would accompany him to San Francisco for his next assignment. The newspaper added: "He achieved notice recently in the battle for the Philippines, press dispatches from the Lingayen area tell of his popularity with the men on his ship because of his bravery and outstanding service in behalf of shipmates wounded when the ship was hit twice."

Repairs to the *Louisville* were completed at Mare Island Shipyard near San Francisco on April 13, and on April 22 she sailed to San Diego for, according to its history, "intensive shakedown and refresher training."

On April 29, the *Louisville* left San Diego for Pearl Harbor and more combat. Paul was relieved one hour before she sailed.

Fifty Years Later

FROM PEARL HARBOR, the *Louisville* sailed to Guam and from there to Task Force 54 where she provided fire support for ground forces on Okinawa. On the evening of June 5, a kamikaze came in low over the island and struck the *Lady Lou* near her #1 stack. After emergency repairs, she returned to her position on the firing line until ordered to Pearl Harbor on June 15 for battle damage repairs. The war ended as the *Louisville* was completing post-repair training and shakedown.

On August 6, 1945, the U.S. dropped a 4.5-ton atomic bomb named "Little Boy" on the Japanese city of Hiroshima, and followed with a second atomic bomb on Nagasaki August 9. The resulting casualties cemented the Japanese defeat, and the emperor officially surrendered August 14. The formal instrument of surrender was signed aboard the USS *Missouri* in Tokyo Harbor on September 15, 1945.

On August 27, with Rear Admiral T. G. W. Settle aboard, the *Louisville* sailed for Guam and Okinawa and from there to Dairen, Manchuria, to supervise the evacuation of nearly 2,000 Allied prisoners of war. Next it was to Tsingtao China, where Admiral Settle accepted the surrender of Japanese vessels in the area.

The *Louisville* escorted these ships to Jinson, Korea, where she was ordered to Chefoo, China. According to the ship's history:

> During the Louisville's stay in Chefoo, the Chinese Commissioner of Foreign Affairs . . . presented Admiral Settle and the ship with a large quantity of brandy, vermouth, beer, and fresh provisions — including 200 live chickens, as a gift from the Chinese Communist Army, in control of that section of China.

In October, the *Louisville* became part of the Yellow Sea Force, operating under Commander Task Group 71.6. After a short period she returned to the United States, proceeding to Philadelphia where on June 17, 1946, she was decommissioned and joined the Atlantic Reserve Fleet.

For her service in World War II, the USS *Louisville* (CA 28) was awarded 13 battle stars.

On September 14, 1959, the *Lady Lou* was sold to a private corporation. She was towed from Philadelphia to Tampa, Florida, and within a year had been cut up for scrap.

On June 1, 1945, Paul reported to the Naval Air Technical Training Center in Norman, Oklahoma, where he served as chief of oral surgery for seven months. While there he applied for transfer from the reserve to the regular Navy. The application was granted with a promotion to commander.

From Norman, Paul and Dorothy moved to the Naval Dental School in Bethesda, Maryland, for advanced medical training and from there to nearly two years of duty at the Naval Air Station in Norfolk, Virginia.

In March 1949, Paul returned to sea in the Pacific, spending eight months aboard the hospital ship USS *Repose*, followed by three years at the U.S. Naval Station in Tacoma, Washington. In December 1952, Paul was assigned to the aircraft carrier USS *Yorktown* for two years.

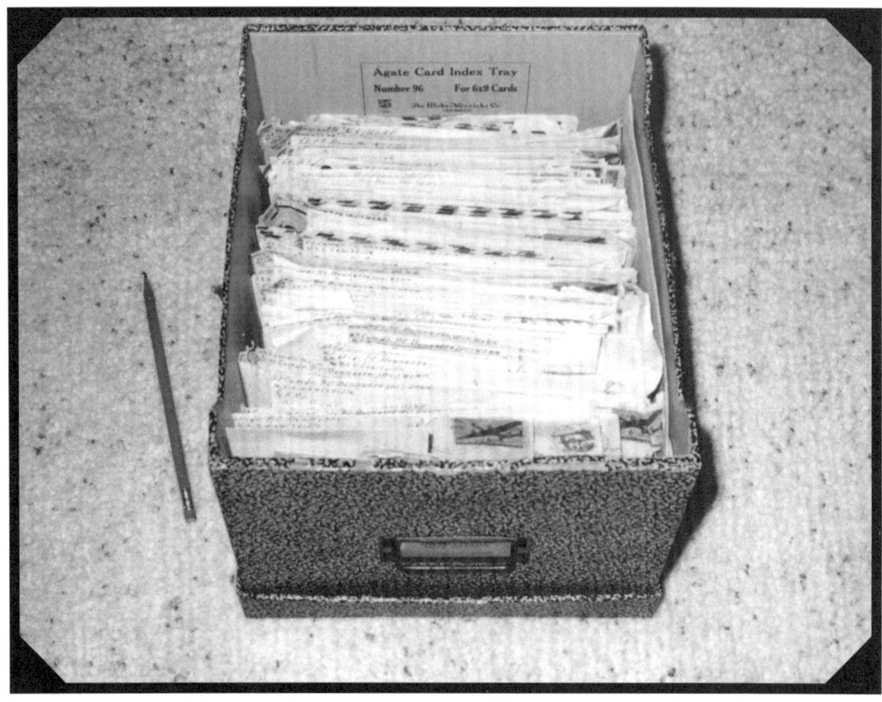

The file box in which the letters to Dotty B were found.

Dotty B and Paul, February 1946, on the Lake Pontchartrain seawall during a trip to New Orleans with Fred and Dorothy Lankard.

Dotty B and Paul at the time of his retirement from active duty in 1964. *U.S. Navy Photo*

In March 1954, I accompanied my parents on a trip to California to join Dorothy for a surprise welcome to the *Yorktown* as she returned from the Pacific. I had never seen the ocean, and I had certainly never seen anything like the mighty *Yorktown* easing to a pier at the Alameda Naval Air Station near San Francisco. We saw Paul before he saw us. He was scanning the crowd with binoculars and did a double take when he spotted not only Dotty B, but me and my parents. For the next five days, Paul and Dorothy showed us San Francisco and I spent many thrilling hours exploring the famed *Yorktown.*

At the end of his last sea duty, Paul and Dorothy went to the U.S. Naval Station in Newport, Rhode Island, followed by six years at the U.S. Naval Dental Clinic at Camp Pendleton, California.

Paul was promoted to captain and spent almost two years at the U.S. Naval Air Station in Corpus Christi, Texas, before retiring from active duty in 1964.

Dorothy and Paul made their final move to San Diego to enjoy familiar Navy facilities and the company of many old friends. After Paul's death in 1970, Dorothy moved to a pleasant apartment where I visited her for the last time in the spring of 1980. A few years later she moved into a nursing home. Her letters complained constantly how boring it was.

Of their many homes over 36 years of marriage, Dorothy and Paul's favorite was the house they had during their six years at Camp Pendleton. Set in the hills above San Clemente, it wasn't large, but it was bright and airy with a patio and garden that overlooked the Pacific Ocean.

Captain Paul Christian Bonnette at the time of his retirement from active duty in 1964.

Index

by Lori L. Daniel